Foreword

How do we capture the essence of the transformational power of e-knowledge? The digital technologies pose a mountainous challenge to all of us trying to explore the possible futures they offer. They combine a new medium with a new delivery system, and each multiplies the effect of the other. The adaptive computer is as revolutionary a way of supporting the way we think and learn as was the invention of writing. The Internet is as pervasive in its communicative impact as was the invention of the printing press. In harnessing the two together, we find ourselves grappling with the equivalent of the invention of writing and the invention of the printing press at the same time. This extraordinary historical convergence must give us pause. And yet the pace of invention never pauses, never gives us the time we need to reflect.

We cannot predict the future, but we do sense that we have the power to shape it. So we need to take time to reflect: on what those possible futures are, which are the more desirable, and what it takes to realise them. The authors of this book set out to help us with that process. On every page you will find them striving to express the ways in which e-systems can be exploited, the benefits they could yield, and what we all, individuals and organisations together, must now do.

Underlying many of the contributions in this book is a debate about epistemology—when the knowledge technologies change so radically, they change not just what we know, but how we come to know it. The contributors here argue that knowledge is contextual, social, relativistic—not a discrete and unchanging object. The e-learning agenda creates the dilemma that while we can atomise knowledge into elements such as 'learning objects', we must recognise that they are there to be shared, contextualised, and negotiated in the social context of the online community of practice.

We will come to a better understanding of the epistemology of e-knowledge as we slowly acquire the habits of the e-Knowledge Economy: multitasking across the different modes of activity, publishing with or without authorship and with or without ownership, managing the tyranny of choice, manipulating the multiple sources of knowledge . . . it will take us a generation to understand the full impact of the new media. Meanwhile, the authors of this volume have succeeded in articulating, through the prosaic combination of writing, graphics, and storytelling, represented in print and PDF forms, the pathways we can use to transform ourselves and our organisations through e-knowledge.

Diana Laurillard

About Diana Laurillard

Professor Laurillard is Head of the E-Learning Strategy Unit at the UK Government's Department for Education and Skills (DfES). She was previously Pro-Vice-Chancellor for Learning Technologies and Teaching at the Open University. Her role there was to ensure that learning technologies achieved their appropriate balance within the full range of learning and teaching methods in the university's courses. She is known world-wide for her widely acclaimed book Rethinking University Teaching, *which recently entered its second edition. The first edition is still used in courses on learning technology all over the world. She has also made a significant contribution to fundamental research on the relationship between student learning and learning technologies, using the notion of a 'conversational framework' to define the learning process for higher education, and then to interpret the extent to which new technology can support and enhance high level conceptual learning.*

Advisory Committee

To support this initiative, we have assembled a committee of professionals recognized as leaders in the e-learning, knowledge management, and international standards movements.

Judy Brown

University of Wisconsin System and executive director of the ADL co-lab is a key figure in the development and deployment of SCORM (Sharable Content Object Reference Model). She provides research and consulting on technology directions for all campuses of the University of Wisconsin System.

Dr. Richard Hames

is one of Australia's most influential intellectuals. A celebrated author, public speaker and futurist, Richard is chairman of The Hames Group (a global network of strategic advisers and knowledge designers), chairman of Australia Tomorrow (an initiative of Renaissance Earth) and a director of the Australian Foresight Institute.

Maria Theresa Martinez

director, Academic Development, Technical Millennium University, part of ITESM is widely involved in Monterrey Tech's e-learning activities that extend throughout the Americas.

Professor Toshio Okamoto

University of Electro Communications, Japan is a full professor in the Graduate School of Information Systems, the University of Electronics and Communications and is a leading figure in the e-learning standards movement in Japan. He is also president of the Japanese Society for Systems and Information of Education.

Dr. Madanmohan Rao

editor, INOMY.com is a well-known commentator on e-business, e-learning, and knowledge development in India. He was formerly the communications director at the United Nations Inter Press Service bureau in New York, and vice president at India World Communications in Bombay.

Dr. Robby Robson

president, Eduworks Corporation, is chair of the IEEE Learning Technologies Standards Committee (LTSC) and is regarded as a leading adviser and practitioner in the field of e-learning standards and products.

Professor James C. Taylor

deputy-vice chancellor, University of Southern Queensland, Australia, and president of the International Council for Open and Distance Education (ICDE), is widely regarded as one of the top experts in the theory and practice of e-learning in the world. He and his university have been recently recognized as leaders in dual-mode university education.

Professor Zhu Zhiting

is vice dean of the College of Online Education at East China Normal University and Director, (Chinese) National Committee of Distance Learning Technology Standardization. He is a specialist in educational technology and a leading figure in the development of e-learning standards and practices in China.

A Guide to Using This Book

- For an overview of key trends and issues in the Knowledge Economy, read the introduction and the brief summaries at the beginning of each chapter. Each chapter also contains a list of terms and concepts.

- This book is designed to make it easier to skim high-level concepts and drill down into the details on items of personal interest. When skimming, pay attention to boxed information, tables, graphics, bolded passages, and section headings.

- Use the online resources at **www.transformingeknowledge.info** at the same time as reading the book to support your learning. Open the site and read along with the book, using the searchable glossary and who's who in e-knowledge, index of topics, full bibliography, case studies, and other resources.

Introduction

Our international team has assembled to produce a manifesto on e-knowledge.

We begin with a simple vision: in the Knowledge Economy, those individuals and enterprises that share and process their knowledge effectively have a great advantage.

To succeed in the Knowledge Economy, most of us will need an order-of-magnitude leap in our ability to create, acquire, assimilate, and share knowledge. Even the manner in which we experience knowledge will be transformed, through technologies and practices that exist today or will soon be available. Between now and the year 2010, best practices in knowledge sharing will be substantially reinvented in all settings—education, corporations, government, and associations and non-profits. That is our vision.

This transformation is underway today. We provide examples of leading-edge enterprises that are currently using e-knowledge to achieve significant savings in the time, cost, and effectiveness of deploying and sharing knowledge. And vignettes and projections of best practices in the future that will use e-knowledge to build and sustain competitive advantage relative to historic market leaders in all fields.

This book traces the three primary indicators of e-knowledge transformation: 1) Internet technologies, interoperability standards, and emerging e-knowledge repositories and marketplaces; 2) enterprise infrastructures, processes, and knowledge cultures; and 3) cascading cycles of reinvention of best practices, business models and strategies for e-knowledge. It concludes with practical, "how-to" guidance on accelerating your enterprise's readiness for e-knowledge in order to mobilize leaders and practitioners around the concept of e-knowledge, and develop an enterprise knowledge strategy explicitly driving business plans.

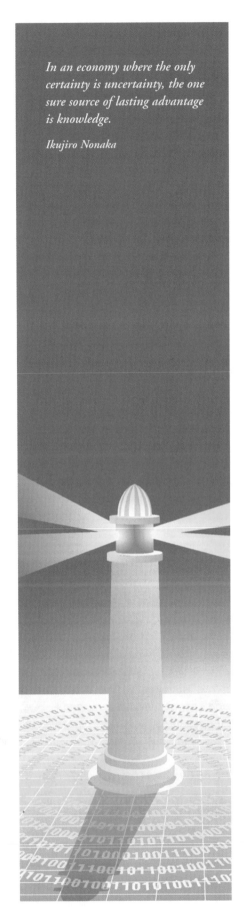

In an economy where the only certainty is uncertainty, the one sure source of lasting advantage is knowledge.

Ikujiro Nonaka

A Revolution in the Sharing of Knowledge

These are complex topics that cannot be left to specialists. *Transforming e-Knowledge* aims to demystify these topics and make them approachable to everyone. To support this effort we have created an online repository of resources, including a searchable glossary of terms at www.transformingeknowledge.info. Use the online resources simultaneously to support your reading.

Across the globe, we see examples of the e-knowledge revolution. From Bombay to Brisbane to Boston, practitioners are heightening their appreciation of the strategic importance of knowledge.

> *Knowledge has become the key economic resource and the dominant —and perhaps the only—source of competitive advantage.*
>
> *Peter Drucker*

Individuals and organizations must fundamentally reshape the manner in which they appraise what they know, what they can do with it, and what they need to know. They must also track best practices when they create, manage, deploy, and leverage knowledge. These new competencies will be compelling sources of competitive advantage in the Knowledge Economy. Over time, technology will be a core component of all knowledge management and learning. The "e" will truly be redundant in reference to e-knowledge management, e-learning, and e-business activities—if it is not already so.

> *What do we know now that we didn't know ten years ago? That learning and knowledge are the result of multiple intertwining forces: content, context, and community.*
>
> *John Seely Brown*

Today, a wide choice of solution providers specialize in the distinct areas of content, context, and community. Within five years, successful solution providers will meet the challenge of covering all three areas, while others will specialize in particular areas. Early adopters and influencers sense that now is the time to participate in shaping these developments. Enterprises that wish to succeed realize that they must act now to start to build and reshape knowledge infrastructures, capabilities, and cultures.

A diverse assortment of learning and training organizations and industry consortia are well positioned to advance this transformation. Poised for leadership and success are standards organizations, content aggregators, and collaborative alliances of knowledge organizations, including libraries, colleges and universities, and professional societies, and associations.

Leveraging technological innovation, solution providers are creating applications that will evolve into powerful and pervasive e-knowledge capabilities. An e-Knowledge Economy is emerging, consisting of providers and users in every sector. All have a stake in the development of policies, protocols, and practices that will accelerate the growth of e-knowledge to meet the knowledge sharing imperatives of the Knowledge Economy. As an e-Knowledge Industry emerges, we can expect a series of "jump shifts" in our best practices for learning and knowledge management and in our ability to harness technological capability.

Jump Shifts in Perspectives, Practices and Circumstances

What is a jump shift? It is a fundamental and disruptive change in our way of doing business. It involves leaping to a higher plane of vision and performance. Jump shifts occur during periods of disruptive technological innovation, such as the e-knowledge disruption we're experiencing today. Today's emerging Knowledge Economy is very different from yesterday's Information Economy. Tomorrow's Knowledge Economy will be different from today's in ways that affect every aspect of learning, knowledge management, and performance for individuals and organizations. The power of this vision is not only that it helps enterprises plan for the future, but that it energizes enterprises to act decisively now, to participate in the jump shifts rather than be left behind.

Jump shifts can take different forms. Jump shifts in vision and perspective enable one to consider a different plane of performance with different practices and values. But jump shifts can also occur in circumstances. For example, it is very likely that within the next few years, the traditional model for scholarly publishing will make a jump shift to an even more unbundled form based on digital repositories and horizontal marketplaces. Our visioning for the future must consider potentials posed by such dramatic changes in circumstances.

Planning from the Future Backward

The essence of foresight-based planning is "planning from the future backward" (Slaughter 2002). Rather than merely extrapolating present knowledge concepts and practices forward into the future, foresight-based planning develops plausible scenarios of the future that capture the potential of current and anticipated trends. Then those scenarios can be pulled back to the present to identify actions and changes in perspective that are necessary to "get there from here." That's planning from the future backward.

Future scenarios can include a range of e-knowledge impacts. Pragmatic changes in e-knowledge can improve the efficiency of existing business and knowledge processes. Progressive changes in e-knowledge can facilitate the reinvention of business and knowledge processes and the underlying knowledge ecology of organizations. At the revolutionary level, e-knowledge can stimulate rethinking of the basic foundations of our enterprises and institutions—colleges and universities, associations, corporations, government agencies, and other enterprises. e-Knowledge scenarios can include permutations and combinations of these impacts.

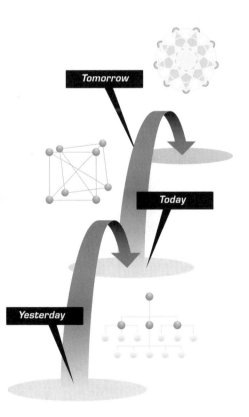

The most successful leader of all is one who sees another picture not yet actualized.

Mary Parker Follett

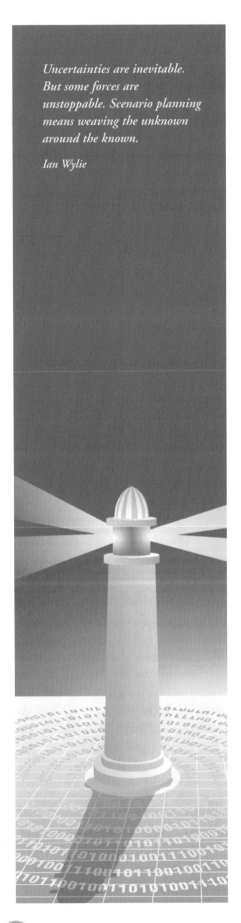

*Uncertainties are inevitable.
But some forces are
unstoppable. Scenario planning
means weaving the unknown
around the known.*

Ian Wylie

A Single Future or Multiple Scenarios?

Even if one accepts the notion that our future holds what for many individuals and organizations will be a revolution in the sharing of knowledge, there is no such thing as "the future" in a singular sense. There are many scenarios for a future state of knowledge sharing. Moreover, these conditions and practices of knowledge sharing will differ in significant ways across the globe. And they will vary dramatically within organizations, communities, and nations, based on the preferences, capacities, and choices made by individuals, enterprises, and governments.

The author of the novel *The Neuromancer,* William Gibson, said "The future is already here; it is just not distributed very well." Meaning that many of the social/economic/technological elements of the future that we will eventually experience already exist today. Those elements have proponents and users. However, the future will be the result of competition between the established order and other possibilities, some of which will require jump shifts. The particular future conditions that emerge will depend on personal and organizational decisions not yet made, technologies not yet invented or not yet deployed at sufficient scale to be influential, and human preferences not yet verified through choosing from real alternatives. So we describe and project futures with humility, not hubris, using the language of scenarios and choice, not monolithic, singular conditions.

Choosing How to Participate in the Knowledge Revolution

It is about choice. As our capacity to share knowledge increases, individuals and organizations will make choices about how they will acquire, process, and assimilate knowledge. The range of choices will be far greater than today. But one fact is clear: those individuals and organizations that achieve a quantum leap in their capacity to acquire, process, assimilate, and share knowledge will enjoy a relative competitive advantage in the Knowledge Economy.

It is also about chance. The uncertainties and imponderables in today's world seem much more daunting than they did in the 1990s. Continuing problems with the economy, political setbacks, and terrorism remind us that progress cannot be guaranteed. An unfortunate confluence of these conditions could seriously retard the development of the Knowledge Economy and a revolution in knowledge sharing.

And it is about readiness. Current owners of large bodies of knowledge resources will attempt to extend and preserve existing paradigms. Under normal conditions, new approaches will be invented by outsiders and deployed despite the efforts of the defenders of the status quo. It pays for organizations and individuals to prepare for the coming paradigm shift in knowledge sharing. This book attempts to provide the insights and recommended actions that will accelerate organizational and individual readiness for e-knowledge.

Today, many of the technologies and practices required for pervasive e-knowledge exist as proof-of-concept pilots or early deployment prototypes. Progressive developments in standards, commercialization, deployment, and acceptance are needed for the e-Knowledge Industry to firmly take root. We believe conditions are favorable for these to occur in large measure between now and the year 2010.

A Manifesto for the e-Knowledge Industry

Tomorrow

Today

The e-Knowledge Industry is at a formative stage in its development. Pervasive and powerful forces described in the table below are driving the emergence of e-knowledge in theory and practice. Yet even leading-edge innovators and organizations are taking fundamentally incremental steps in vision and practice. It's time for practitioners and policy makers to make a jump shift in vision.

These potential forces provide the basis for raising expectations, elevating perspectives and mobilizing energies for the e-Knowledge Industry and for transforming the ability of organizations and individuals to create, manage, repurpose, combine and experience knowledge.

This book aims to support and articulate the need for this transformation. We endeavor to explain the meaning of these developments in terms that are clearly understandable to policy makers, organizational leaders and managers, and educators and learning/training professionals in all settings. We illustrate how this transformation will touch virtually every learning and knowledge management enterprise. The focus is on understanding the implications of these developments for the various contexts—technical, process, standards, cultural, and political—where there is interplay of knowledge management and learning. Moreover, the focus is also on both insight and concrete advice on how to accelerate individual and organizational readiness for e-knowledge. Put simply, *Transforming e-Knowledge* aims to be a manifesto for the emerging e-Knowledge Industry.

The table on the following two pages summarizes the topics and ideas that follow. Scan them now and revisit them as you proceed through the book.

Forces Enabling and Stimulating the e-Knowledge Industry

Investments in infrastructure and best practices by 'early adopters' of e-knowledge (e.g. associations, governmental agencies, corporations, universities) deliver results that encourage wider adoption, and also facilitate new generations of enterprise applications.

Global enterprises increase competitiveness by developing faster ways to manage their knowledge and their strategic learning, creating tools that non-experts can use.

Growth in expert networks and easier, more productive participation in communities of practice push e-knowledge practices and competencies.

Increasing sophistication by users, who develop an appetite for services that provide significant gains in their capacity to access and assimilate knowledge.

Advances in Internet and intranet-based capabilities enable jump shifts in creating and accessing knowledge stores.

Innovations in mobile communications provide ubiquitous access to perpetual learning solutions as well as new ways to meet demands for e-commerce any place or time.

Insight into new and more effective ways of experiencing knowledge drives innovation.

Increased understanding about how to deploy international standards in ways that ensure useful return on investment (e.g. through interoperability) stimulates continued investment.

Yesterday

An Information Economy where most knowledge is proprietary and hoarded.

Convergence is heralded in the wake of developments in telecommunications, computer networks, and information technology.

Value and supply chains for knowledge are embedded in proprietary sources of knowledge.

Content is king. Learning silos and academic publishing silos exist. The metaphor for traditional learning is program delivery. Distance learning is isolated from other forms of learning and knowledge management.

Traditional learning is expensive, due to cost of content and other resources and faculty involvement at all stages.

Tactical learning is a response to specific needs and skills gaps. Learning practices differ across the enterprise.

Today

An emerging Knowledge Economy where the power of shared knowledge becomes evident. Traditional power relationships relating to knowledge begin to erode.

Networked webs and the proliferation of mobile telecommunications advance the practice of networked knowledge.

Value chains for content begin to be unbundled and disintermediated (eliminating the middleperson), harnessing the malleability of all things digital.

Content and context are equally important. "Distance" and "traditional" learning are enhanced through e-learning, using the metaphor of interactivity. Traditional scholarly publishing models begin to be unbundled.

e-Learning is used to digitize existing models and begins to reinvent cost, availability of content, and roles of faculty, mentors, and learners.

Integrated learning is shared across the organization, introducing consistent practices and infrastructures.

Tomorrow

A mature, fully developed Knowledge Economy that rewards knowledge sharing and the proliferation of knowledge. Pervasive access to knowledge changes many power relationships and even societal assumptions and practices.

Computing and networks become pervasive, enabling the "mobilization" of knowledge to take account of the location of users and their needs at each location.

Value chains become "value nets" as content is unbundled and available from many sources. The cost and nature of content change.

Content, context, and community are structured and interpenetrating. Interactivity drives learning. The use of knowledge management to support learning is a major breakthrough. New publishing models emerge.

Economic models of learning are fully reinvented. The cost of e-content declines and usage soars. Faculty, mentor, and learner interactions are reinvented.

Strategic, enterprise-wide learning uses directed and autonomic learning to respond rapidly to organizational challenges. Who can **do** what is more important than who **knows** what.

Yesterday

Rudimentary standards for computer-based training (CBT) are developed.

Organizational infrastructures are introduced for using digitized knowledge.

Content is held in proprietary channels—courses, books and corporate repositories—that are impermeable, vertical silos.

Formal knowledge management is practiced by selected, knowledge-centric organizations.

Users acquire knowledge in fixed locations tied to physical repositories and links to networks.

Today

Clusters of international standards groups create the first generation of standards for learning objects and e-content repositories.

Early generations of integrated portals, enterprise resource planning (ERP) systems, learning management systems, learning content management systems, and knowledge sharing tools.

New repositories and models of sharing content are under development—e.g., **MERLOT** and the **Advanced Distributed Learning (ADL)** co-lab, plus the **SPARC** model for institutional repositories.

The practice of knowledge management expands as tools develop and knowledge ecologies are understood. Insight develops on making communities of practice both effective and reflective.

Mobile devices and wireless networks are enabling users to acquire, create, and store knowledge anywhere and any time.

Tomorrow

Iterative cycles of standards development continue, creating truly scaleable, interoperable standards for digital content, its access, and transmission.

Powerful, open (yet secure) enterprise application infrastructures and solutions support knowledge sharing and reinvention of business processes, organizational dynamics, and knowledge cultures.

Robust, open content marketplaces create horizontal channels for exchanging content and aggregating supply and demand.

Enterprises actively shape their knowledge ecologies. Knowledge management is practiced throughout all organizations, fused with learning. Communities of practice are the key strategic organizational unit in the Knowledge Economy.

Pervasive information and communication technology (ICT} environments will enable people to experience knowledge any time, any place, and in new ways. Knowledge sharing acquires **amenity**. Leading-edge knowledge users experience an order-of-magnitude leap in their capability to acquire, use, and share knowledge.

Contents

CHAPTER 1

What is e-Knowledge?

- Understanding e-Knowledge
- Pioneering Examples of e-Knowledge
- Pervasive Technology Changes How We "Experience" Knowledge
- Beyond Existing Concepts of e-Knowledge

Knowledge is interpreted content, available to a member of a community and understood in a particular context. Digital representations of content and context become e-knowledge through the dynamics of human engagement with them. The digital elements of e-knowledge can be codified, combined, repurposed, and exchanged. Knowledge is both a thing and a flow, shifting between explicit and implicit states and between different meanings in different contexts. The original concept of knowledge management has evolved to a broader notion of knowledge ecology. e-Knowledge is changing the traditional value chain to a value net. It is also creating opportunities for marketplaces for digitized content, context, and narrative. The e-Knowledge Industry may democratize the provision and use of knowledge, reshape power centers, recalibrate the economics of publishing and enable new roles.

Pioneering examples of e-knowledge are presented in corporations, universities, associations, government, and health care settings.

Mobile, ambient technology is changing the dynamics of how we will live, work, and learn. Such technology environments will revolutionize everything about the "knowledge experience": place, use of time, nature of interfaces, intensity of engagement, reliance on just-in-time knowledge and agents, ability to multi-task, and the amenity of the knowledge experience. These new experiences will shape behaviors, practices, and social groupings for knowledge sharing.

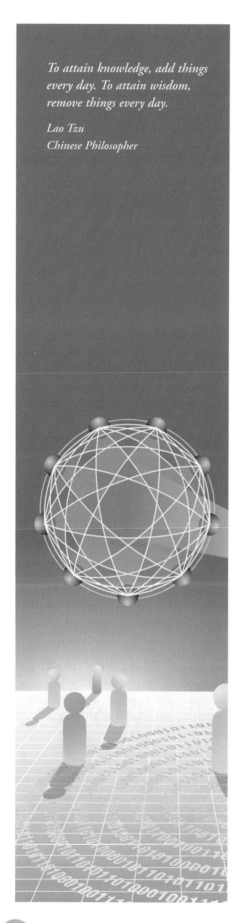

To attain knowledge, add things every day. To attain wisdom, remove things every day.

Lao Tzu
Chinese Philosopher

Terms & Concepts

Information and Communications Technology (ICT): Enables e-knowledge and the reinvention of e-knowledge processes.

Data: A collection of unorganized facts and/or figures.

Information: Data that has been organized in such a way that it achieves meaning, in a generalized way.

Knowledge: Information that is presented within a particular context, yielding insight on application in that context, by members of a community.

e-Knowledge: Digital representations of content and context become e-knowledge through the dynamics of human engagement with them.

Value Chain: A chain of activities and relationships that adds value to business processes. e-Knowledge enables the unbundling and reinvention of traditional value chains for learning and knowledge management and the enterprise activities that depend on them. The traditional value chain can become a **value web** in tomorrow's e-knowledge environment.

Content: Objective information, sometimes codified knowledge, sometimes a fusion of data, information, and knowledge that is used to support learning, business applications, and processes.

Context: The setting and conditions in which the content is or can be applied. Content is given different meaning by differing contexts.

Community: The formal and/or informal groupings in which people function when they experience e-knowledge.

Explicit Knowledge: Objective knowledge codified and captured in textbooks, manuals, process descriptions, learning objects, and topical content repositories. Typically, the 'what' of knowledge.

Tacit Knowledge: Insights, intuitions, and subjective knowledge that constitute the intellectual capital of most organizations. Advanced knowledge management focuses on tacit knowledge. Typically, the 'how' (process) of knowledge acquisition and application.

Knowledge Management (KM): The practice of nurturing, collecting, managing, sharing, and updating the knowledge resources of an enterprise

e-Knowledge Marketplaces: Repositories that are set up to encourage and enable the exchange of the elements of e-knowledge. Over time, horizontal marketplaces will cut across industry, disciplinary, and enterprise boundaries.

e-Knowledge Industry: The full range of enterprises that provide and/or use e-knowledge constitutes the e-Knowledge Industry.

Intellectual Capital: The sum and synergy of an organization's knowledge, experiences, relationships, processes, discoveries, innovations, and market presence

The Semantic Web: (An initiative of the World Wide Web Consortium). In the Knowledge Age, networked information will develop from both the syntax and the semantics of e-knowledge. Computer applications will be able to handle meaning and context from metadata (data used to describe the content of knowledge objects).

Understanding e-Knowledge

We begin with a definition of knowledge. In simple terms, knowledge is information and insight understood in a particular context. Its dynamic and contextual nature has led Peter Drucker, the creator of the term "knowledge worker," to assert that " the nature of knowledge is that it makes itself obsolete" (Ruggles and Holtshouse, 1999). Because the combination of knowledge and its context are continuously changing, common sense suggests it must be linked with processes of perpetual learning.

The context of knowledge is especially critical in today's global marketplace. Individuals and organizations must deal with multiple contextual meanings to an extent that would have seemed obsessive only ten years ago. Our approach to knowledge and learning draws from contexts and settings from across the globe. For example, consider the Chinese context where the term *guanxi* focuses on the importance of relationships or networks between people rather than organizations. Knowledge management and learning in such a setting expresses different dynamics than mainstream Western approaches.

In this book, we use a diversity of lenses through which to understand the facets of knowledge and its interaction with learning. The first lens is the simple value chain that represents the relationships between data, information, and knowledge. Other lenses make use of the relationships between knowledge and strategy, organizational change, networks, and economics (including supply chains and demand chains for knowledge).

Networked information and communications technology (ICT) has put the "e" in e-knowledge. But e-knowledge involves much more than merely digitizing and passing around everything we know using present concepts, structures, and proto-cols. As it develops, e-knowledge is creating new standards, structures, processes, best practices, business models, and strategies for creating and exchanging data, information, and knowledge.

Books, manuals, process descriptions, and detailed operating procedures have long served as repositories of what organizations know and what they do. In addition, the associated procedures and insights historically have been shared with others through education, training, and apprenticeship programs, both formal and informal. Digitization of resources and sharing through computer and telecommunications networks are making a wide range of repositories of potential knowledge available and accessible in ways never before possible.

Every day brings technical advances that make it easier to store, transmit, and share many kinds of information in digital form and at high speed. It becomes increasingly feasible to routinely capture one's daily experiences and their contexts for later analysis and perhaps incorporation in organizational processes. In principle, most, if not all, of that information could be a source of knowledge for others.

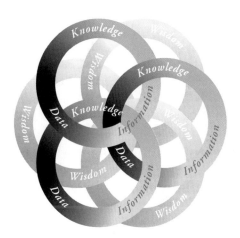

The Value Chain of Knowledge

Data *is a collection of unorganized facts and/or figures.*

Information *is data that has been organized in such a way that it achieves meaning, in a generalized way.*

Knowledge *is information that is presented within a particular context, yielding insight on application in that context.*

Wisdom *is the reflective or realized insight resulting from successful application and/or synthesis of knowledge. It is a higher plane of understanding that exists beyond the "simple value chain of knowledge." However, there is no agreement among the knowledge management community on what truly constitutes wisdom.*

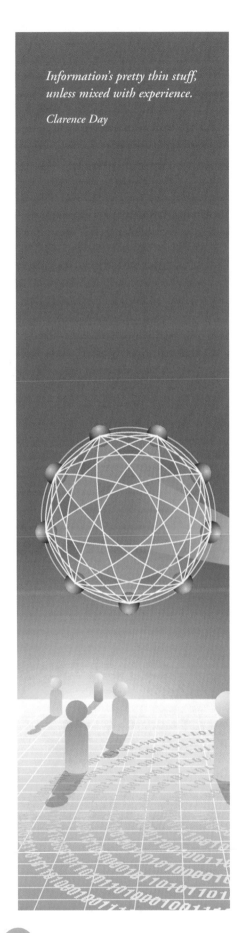

Repositories of Knowledge Resources

People

Books, texts, manuals, and other media

Libraries (physical and digital)

Courses and other learning experiences

Organizational processes and contexts

Training and apprenticeship programs

Professional knowledge and tradecraft of individuals, working groups, and associations, both formal and informal

News services

Some information can be shared directly, embedded in distinct courses, planned learning experiences, and other forms of communicating and sharing. Other information must be repurposed or otherwise transformed, through "data mining" or other types of filtering and aggregation, that expose significance in the information. "Sense making" is performed by humans using these tools. One person's information can become another person's knowledge, and vice versa, but not without overcoming some barriers in current practice.

> *It's impossible to calculate the full value of a given piece of information to all the people who might possess it.*
>
> *Richard Hunter, 2002*

Overcoming Obstacles to Digitization and Sharing

Obstacles still remain to the effective sharing, exploitation, and creation of knowledge. The first obstacle is not fully appreciating the elements of latent potential in each source of knowledge. The second is representing the results to others in a form that is accessible, easily comprehensible, and useful, even if others are separated by time or distance from the source of the knowledge. This representation of content and context is what we call e-knowledge. One important aspect of e-knowledge is being able to unbundle content in ways that facilitate subsequent editing and recombination. Another aspect is being able to identify other contexts in which content might be relevant if it can first be generalized from its original form then repurposed to suit the new context. The capacity to combine learning content in useful ways is also significant. As yet, few organizations can do those things well, if at all. Even organizations having developed such capability face significant problems in exploiting their advantage. For example, historically publishers have bought and sold exploitation rights on a geographic basis: country-by-country with different pricing structures in each market. That business model is incompatible with forays by those same publishers into e-publishing via the Internet where the market is worldwide. Reconciling those two business models (traditional and digital) is proving problematic. Issues of publisher prerogatives and intellectual property rights have complicated the combination of content from different publishers, even under the most favorable conditions. At worst, publisher prerogatives have scuttled most cross-source content exchanges and combinations of intellectual property from different publishers.

Advances in ICT, coupled with greater flexibility within and between organizations, are providing the means to overcome these barriers and transform the practice of combining and sharing of knowledge. The technology is not just making content exchange more efficient, it is enabling the emergence of e-knowledge and an industry dedicated to its creation, storage, enhancement, updating, combination, and exchange. These concepts and the associated technologies and standards enable processes that have never before been possible, such as instant, automated, Web-based negotiation of copyright clearance to use third-party material in e-content.

e-Knowledge Requires the Codification and Exchange of Digital Content

e-Knowledge is rendered from digital content where "content" itself can take many forms depending on the user or application—as data, metadata, transactions, performance logs, structured and unstructured information, etc. Following on, one person's "information" may be another's "knowledge" due to the intrinsic malleability of things digital. Digital content becomes e-knowledge through the dynamics of human engagement with it. It is easily repurposed and recombined with other e-knowledge. All the while, the intellectual property rights of e-knowledge can be monitored, metered, and charged to users.

e-Knowledge includes two distinct types of knowledge that can be rendered digitally:

- *Explicit knowledge* is knowledge that is transmittable in a formal, systematic manner. It consists of objective content (structured information and codified knowledge). In digital form, it is derived from all kinds of sources—from databases to information "atoms," from purposed modules and aggregations of content that can be stored, shared, described, combined, repurposed, syndicated, metered, and exchanged for fee or for free. These sources are available in a full spectrum of forms and characteristics, ranging from highly granular (paragraphs, individual images, video clips), to chapters and topics, to full texts and anthologies. *When such content is modularized and coupled with learning objectives, it is typically referred to as "learning objects" or "knowledge objects."*

But the lumping of digital resources into modular objects also demands that attention is given to the details of ensuring that the learning objects can be learned from. This involves understanding the organizational routines, tradecraft, and other inputs that give learning objects meaning in particular contexts. Providing these details will be the "new frontier" of learning object exchanges and marketplaces. It brings the prospect of mining those details to determine generalized ways to re-purpose learning objects to suit new contexts. It also makes more feasible the routine association with learning objects of data on their effectiveness for learners, both when used by themselves and when combined with other learning objects.

e-Knowledge is digitized content and context that can be "atomized," repurposed, updated, recombined, metered, and exchanged. e-Knowledge includes explicit knowledge and means of dealing with aspects of tacit knowledge, such as its transfer. e-Knowledge enables the development of processes and marketplaces for the exchange of digital content that have never before been possible.

The e-Knowledge Industry consists of all of the parties involved in the creation, storage, enhancement, combination, and exchange of e-knowledge.

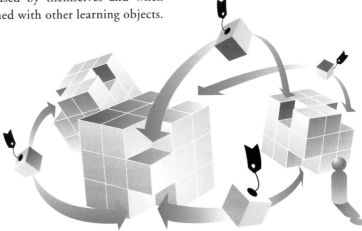

• *Implicit or tacit knowledge* is subjective, experience-based knowledge. Typically, it is not easily expressed in words, sentences, and formulae. It is highly context specific. It includes, but is not limited, to beliefs, values, tradecraft, mental models, and technical skills. Tacit knowledge resides in formal and informal networks of experts and communities of reflective practice. Some of this knowledge can be codified, made explicit, and migrated into content repositories and marketplaces. Most is accessed through person-to-person knowledge sharing or social interactions. New opportunities for sharing are made possible through pervasive, secure, online interactivity through communities of practice. Practitioners are developing heightened appreciation for the importance of such vibrant sources of tacit knowledge.

Tacit knowledge includes the informal knowledge that exists through common practice and is shared via e-mails, communities of practice, expert networks, and other permutations of online interaction. As organizations develop their e-knowledge competencies, they enhance their capacity to nurture, harvest, and use informal, tacit knowledge.

The policies, practices, competencies, networks, communities, and marketplaces for exchanging explicit and tacit e-knowledge are developing today. Their refinement to handle continuously revised knowledge will catalyze and drive the revolution in learning and knowledge management tomorrow.

The nature of knowledge is that it makes itself obsolete.

Peter Drucker, 1999

Interactions Between Tacit and Explicit Knowledge

By definition, knowledge is dynamic, not static. Knowledge continuously changes meaning and form. Whether knowledge is held by individuals, organizations, communities of practice or networks of organizations, the content, context, and community in which it is used are always changing.

It is especially critical to understand how elements of explicit and tacit knowledge can transcend their current states through progressive cycles of conversion. Ikujiro Nonaka (1999) has captured the essence of the relationships and interactions of tacit and explicit knowledge in four modes: socialization, externalization, combination, and internalization. These knowledge conversions are portrayed in the figure to the right.

Depicting the Interactions Between Tacit and Explicit Knowledge

In their work on the integration of e-learning and knowledge management, Woelk and Agarwal (2002) have schematically represented the transitions of knowledge between Nonaka's four phases. They have added a fifth phase, cognition, in which the knowledge seeker makes sense of tacit knowledge in context through applying it to a business problem.

Understanding e-Knowledge as a "Thing" and a "Flow"

In recent years, practitioners have begun to understand the complexities of modeling knowledge in all its forms. In consequence, the assumption of a clean delineation between tacit and explicit knowledge and the migration of knowledge between different states is questionable. The emerging ecology of knowledge representation suggests that knowledge exists as both a *thing* and a *flow* at the same time. The "thing" is knowledge that is "known" (the "know-what") and can be formally shared and used. The "flow" is the changing contexts or passage of knowledge through the informal structures of organizations where communities of practice and others make sense of it and convert it from "knowable" to "known." To accept this paradox, practitioners must accept that in the uncertain conditions that characterize most real-life settings, knowledge is continuously changing,

Knowledge Management Phases

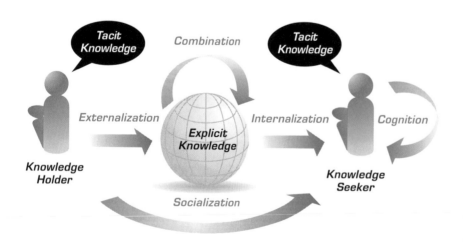

Interactions Between Explicit and Tacit Knowledge

Tacit and explicit knowledge are not totally separate. Rather they are mutually complementary. They interact and exchange with each other in the creative activities of human beings. Our model of dynamic knowledge creation is anchored in the

assumption that human knowledge is created and expanded through social interactions between tacit and explicit knowledge. We call this interaction knowledge conversion.

Ikujiro Nonaka, 1999

The most profound technologies are those that disappear. They weave themselves into the fabric of everyday life until they are indistinguishable from it.

Marc Weiser

TACIT KNOWLEDGE

Socialization (TACIT TO TACIT)

Converting tacit knowledge to other tacit forms such as shared mental models and technical skills acquired through shared experiences. Apprentices learn through observation, imitation, and practice. On-the-job training. Advanced tradecraft among teams of practitioners.

Internalization (EXPLICIT TO TACIT)

Converting explicit knowledge to tacit, thereby internalizing it to the individual. Embodying explicit knowledge through learning by doing. If shared with others, this tacit knowledge can become part of the tacit knowledge base through shared mental models or technical know-how.

Externalization (TACIT TO EXPLICIT)

Conversion from tacit to explicit knowledge. This is the process of articulating tacit knowledge into explicit concepts or language. This is highly important to knowledge creation. Tacit knowledge is made explicit, captured in metaphors, stories, analogies, concepts, and models.

Combination (EXPLICIT TO EXPLICIT)

Combining different elements of explicit knowledge. Combination and systematization of concepts through symbols such as language or figures is achieved through media such as documents, meetings, telephone conversations or computerized information. ICT is a powerful tool in combination and has been the focus of much of knowledge management.

EXPLICIT KNOWLEDGE

Adapted from: Ikujiro Nonaka, "The Dynamics of Knowledge Creation," The Knowledge Advantage, 1999, p.66-68.

flowing between different states of chaos, complexity, and knowability. What is "known" at any time depends on the management of content, context, and narrative. Under such conditions, organizations need to manage the different kinds of knowledge using different tools and techniques (Snowden, 2002).

Only when tacit and explicit knowledge interact can innovation occur.

Ikujiro Nonaka, 1999

This conception of knowledge recognizes that organizations consist of different **knowledge habitats**, each of which has different contexts and rules. These include the **formal organization, formal communities of practice, shadow or informal organizations, and temporary teams** dealing with environments recognized to be chaotic and turbulent (many organizations operate in such environments but few seem to accept this). The practice of knowledge management is dealing with these complexities with greater sophistication and understanding. The concept of knowledge management has been superseded in some circles by the more metaphorical **knowledge ecology**.

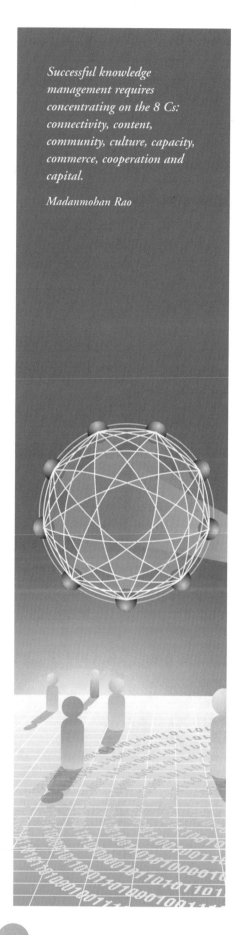

Successful knowledge management requires concentrating on the 8 Cs: connectivity, content, community, culture, capacity, commerce, cooperation and capital.

Madanmohan Rao

In the third generation, we grow beyond managing knowledge as a thing to also managing knowledge as a flow. To do this, we will need to focus more on context and narrative than on content.

Dave Snowden, 2002

Knowledge Management Through Five Lenses

There can be many lenses through which to discern knowledge and its management. These different lenses incorporate a range of perspectives and differentiate between the purposes and motivations shaping knowledge management at various levels. A broad classification scheme would distinguish between:

- *Personal knowledge management* (individual dispositions and behaviors);
- *Organizational knowledge management* (multi-national corporations, small-to-medium enterprises, governments, non-government organizations, educational institutions);
- *Sectoral knowledge management* (economic sectors such as information technology, pharmaceuticals, agriculture, indigenous culture, etc.);
- *National knowledge management* (national policies for stimulating innovative cultures within industry); and
- *Cultural knowledge management* (transcends and spans organizational, sectoral, and national boundaries).

In terms of outcomes, knowledge management could further be classified into outcomes that improve *efficiencies* and outcomes that stimulate *innovation*.

An International Standards Movement Has Developed

Perhaps the most visible activity in the e-knowledge world involves a comprehensive process of international collaboration in the development of standards and specifications for systems to manage and exchange learning content, process organizational knowledge, and support e-business transactions. Standards developments in applications interoperability have also advanced the growth of so-called "Web services" which will facilitate the development of seamlessly and easily integrated applications infrastructures.

The standards movement has been facilitating the birth of durable and transactable e-knowledge. The complex work of these standards groups has been far too arcane to engage the detailed attention of most professionals who are responsible in their organizations for knowledge management and learning. *But the strategic implications of standards for implementing processes, networks, and marketplaces for e-knowledge are clear: such standards assist in building and maturing e-knowledge marketplaces while also stimulating innovation in the use of transactable e-knowledge.* These issues should feature prominently in the planning of every enterprise for which knowledge is essential to competitive advantage.

Today's Vertical Channels for E-Content

Traditional Publishers and Direct-to-Digital Publishers—traditional publishers like Harcourt Brace, Pearson, Thomson and new direct-to-digital publishing enterprises

Course and Learning Management Systems—course materials held by WebCT, Blackboard, Click2learn, Outstart, and other applications

Universities and Colleges—university presses plus faculty course materials

Professional Societies and Associations—trade publications plus tradecraft-rich bodies of knowledge

Corporate Learning and Knowledge Management—private channels for proprietary content, off-the-shelf content, internal documents, white papers, and specifications

Components of Tomorrow's Horizontal Channels For e-Knowledge

Content/Context Repositories—discipline- and institution-specific repositories, plus marketplaces that aggregate content repositories into a meta-marketplace

Content Creation Tools—tools for creating and managing content/context through Learning and Content Management Systems (LACMS)

Value-Added Content Services—additional services that enhance the value of content and codified context in learning objects

Exchange Infrastructure—the marketplace exchange service that enables metering, repurposing, combining of content by demand aggregators, and direct users

Demand Aggregation/Syndication—enterprises that aggregate demand for e-knowledge, such as colleges and universities, professional societies and associations, and corporate learning (e.g., Emerald Now)

Aggregators are enterprises or organizations that aggregate or package learning content, such as MERLOT and Emerald Fulltext. Aggregation is also occurring at the institutional level, providing concentrations of intellectual capital.

Adapted from: Patrick McElroy, A New Paradigm for Acquiring, Managing, and Distributing Content in Higher Education Institutions, 2002.

The major standards efforts have involved participation by government, educational, and commercial enterprises. Early focal points have included standards for describing content and ensuring that it will work with other content and with all delivery systems ("interoperability" standards). Relevant groups include the IMS Global Learning Consortium, ADL, IEEE LTSC, Dublin Core, and MPEG. More recently, process standards have gained attention (WfMC and GKEC). In addition, the publishing, media, and technology industries have focused on standards for digital asset management—PRISM, XMCL, ebXML, XrML, ODRL.

At the end of the day, the standards developed by these groups, while important for implementers, may prove less significant for organizations than the visibility they have given to the requirements and potentials of the emerging e-Knowledge Industry. Moreover, they have been a powerful force for the development of a truly global perspective to the e-Knowledge Industry. In addition, while working together to develop learning object standards, professionals in these fields quickly discovered the *tactical* importance of mobilizing and unifying the energies of professionals in e-learning and knowledge management. Partnering with one another, they have achieved greater visibility than either e-learning or knowledge management would have achieved acting alone. Over time, the *strategic* importance of fusing e-learning and knowledge management will become abundantly clear to policy makers and practitioners alike.

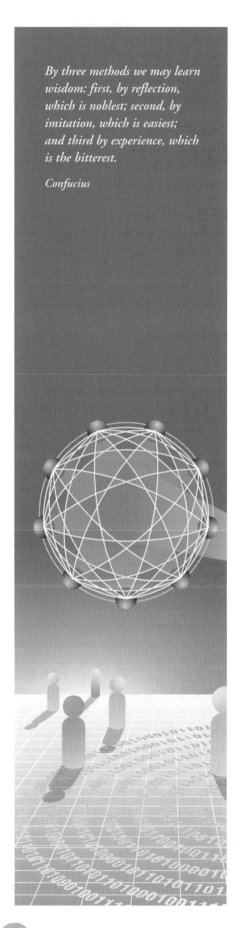

By three methods we may learn wisdom: first, by reflection, which is noblest; second, by imitation, which is easiest; and third by experience, which is the bitterest.

Confucius

Digital Marketplaces for e-Knowledge are Gestating

Today, proprietary, vertical channels for distributing e-knowledge have been initiated by traditional publishers, direct-to-digital publishers (purely digital), learning management system providers, and others. Globally, hundreds of different channels have developed using their own content repositories, proprietary authoring tools, and learning management systems. These channels have failed to attract a groundswell of users sufficient to effect cultural change. And they won't until proprietary silos are replaced by open, interoperable, and scaleable marketplace mechanisms for e-knowledge. These mechanisms will create "horizontal" channels that enable the combination and repurposing of content held by different publishers, learning content management systems, and digital content repositories in general.

Today's vertical channels are merely an evolutionary step in the migration path toward horizontal channels based on more robust, interoperable mechanisms for knowledge sharing. Today, the knowledge industry is very much like the computer industry in the 1980s as described by Andrew Grove (1998) in his book, *Only the Paranoid Survive*. The vertical, proprietary channels in the computer market were transformed by the shift to a horizontal computer marketplace that enabled cascading innovation, fast growth, keen competition, and reductions in price.

In the not-so-distant future, advances in e-knowledge will enable the creation of horizontal marketplaces in the Knowledge Industry. They will facilitate the seamless exchange of formally rendered, explicit, and tacit knowledge, slashing across today's publishing and intellectual property boundaries, while metering and paying for the use of intellectual property. Innovation, competition, growth, and cost reduction are likely to thrive as well.

The Power of e-Knowledge: From Value Chain to Value Net

The fundamental value chain of the Knowledge Economy is familiar and proven: the related and bi-directional processes of computation, cognition, context, and communication that create the hierarchy of data, information, and knowledge. Yet as leading-edge practitioners have applied network-based tools of knowledge management and sharing, they have discovered several transformative new insights.

First, e-Knowledge Chunks are Malleable, Expandable, and Fungible. e-Knowledge tools enable the unbundling, reprocessing, and repurposing of data, information, and knowledge in ways that can render them into other forms. Data becomes information when organized in a way to give it meaning; information is codified as knowledge when presented within a context. We say more on this subject later when we discuss new ways of experiencing e-knowledge. Conversely, codified knowledge can be decontextualized and disaggregated to form data-like chunks of content that can then be re-aggregated or re-purposed. The tools of e-knowledge can be used to combine content and context to create knowledge chunks that are malleable, expandable, and fungible (see graphic page 15).

Digital publishing technologies and extensive global networking—coupled with an increasing volume of scientific research and decreasing satisfaction with a dysfunctional economic model—change the fundamental structure of scholarly publishing by allowing its various components to be de-linked, both functionally and economically. When the functions are unbundled and begin to operate separately, each can operate more efficiently and competitively.

Raym Crow

Second, e-Knowledge Tools Enable the Reinvention of Processes and Relationships. e-Knowledge has a fundamental characteristic in common with e-business. The core principle of e-business is to change the way that enterprises conduct business, whatever that business may be. This translates into reinventing and transforming core processes, relationships, and cultures. Similarly, e-knowledge is about the use of technology to transform processes and relationships pertaining to the creation, nurturing, and management of knowledge. Over time, e-knowledge will create a breed of knowledge-sharing processes, relationships, and cultures that are much more than just more efficient versions of existing practices.

> *If we apply knowledge to tasks we already know how to do, we call it productivity. If we apply knowledge to tasks that are new and different, we call it innovation.*
>
> *Peter Drucker, 1999*

Third, e-Knowledge Transforms Value Chains into e-Knowledge Value Nets. The traditional view of the value chain follows the linear progressions of an Industrial Age product cycle. But the Knowledge Age has been changing all that: *disaggregating* and *disintermediating* traditional value chain relationships and *reintermediating* new relationships between market players. Don Tapscott (2001) introduced the term *polymediation* to herald the emergence of entirely new business entities and opportunities enabled by "digital capital." The richness in relationships combines vertical and horizontal supply chains to create what Patrick McElroy (2002) characterizes as a *"value net"* in referring to the e-knowledge space. This metaphor of a value net aptly captures the multi-dimensional, multi-directional opportunities for value creation, knowledge enhancement, and sharing in our e-knowledge future.

Power in the Printed Knowledge Age

Owners of various supply channels set the rules and control supply.

Demand aggregators have limited clout.

Digital publishing and print-on-demand are controlled by owners of vertical channels who set the rules and the practices.

New players cannot break into existing channels.

Power in the e-Knowledge Age

New supply channels empower the individual provider—faculty, researchers, practitioner—and communities of providers.

Demand aggregators enhance their clout, building on the power provided by their relationship with learners/consumers.

Traditional providers are "disintermediated" by individual faculty and learners using the marketplace to create digital products.

New organizational forms (formal and informal) evolve to support the creation and sharing of knowledge—communities of practice.

The e-Knowledge Industry Develops and Grows

The e-Knowledge Industry consists of the individuals and enterprises that create, store, and exchange digital content, add value to it, and/or aggregate content, and serve demand for e-knowledge. The e-Knowledge Industry includes publishers, new media companies, content developer companies, professional societies and associations, companies, colleges and universities, and other knowledge-creating enterprises. In addition, individual professionals, faculty, and practitioners are empowered by the emerging influence of e-knowledge to create their own content, knowledge, and insight and offer it for exchange.

Democratization, Empowerment, and New Choices.
In a very real sense, the e-Knowledge Industry is a powerful engine for democratization and empowerment. In the Information Age, publishers, colleges, and universities controlled the supply of vetted content. In the e-Knowledge Age, new market mechanisms will emerge, including free sources of content, context, and insight. Marketplaces will enable individual professionals, practitioners, faculty, and others to create and supply e-knowledge resources to augment the traditional supply channels.

New Roles, Responsibilities and Players.
The e-Knowledge Industry will provide new roles and responsibilities for existing players and encourage new players to come to the table. *e-Knowledge suppliers and aggregators* will be able to provide their content and encoded contexts to a wider range of audiences than offered through traditional vertical channels. *Value-added e-knowledge partners* will enrich content and context, providing a variety of useful services. *e-Knowledge demand aggregators* will be able to leverage their market power through aggregating demand among their clientele.

e-Knowledge users will include individuals and organizations. Their influence will be dramatically enhanced in the e-knowledge marketplace economy.

A Changing Enterprise Landscape.
Which organizations and enterprises will fill these roles over the next ten years? Existing learning, publishing, and knowledge management organizations? New subsidiaries of existing enterprises? Totally new enterprises? New kinds of communities of practice that cross traditional organizational boundaries? Cooperatives of free agents or amorphous peer-to-peer networks? New strategic alliances and collaborations? Only time will tell, and the outcomes may be surprising. The enterprise landscape of the e-Knowledge Industry in ten years time will likely be very different from the clusters of organizations and individuals that aspire to be major players in e-knowledge today.

Players in the e-Knowledge Industry

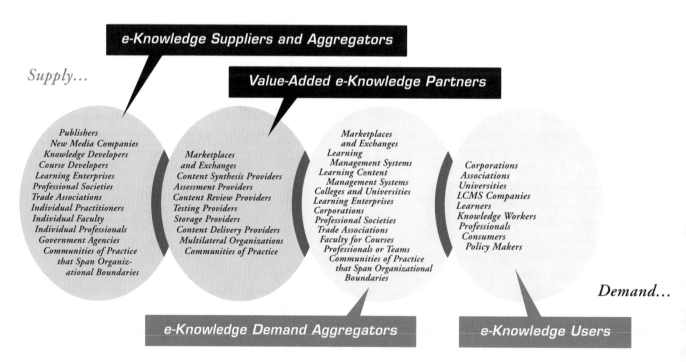

Adapted from: Patrick McElroy, *A New Paradigm for Acquiring, Managing, and Distributing Content in Higher Education Institutions,* 2002.

Pioneering Examples of e-Knowledge

- *Pervasive Computing Transforms Approaches to Elder Care*
- *Professional Society as Indispensable Knowledge Resource*
- *Universities Leverage Their Knowledge Resources*
- *Industry-wide Knowledge Sharing Enables German Industry to Compete*
- *Making e-Government Work*

Pervasive Computing Transforms Approaches to Elder Care

An e-knowledge approach can be combined with pervasive computing to improve our understanding of aging, to improve elder care, and to make some aspects of our own aging less problematic. Pervasive computing makes possible the collection of detailed, moment-by-moment data on user actions and contexts, wirelessly, anywhere and anytime. A global community of organizations is using this approach to gather data on the lives and needs of the elderly with a view to increasing their autonomy and quality of care.

One of the data capturing pioneers is Elite Care's Oatfield Estates in Milwaukee, Wisconsin, which has built pervasive computing into its living spaces. Residents carry dual-channel radio frequency locator tags that serve as their apartment key and emit periodic infrared pulses to the sensors in each room. Beds have embedded weight sensors. Each apartment has motion and health vitals sensors plus a networked computer with touch screen interface, enabling communication through e-mail, word processing, audio for speech recognition, and video conferencing using webcams. These systems and sensors feed personalized databases on each resident. Caregivers use these databases to monitor personal health, activity levels, and interactions with medical attention and status of medication. Managers use this knowl-

edge base to monitor staff performance. Residents use the personal history data, both theirs and others, to foster social interactions with other patients. This environment has changed the way that residents live. They have greater control and autonomy, knowing that if they become disoriented and wander, require emergency help, or fall behind in their medication, assistance will be forthcoming immediately. Caregivers and medical personnel do not need to manually record and enter patient data; they have access to a far richer knowledge base on each patient, easily accessed and arrayed.

While these developments bring immediate benefit to residents, their families, and caregivers, our primary interest is in the implications for e-knowledge. From the perspective of health professionals and policy makers, the data collected in such schemes can be merged with data being collected globally on patient health, activity, and care. Multiple analyses can be undertaken, ranging from pattern determination (e.g., as in epidemiology) to codification of "what works" in elder care, in repositories of grounded knowledge and tradecraft that can be used by caregivers and medical educators.

More futuristically, new forms of assisted living can be envisaged in which pervasive computing is combined with intelligent agent technology to compensate for declining cognitive facilities. An example is the difficulty that many people have in retaining their skill base and tacit knowledge as they age. Even when we are young, our ability to perform a task fluidly and automatically typically declines if we do not practice the task frequently. We become rusty. This loss of competence in relation to rarely-used knowledge may become more problematic as we age. Pervasive computing offers the prospect of regaining that knowledge on demand.

The important thing is not to stop questioning.

Albert Einstein

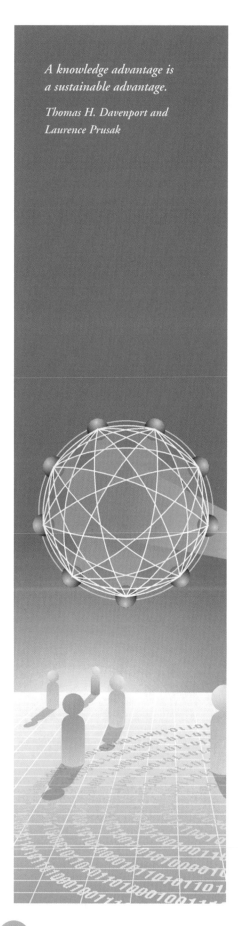

A knowledge advantage is a sustainable advantage.

Thomas H. Davenport and
Laurence Prusak

Pervasive computing provides mechanisms to capture and replay every aspect of what we know and what we do. This has implications for people throughout their lives. Important applications in elder care include empowering older people and enlarging the knowledge base of "what works" in assisted living.

In a possible scenario, our individual retirement plans would go beyond financial considerations to include provision for cognitive augmentation. If we learned a skill that we wanted to have available to us years later, we would use pervasive computing to assemble rich data on our peak level of performance on that skill. This could be possible through the combined use of webcams and data gloves. Webcams can capture video records of that performance from multiple vantage points (including what we see when we perform a task). Data gloves can capture data on how our hands and fingers move during performance of a task. The various data streams can be analyzed by "remembrance" agents to identify key elements that could be replayed years later to stimulate recall of the elements of that skilled performance. For example, recordings from data gloves might be replayed through force-feedback ("haptic") gloves to convey how it felt to perform the task. Prospectively, this could be shared with others immediately (to demonstrate what a skill entails), and used by us in later life (to re-establish our original level of competence).

As an indication of the wider implications, eldercare environments that use pervasive ICT are being progressively improved by outlinks from patients' facilities to their families and others. One result is that families can participate in the monitoring of their loved ones' progress, activities, and condition. They can also provide more frequent contact and interactivity through electronic communication and large-screen visual displays that enable resident and family to see one another. An unexpected outcome has been the involvement of elder care residents in family history projects and oral history projects involving children, grandchildren, and great- grandchildren. Such developments will be facilitated if pervasive computing is used routinely to capture day-to-day experiences in a whole-life diary.

Professional Society as an Indispensable Knowledge Resource

The American Association of Pharmaceutical Scientists is a professional society serving 4,000 pharmaceutical scientists as members and another 50,000 customers. AAPS has evolved a knowledge portal that members and non-member customers use to access the latest findings in research and practice in pharmaceutical science. Using the portal, users can create "my professional journal" using the portal's personalized search capabilities to assemble relevant data (author, title, key terms, etc.) on all recently published articles in topic areas that they can enumerate. Such data is typically stored as "metadata" following standards. Subscribers can extract not just the metadata/abstract, but the entire article—or in future, just key portions of it. AAPS began by digitizing its own journals, but has since added links to other scientific journals, including 20 from Elsevier. The personalized portal also features a specialized news service dealing in new developments in the field.

The future for the American Association of Pharmaceutical Scientists is to fuse education and knowledge experiences together so its members will be learning whenever they access the digital body of knowledge or use the portal to experience new developments in the field.

Jack Cox, CEO, American Association of Pharmaceutical Scientists, 2002

AAPS also has deployed communities of practice in both established and emerging subdisciplines in pharmaceutical sciences. It has a formal structure of scientific "sections" that provide content and program materials for AAPS's meetings and publications. AAPS also fosters the organic development of self-forming discussion groups in new, hybridized areas of interest, providing enterprise support as the groups achieve critical mass and demonstrate sustainable interest. At any one time, it has as many as 25 such groups incubating. A recently formed group on "Nutriceuticals" combines subject matter content spanning five sections, and focuses on the field of natural health products that desperately requires scientific, government, and public scrutiny. These communities of practice contribute to the perpetual development of new findings and insights in the field and to the development and learning of participating members.

AAPS has digitized and repurposed many of its learning materials into online resources, CDs, and other media. In addition to its formal programs and exchanges of information, AAPS creates many opportunities for meetings, seminars, and other face-to-face venues. In these settings, the formal programs are only half the value; the in-the-hall conversations between scientists sharing their latest insights or synthesis of new developments are equally value laden. In the future, AAPS sees its publishing and education programs fusing together. In this rapidly developing field

of pharmaceutical science, just-in-time knowledge on the latest developments is the vehicle for perpetual learning.

Universities Leverage Their Knowledge Resources Through Alliances

Alliances of universities for this purpose are not new. Achieving commercial success is another matter. The first generation of e-learning alliances, set up during the dot.com era with hopes of developing new income streams for universities, spent a great deal of money with little financial return. The lessons learned led to the establishment in the UK of a public-private partnership, e-Universities Worldwide Ltd ("e-U"). This is a collaborative alliance of knowledge organizations, including colleges and universities. The primary purpose of e-U is to enable UK providers of higher education to participate in the global e-learning market on a better basis than would be possible if they operated individually.

Initiatives such as the e-U show the way for universities to collaborate to exploit and share their knowledge to the benefit of all parties.

The chances of success have been raised by insistence on the establishment of:

- a common technical platform, jointly developed by a leading vendor (Sun) and compliant with all relevant standards, to ensure that no technical obstacles exist to developing courses in one institution and running them at another institution;
- a shared knowledge base on the effective use of that platform to meet needs in particular disciplines or to meet generic needs;
- processes to ensure that courses meet international standards of quality and are appropriately certified and recognized;
- development funds that individual insti-

If you can imagine it, it probably will happen. If you can imagine it, it probably already exists, somewhere.

Bruce Judson

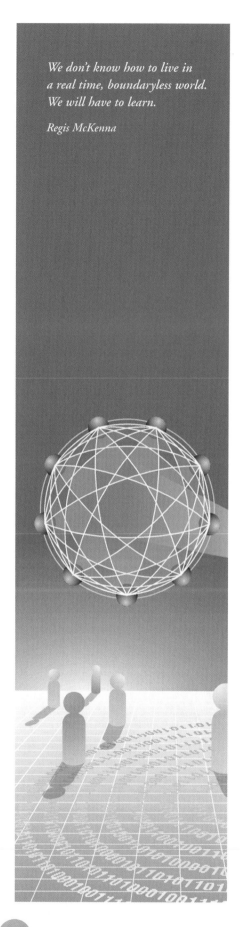

We don't know how to live in a real time, boundaryless world. We will have to learn.

Regis McKenna

tutions or consortia can bid for, to enable them to create or modify courses;
- business plans for each course;
- support for marketing globally, with options that include using e-Universities Worldwide as a shared brand, or marketing courses using the name of the originating institution(s); and
- a shared knowledge base on experiences in strategic positioning of courses and in marketing courses and managing their presentation, directly or through local agents.

Taken together, those approaches should help universities to determine the likely market for a proposed course, develop and update the course in a timely and cost-effective fashion, and maximize the market for their course and any derivatives of it.

The kinds of knowledge resources that are available to be leveraged in this initiative include *process knowledge* (know-how regarding the development of e-learning material); *subject-matter knowledge* (know-how regarding user needs in particular subject areas and for particular purposes); other *intellectual property* (ranging from research-derived knowledge, captured in patents or otherwise disclosed to specialist audiences, but potentially available for use in e-knowledge courses, products, and services); and *primary resources* (ranging from world experts who may be willing to participate in on-line discussions between students and mentors, to access to digitized versions of knowledge assets held in university museums and libraries).

We anticipate that initiatives such as the e-U will result in the development of follow-on opportunities, in which universities can work with third parties (e.g., publishers, corporate, universities) to become **e-knowledge suppliers** to a wider range of audiences than they can reach through their traditional channels. They may also be able to enrich the content and context of the offerings from other universities.

Industry-wide Knowledge Sharing Helps German Industry to Compete

The Fraunhofer Institute (Europe's largest R&D organization, with laboratories across Germany) is coordinating national strategy on knowledge-based manufacturing. Its goal is to enable companies in Germany and other parts of the European Union to compete more effectively across the world. Relative to the United States, for example, the key commercial challenges they face are an unfavorable exchange rate and an historic difficulty in getting sufficient return on the investment they make in designing new products. Their public strategy is to use knowledge management to tackle the second of these challenges. They aim to make it easier and more affordable for even small manufactures to incorporate innovations in their products that users will value (such as modifications tailored to each user.) By reducing the time-to-market of those innovations the initiative could maximize the time they can be competitive in the marketplace.

In a pilot project ending in 2001, German industry and the German government committed the equivalent of about US$30 million to a national project, coordinated by the Fraunhofer Institute, to explore ways to speed up the effective use of knowledge about advances in manufacturing. The approaches used included studies of knowledge codification and sharing at every stage in manufacturing, and the role of partner organizations, such as universities and training organizations, in the associated communities of practice.

German industry has invested the equivalent of US$30 million to a national project to explore ways to speed up the effective use of knowledge about advances in manufacturing. Larger follow-through projects are envisaged at the European level.

Those studies led to insights into some of the ways in which knowledge flows and organizational routines develop, both within individual companies and within supply chains. Perhaps more interestingly, they suggest that knowledge that is in scarce supply, such as the knowledge of leading designers, can be used within a community of practice to raise awareness of best practice and to then augment the capabilities of others. In this way, even modestly-trained staff can set more valued targets for themselves and can reach them.

Larger, follow-through projects are envisaged at the European level. Such ventures offer the prospect that entire segments of manufacturing industry could make use of shared libraries of expertise in key areas such as computer-aided design and manufacture, coupled with shared facilities for describing their capabilities, their products, and even individual components in sector-wide databases. Every part of this initiative requires consideration of the details as well as the vision. There has to be agreement about the sharing of knowledge and about the technical details of how knowledge will be described so that it can be updated, shared, and accessed via wide-area networks to be used both by computers and by human users. The role of standards is crucial here.

Today's high-wage economies, such as high-technology manufacturing, will not be sustainable unless they can make better use of knowledge about best practice and can meet global performance levels for the time and costs of operations. Agreement about the details of knowledge-sharing, and in particular the standards to be used to describe and share knowledge, is now seen as a key element in the success of knowledge-intensive organizations that work with other enterprises to develop products and services.

Making e-Government Work

As pervasive computing begins to impact all societies and economies, it enables not just new learning and knowledge management capabilities, but it also triggers the growth of government services.

For example, Michigan.gov, the State of Michigan's government services portal, has been widely acclaimed as raising the bar in terms of e-government. It has achieved this through delivering integrated access and clear benefits to all stakeholders—government departments, businesses, and citizens of the state. It has also achieved this through vision, leadership, and a willingness to transform the business processes of government by closely aligning the expertise required (at all organizational levels) with a strategic plan for service delivery. Giving customers what they want has been key, and so has recognition that transformation is an ongoing process.

With cost-savings and benefits to the customer in terms of timeliness and trusted information, Michigan.gov delivers everything from fishing licenses and camping ground reservations to schedules of legal hearings to comprehensive schooling directories, the granting of e-scholarships and personalized portals.

e-Government is integrating services delivery, thereby creating new experiences for citizens such as one-stop shopping for information and services. But even greater strides are being made in developing knowledge communities that enable government departments to resolve cross-cutting issues and engage with other departments and customers/citizens in formulating policies and services.

Meanwhile, and on a much grander scale, the UK Government is now consolidating a knowledge management framework that spans all levels of government and recognizes "knowledge communities" as the key to moving forward. The framework is building upon the earlier success of its e-Envoy's Knowledge Network. Launched in late 2000, the Knowledge Network has achieved a significant milestone in delivering real-time knowledge sharing between government departments. Efficiencies are not just being delivered in terms of timeliness but also in the handling of issues that require cross-departmental input and rationalization. Importantly, key industry players such as IBM, Cable and Wireless, and Lotus have also supported this initiative.

In a similar way to the UK's e-Envoy, the Australian National Office for the Information Economy is leading the introduction of integrated government service delivery. After launching a comprehensive Government Online Strategy in early 2000, it is now concerned with moving to the next phase of online services development. The issue is no longer about establishing government agency presence online but in delivering a return on investment through ensuring all stakeholders derive benefit from interoperable services.

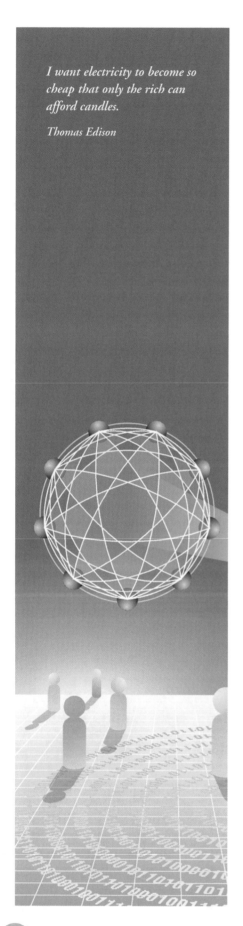

I want electricity to become so cheap that only the rich can afford candles.

Thomas Edison

Pervasive Technology Changes How We "Experience" Knowledge

What does it mean to "experience" knowledge? The answer can be both complex and highly personalized. Today, we experience knowledge through iterative cognitive processes of definition, search, interpretation, understanding, and assimilation. In these processes, we select from a wide and diverse range of sources, tools, and interactions. Engaging knowledge is largely a conscious, willful process.

Wireless will make computing more sociable. Instead of going to some corner or finding some special place to log on, you can stay where you are, with other people, while you connect. It becomes a shared activity, like watching television, rather than an individual one.

Esther Dyson, 2002

The Experience Can Be as Important as the Knowledge Gained

The experience of engaging knowledge is often equally as important to the knowledge seeker as the actual enhancement and/or application of knowledge achieved—sometimes more so. We have each developed our own approaches for searching for, acquiring, engaging, and assimilating knowledge from a range of sources. The experience of engaging knowledge has been shaped by social and organizational norms, past experiences, personal preferences, and other factors. Individuals select a particular mixture of knowledge-engaging experiences based on the process's effectiveness and the satisfaction they achieve through the experience. Years of knowledge seeking develops ingrained habits of mind, body, and spirit that can be difficult to re-pattern.

Limitations to Experiencing Knowledge—and Overcoming Them. The effectiveness and efficiency of knowledge management experiences have been limited by the personal ability of individuals to process knowledge. At the same time, they are constrained by the limitations of the technical interfaces and support systems that enable the individual to access knowledge, sort and sift through alternative sources, and select and assimilate the knowledge suited to their needs and/or preferences.

The first generation of e-knowledge exchange looks and feels like more highly digitized versions of yesterday's knowledge resources. Today's state-of-the-art of knowledge repositories, search engines, intelligent agents, expert evaluations of knowledge resources, syntheses of knowledge, and community of practice support tools represent prototypes of the knowledge marketplaces of tomorrow. They demonstrate proof of concept but not a quantum leap to a new level of knowledge engagement experience.

While PCs and workstations have come under some criticism for "tethering" knowledge workers to their desks, wireless technologies may be the perfect answer for mobilizing the workforce by letting them capture and harness key information and knowledge attributes wherever they are, whenever they want, and however they want. Strategies focused on knowledge mobilization via handheld devices and wireless networks—ranging from pocket PCs and cell phones to WLANS and RFID tags—can take knowledge management to an entirely new plane of performance, putting road warriors and field workers in the center of the information and communications world via mobile portals and on-demand expert services."

Madanmohan Rao, 2002

What will move us to that new level? We need to make life simpler for learners and for teachers/mentors. We can help them to make far more sense of the world and to deploy far more of their taken-for-granted knowledge (like their ability as children to make intuitive judgments using feedback from their eyes and their hands as they build a model from a kit of parts). In education today, it is all too common to be faced by an over-full syllabus of doubtful worth, including many tasks that make little sense or have already been mastered , hence the prevalence of rote learning and surface (rather than deep) learning. The incidence of such pathologies will decrease hugely if teachers and learners have ready access to ways to simplify the world and to speed up our coming-to-grips with new information.

Tools now exist to reduce complexity and increase our understanding of what we do. Educationalists take surprisingly little account of this. By contrast, industry is quick to adopt such tools, since they can simplify tasks that were previously the province of world experts but are now possible for less-skilled people, at speed. An example is drug design, where chemists want to know whether it would be easy or hard to synthesize a prospective new molecule from possible pre-cursor components. They can tell this if the available data gets presented in ways that allow them to use sight and touch. Drug design then becomes almost analogous to a child playing with Lego™ bricks. Chemists can look at the shape of each possible component, juxtapose them to see if they look as if they might fit, then wear feedback gloves to see whether the components "snap" together.

Such visualization tools provide an illustration of emerging and more powerful ways to engage quickly and effectively with data, information, and knowledge. Quantum leaps in the knowledge experience await the deployment in education of a combination of ready access to tools that increase our engagement with the knowledge that our society needs us to have, plus tools that allow us to more readily share knowledge, spot gaps in our knowledge, and then find suppliers of that knowledge (or if necessary, create new knowledge). Wide access to such tools is becoming more and more likely because of several trends: the commodification of those tools is making them affordable; the emergence of pervasive technology environments; new capabilities of the World Wide Web, including the Semantic Web; and, the next generation of knowledge-sharing tools. These advances will enable knowledge sharing to achieve the accelerated ease of use necessary for true transformation to be achieved.

Achieving Amenity in Knowledge Sharing. This less-than-revolutionary performance of first-wave technologies is a familiar pattern. History has shown that transformative deployment and application of technology takes time. In the near future we can expect faster, better, cheaper, and more engaging versions of knowledge-sharing technologies, infrastructures, and protocols to emerge. Even more importantly, the technology will become convenient, easy, and reliable. But it will be over time that knowledge sharing environments will achieve ***amenity.*** John Seely Brown asserts that when technology achieves amenity, it becomes invisible. It becomes part of the user's world, and the user is absorbed into its world, easily, and seamlessly.

W. Brian Arthur has observed that the Knowledge Revolution is in the early stages of amenity-building. Arthur points out that it took automobiles roughly half a century to reach amenity through the

In theory there is no difference between theory and practice. In practice there is.

Jan L.A. van de Snepscheut

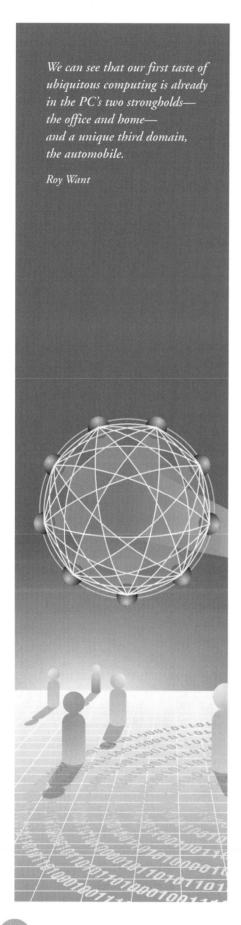

We can see that our first taste of ubiquitous computing is already in the PC's two strongholds—the office and home—and a unique third domain, the automobile.

Roy Want

development of highway infrastructures, rules, and protocols, safe and easy-to-use equipment, and a host of other amenities of driving. Other, earlier revolutions like steam power and railroads followed similar patterns.

A revolution doesn't really arrive until we structure our activities around the new technology—and the new technology adapts to us by becoming easy to use.

W. Brian Arthur, March 2002

Pervasive Computing

The predominant vision of ICT has focused on the development of mobile personal digital devices. Laptop and notebook computers, personal digital assistants, mobile telephone, and evolving generations of hybridized devices have enabled individuals to carry knowledge around with them and plug into wired or wireless networks to access knowledge repositories and communications. Every day, mobile digital devices are extending the capacity of individuals to communicate and engage knowledge anytime, any place.

An alternative vision of ICT development holds even greater promise for transforming the knowledge experience. The late Marc Weiser and his colleagues championed the vision of **ubiquitous computing** in which cheap, low-power computers with convenient displays are embedded into our everyday environments—homes, work, schools, automobiles, and public places. These devices are linked by wired/wireless networks and supported by applications software. This ubiquitous atmosphere of computing will pervade common places and interact with personal digital devices and/or computing devices carried or imbedded in clothing. Pervasive computing will include sensing and recognition technologies that can deal with many inputs, including data, acoustics,

image, motion and gestures, light, heat, moisture, and pressure. New kinds of unobtrusive interfaces between the physical and virtual world will be deployed to support these environments.

Pervasive computing could be the migration path for blending the physical and virtual worlds, achieving amenity. It will support many kinds of interfacing/communications—including speaking, gestures, and writing, not just keyboard and mouse through graphical user interface. Many inputs will be sensed automatically with no required human action or intervention. New kinds of **ambient displays** will be less demanding of our attention, enabling us to engage knowledge peripherally or even subconsciously. Supported by new developments in the World Wide Web, pervasive computing will dramatically change the manner in which we experience knowledge.

The most profound technologies are those that disappear. They weave themselves into the fabric of everyday life until they're indistinguishable from it.

Marc Weiser, 1991

Demonstration environments for pervasive computing have been developed for workplaces like Xerox PARC, homes, and museums. As individuals enter these environments, they are immediately recognized and authenticated, thereby triggering the availability of communication and/or knowledge resources. The individuals can engage a variety of displays ranging in size from an inch (pagers, phones and small, embedded devices), to a foot (screens of notebook computers, personal digital assistants of various kinds) to a yard (smart whiteboard-like devices). The engagement can be any combination ranging from peripheral to fully focused, using keyboard, speech, gesture, or other means.

New Terms and Concepts

Mobile computing is the use of mobile devices, such as laptop, notebook computers, or personal digital assistants to engage in communications and computing wherever the devices can access wireless networks.

Pervasive computing, or ubiquitous computing, involves an interconnected archipelago of computing devices embedded in environments and communicating with one another and with mobile computing devices.

Ambient computing refers to the characteristic of pervasive computing that makes it an integral part of the environment, surrounding, encompassing and available.

This is today. Tomorrow's pervasive knowledge settings will significantly extend the comfort level of today's knowledge user. The film *Minority Report* provides a stunningly dramatic representation of how individuals in the mid-twenty-first century may be able to use pervasive knowledge environments to engage, manipulate, and assimilate a virtual avalanche of knowledge in pictorial, graphical, text, and audio forms. In the movie, investigators are able to stand before receptor screens and, using sensor-studded gloves, manipulate, arrange, and combine images, text, and other information on a just-in-time basis. In minutes, they investigate, analyze, synthesize, and launch action that would take hours or days using today's techniques of knowledge management and decision support. Most of the technologies needed to implement this already exist and the remainder are under research and development. No person watching this representation can doubt that the patterns and cadences of the knowledge experience are on the threshold of the Knowledge Age equivalent of a sea change.

Revolutionizing the Knowledge Experience

So, how will we *experience* knowledge ten years from today—a world of pervasive computing, the Semantic Web, content marketplaces, and tradecraft-rich communities of practice?

Places to Experience Knowledge. Today, mobile computing and wireless communication with cellular telephones enable us to communicate, compute, and use knowledge anyplace with wireless service. But limitations in bandwidth, existing interfaces, and our lack of insight into how best to use wireless environments limit the nature of the knowledge sharing experience. Wireless environments are at the pilot stage of development, but they hold great promise for enabling new kinds of work and learning experiences in the near future.

In our future knowledge sharing environments, we will be able to engage in robust wireless knowledge sharing virtually anywhere with greater bandwidth and genuine amenity. Pervasive computing environments will be available in environments such as our automobiles, schools, homes, workplaces, and museums; other public settings like malls, community centers, and government service centers will provide pervasive computing capabilities in selected areas.

The film *Minority Report* also provided an unnerving snapshot of the potential intrusive nature of pervasive technology environments. Passersby in shopping areas were recognized and accosted by personalized advertisements for goods and services, based on past shopping preferences and other personal insights. In *World Without Secrets,* Richard Hunter points out the difficulty of maintaining privacy in the coming world of ubiquitous computing. In a world of pervasive knowledge sharing, we will all want to have the capacity to cloak our identities at certain times we choose.

The technology required for ubiquitous computing comes in three parts: cheap, low-power computers that include equally convenient displays, software for ubiquitous applications and a network that ties them all together.

Marc Weiser

Pervasive Ambient Environments

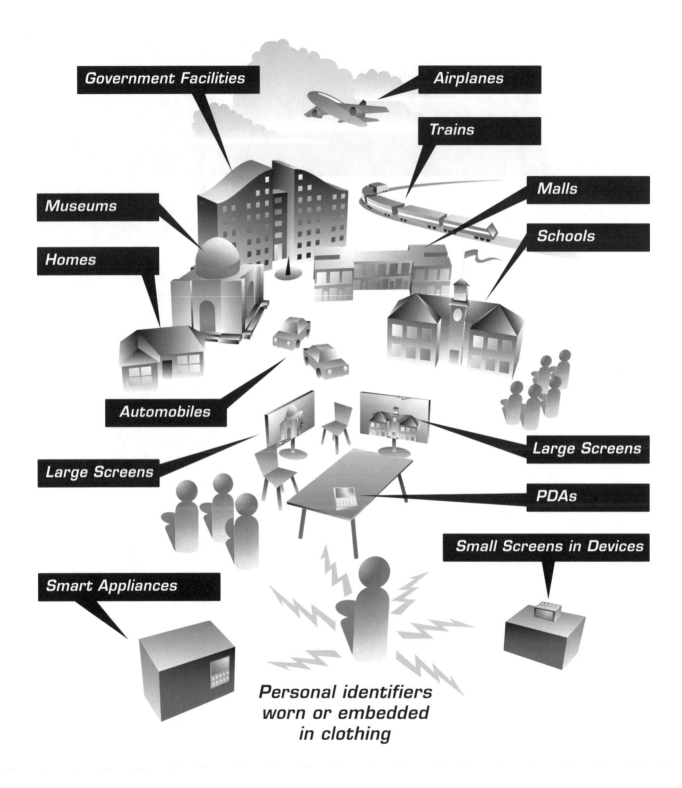

Changing How We Experience Knowledge

Dimensions	Today's Experience	Future Experiences
Places to Experience Knowledge	*Mobile computing/communication with laptops, PDAs, and cellular telephones enable communication, computing, and sharing knowledge anyplace served by wireless. Current bandwidth limitations restrict what can be shared.*	*Almost everyone will engage in robust wireless knowledge sharing virtually anyplace with greater bandwidth and amenity. Pervasive computing environments will exist in selected public and private settings—homes, offices, cars, and parts of museums, malls, and government facilities.*
Interface with Knowledge Sources	*Most people share knowledge through traditional interfaces—conversation, books, and other physical representations. GUI interfaces with laptops, PDAs and cell phones provide access to digital explicit knowledge.*	*People will experience far more numerous, capable, and high amenity interfaces with digital resources. They will interact through speech, handwriting, gestures, and/or keyboarding. Output will be received via mobile, ambient, and personal displays. More graphics, simulations, schematics, and syntheses will be available.*
Intensity of Engagement with Knowledge Sources	*Today's knowledge sources require concentration on keyboard/mouse and GUI display. Full attention is required.*	*Future knowledge users will engage knowledge in a variety of intensities ranging from ambient/peripheral to directed/highly engaged. Knowledge users will deploy agents and knowledge management tools to support their engagement. The physical act of engaging knowledge will be more intense, enabling users to engage, manipulate, and combine an avalanche of images, text, audio, and other media.*
Time Sequence for Accessing Knowledge	*Knowledge search, acquisition, and synthesis all take time. Just-in-time knowledge access is possible for simple knowledge from known sources.*	*Users will access an increasing range of knowledge on a just-in-time basis, including complex knowledge combinations. The shelf life of knowledge will decline.*
Reliance on Agents, Expert Advice, Synthesis	*Today's first-generation intelligent agents and digital repositories are not widely used. No content marketplaces are fully operational yet.*	*Many knowledge users rely heavily on plentiful, powerful agents. Heavy usage of marketplaces, peer reviewed knowledge repositories, and syntheses of expert opinion.*
Ability to Multi-Task Knowledge Streams	*High "coefficient of friction" in processing knowledge and multi-tasking. Personal knowledge bandwidth gets filled quickly. Individuals are limited in their capacity to process and share knowledge.*	*Time, effort, and "coefficient of friction" of knowledge processing are dramatically reduced. Various modes and levels of intensity of engagement expand options for multi-tasking.*
Amenity of the Knowledge Experience	*Traditional means of acquiring knowledge have achieved amenity— books, conversation, other print media, TV, video. Digital means of knowledge processing are difficult to use and distinct.*	*Engagement of digital knowledge will fully achieve amenity and integration into the daily lives of active knowledge navigators.*

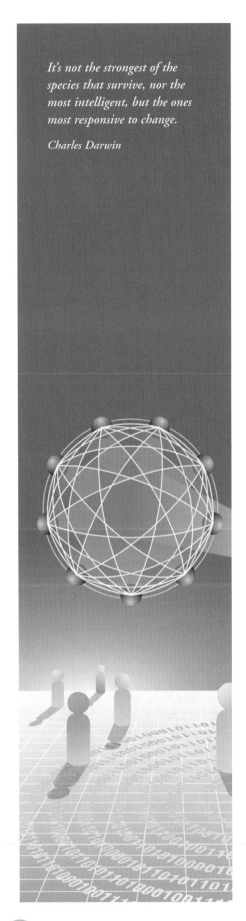

It's not the strongest of the species that survive, nor the most intelligent, but the ones most responsive to change.

Charles Darwin

Interfaces with Knowledge Sources. Today, knowledge is made available through conversation, books, other physical representations, and graphical user interfaces with digital sources of explicit knowledge.

In the future, individuals will enjoy more numerous and capable interfaces with digital resources. The range of interface options with digital knowledge will increase dramatically. Individuals will communicate with digital devices through speech, handwriting, gestures, and/or keyboarding. Output will be received on a wider variety of ambient, mobile, or personal displays. Moreover, the communication with digital resources will encompass tacit and explicit knowledge, conveyed in images, speech, text, graphics, and multiple media at once.

A far richer combination of schematic, graphics, simulations, and syntheses of knowledge will be used to array knowledge relationships. Individuals and groups working on projects will be able to arrange, display, and manipulate complex combinations of knowledge in a variety of amenable ways. Previous generations developed skills in manipulating and presenting knowledge. Future generations will hone greater skills in analyzing, reframing, utilizing, and sharing knowledge—at a faster pace and in real time.

Intensity of Engagement with Knowledge Sources. Today's prevailing model of engagement with digital knowledge resources requires concentration on a keyboard and mouse communication through a GUI display. Attention is required and actions taken on the body of knowledge are consciously directed.

In our Knowledge Age future, individuals will engage knowledge sources in a variety of modes ranging from ambient/peripheral to direct/highly engaged. Moreover, the capability to deploy agents to perform knowledge searches and aggregation will facilitate brief periods of engagement fol-

lowed by movement to other tasks while the searches and aggregation are conducted. The physical act of engaging knowledge will be more intense, enabling users to engage, manipulate, and combine an avalanche of images, text, audio, and other media.

Time Sequence for Accessing Knowledge. Today, most knowledge is pre-acquired and collected for decision-making, product development, and policymaking. The shelf life of decisions is set by the timeframes for change in the environment and timeframe to assemble knowledge necessary for decisions.

In our future, we will develop the capacity to seek and manipulate knowledge with great fluidity and speed. To a far greater extent than today, users will acquire and use knowledge on a just-in-time basis. Plain language communication with expert/executive data warehouses will become common practice for managers, analysts, customer service representatives, and even consumers. Alternative sources and perspectives can be considered, selected, and/or abandoned rapidly. The shelf life of need-to-know knowledge and the time to make knowledge-based decisions will decline dramatically. The knowledge assimilation and decision-making experiences will fuse and change substantially.

Reliance on Agents, Expert Advice, Synthesis. Today's generation of agents and search engines are puny in comparison with the knowledge-seeking tools and the knowledge repositories that will emerge over the coming five to ten years. In our future, these agents will be pervasive, powerful, and plentiful. Moreover, the knowledge repositories and marketplaces they access will be extensive and easily used.

Having all the information in the world at one's fingertips is a curse, not a blessing, for most individuals. Consequently, most individuals will rely heavily on vetted (refereed) sources of information, proven marketplaces, and syntheses of insight provided by recognized experts. Even when they use agents to collect knowledge and insight, many individuals will direct the agents to favor vetted sources.

Ability to Multi-task Knowledge Streams.
Today's knowledge navigators quickly fill their personal knowledge-processing bandwidths. Multi-tasking is limited severely by the state of today's knowledge tools.

The combination of high amenity interfaces, ambient resources, agents, and peer-reviewed knowledge marketplaces will dramatically reduce the time required for knowledge search and synthesis. Knowledge navigators will be able to draw upon more streams of knowledge at one time without overwhelming their limited attention capacity.

Amenity of the Knowledge Experience.
Amenity has been achieved by traditional means of acquiring and sharing knowledge—conversation, books, newspapers, other print media, television, video, and the like. These media usually fit seamlessly into our lives. On the other hand, today's experience of engaging digital knowledge is still uncomfortable and distinct from one's other activities.

In our future, engagement with digital knowledge will acquire amenity. The physical interfaces, means of interacting, languages, and other aspects of the knowledge experience will be familiar and easy. In some cases they be peripheral, indistinguishable, even involuntary. For knowledge denizens buying into accelerated knowledge sharing, pervasive interactivity and knowledge engagement will be as much a part of life as breathing.

The Challenge of Accommodating Different Knowledge Experiences

As we enter this brave new world of quantum leaps in the velocity and acceleration of knowledge assimilation, a

variety of challenges will emerge. The greatest will be the divide between what Marc Prensky labels "digital natives" (net or digital generation people), who are comfortable with using digital tools to accelerate ways of experiencing knowledge, and "digital immigrants" (some generation X people and most Baby Boomers), who are programmed to experience knowledge in slow, sequential, and long-shelf-life ways. As digital natives embrace the new ways of experiencing knowledge, think of the existing gaps that will become chasms in our organizations—between managers and front-line workers, between faculty and learners, between boards of directors and staffs. To a greater extent than we previously thought, people can acquire new ways of thinking and experiencing knowledge. But it is hard work. The easy part of the e-knowledge revolution will be developing the infrastructures, tools, processes, and competencies for e-knowledge use among the ***digerati.*** The harder task will be for organizations to enable and incentivize both digital natives *and* digital immigrants to embrace new ways of experiencing knowledge.

New Experiences Shape New Behaviors, Practices, and Social Groupings

How will new ways of experiencing knowledge change the behavior and social patterns of knowledge-seeking individuals and enterprises in the Knowledge Age? And how could that lead to new social and economic structures and processes based on knowledge? The following practices of people on the leading edge of the Knowledge Age may yield some clues.

Swarming. Preteens in Finland, young professional in Korea, and Senate staffers in Washington D.C. all have one thing in common: they swarm. Swarming is the behavior pattern of groups of amorphous groups of cell phone users who communicate to one another about where the best

The real danger is not that computers will begin to think like men, but that men will begin to think like computers.

Sydney Harris

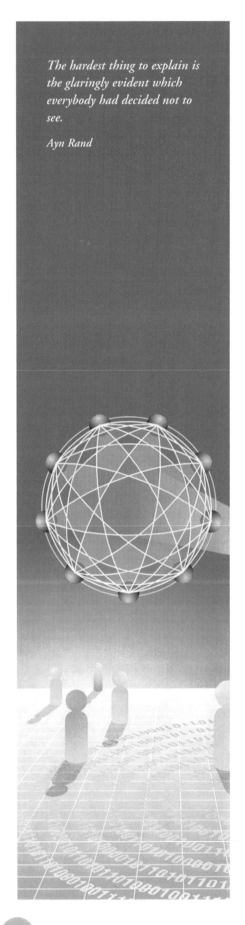

The hardest thing to explain is the glaringly evident which everybody had decided not to see.

Ayn Rand

Digital Natives (Net or Digital Generation)	Digital Immigrants (Baby Boomers, Some Generation X)
• Receive information fast, use Internet as first source	• Slower processing of information, use Internet after other sources
• Parallel process, multi-task	• Sequential processing, focus on single tasks
• Prefer to understand data through non-verbal interactions, such as simulations	• Prefer to understand data through use of hard-won expertise in data manipulation via spreadsheets and similar tools
• Prefer graphics before their text	• First text, then graphics
• Random access via hypertext	• Step-by-step access
• Prefer to access problems through games rather than "serious "work	• Work and learning are serious endeavors

Adapted from: Marc Prensky, Digital Natives, Digital Immigrants, *2002.*

party is, what movie they all want to see, or which of several meetings they need to attend, then swarm together in response to the information. It's all about finding the best experience. Networks of swarmers are leaderless, responding to information and interactivity. Swarming can be frivolous or deadly serious. In Edinburgh, a network of avid female swarmers descends on whatever local nightspot Prince William is reported to be patronizing. On the other hand, Philippine President Joseph Estrada was done in by "smart mobs" organized by swarming for the purpose of protesting his massive corruption. The U.S. military has even commissioned a study on "Swarming and the Future of Conflict." Swarming occurs in both physical (cell phone or pager messages stimulate the swarm) and virtual (e-mail or IM messages attract virtual visitors) environments.

Blogging and Klogging. Blogging is short for "Web logging," a practice that's taken off in the past year or so, and now involves hundreds of thousands of practitioners. Bloggers create a personal Web page with notes, comments, news-feeds, and ideas on things they consider important.

They update these notes and ideas frequently and engage interested viewers to converse back-and-forth on those points. While some blogs aren't much more than online diaries, others include interesting insights and tradecraft, and knowledge relating to a person's job. These so-called "knowledge blogs," or *klogs,* begin to look like something that could be a valuable component of a knowledge network of community of practice. They may be especially useful as a mechanism for surfacing new ideas, which the community of practice could evaluate and promote for further consideration.

Peer-to-Peer (P2P) Interactions. The most well known example of P2P music exchange software is Napster, which enables distributed users to share the music contained on their machines with a distributed network of other others/contributors. Other examples of P2P functionality include the Intel Philanthropic Peer-to-Peer program which linked two million PCs around the world to support medical research. The Groove provides encrypted, shared space that can be used for workgroup collaboration among distributed, P2P participants in communities of practice, corporate sales forces, or other dispersed groups of users. P2P interactions are a key element of communities of practice and will be a central feature, in some form, of tomorrow's knowledge sharing environments.

In the area of P2P technologies for learning, the Knowledge Management Research Group in Stockholm have participated in the development of Edutella, a search service based upon context descriptions. It is an educational application that is a prototype for learning on the Semantic Web and designed to enrich the Semantic Web with a "Conceptual Web." Its "driving vision is a learning web infrastructure which will make it possible to exchange/annotate/organize and personalize/navigate/use/reuse modular learning resources, supporting a variety of courses, disciplines and universities." (Nilsson, et al. 2002).

Sources and Reading on "Experiencing Knowledge" and Changing Behaviors and Practices

W. Brian Arthur. 2002. Is the Information Revolution Dead? If History Is a Guide, It Is Not. *Business 2.0,* March, 65–72.

John Seely Brown. 2000. *The Social Life of Information.* San Francisco: Jossey Bass.

Joel Garreau. 2002. Cell Biology: Like the Bee, This Evolving Species Buzzes and Swarms. *Washington Post,* July 31.

Jennifer Hoffman. 2002. Peer-to-Peer: The Next Hot Trend in e-Learning? *Learning Circuits,* February 16.

Intel Philanthropic Peer-to-Peer Program. www.intel.com/cure/overview.htm

Mikael Nilsson, Matthias Palmér & Ambjörn Naeve. 2002. Semantic Web Metadata for e-Learning—Some Architectural Guidelines. *WWW2002 Proceedings.* kmr.nada.kth.se/papers/SemanticWeb/p744-nilsson.pdf

George Partington. 2002. Blogging: Electronic Postings and Links Push Information to the Surface. *Worldcom.com,* July 26.

Otis Port. 2002. The Next Web. *Business Week,* March 4, 96–102.

Marc Prensky. 2001. Digital Natives, Digital Immigrants. *On the Horizon,* November/December.

Mikela Tarlow. 2002. *Digital Aboriginal—The Direction of Business Now: Instinctive, Nomadic, and Ever-Changing.* New York: Warner Books.

Knowledge workers will depend on vibrant communities of practice and peer-to-peer networks to engage in a rapid-fire, perpetual exchange of ideas and insights involving their tradecraft. Tacit knowledge and insight will be cultivated and shared to a greater degree and with greater velocity than is possible today. New ideas will churn and be evaluated by the community.

Evolving New Behaviors to Support e-Learning and Knowledge Management. The future social/collaborative/community environments and behaviors of the Knowledge Age will evolve over time, shaped by the "pull" of knowledge seekers needs, rather than the "push" of technologists or dot.coms' latest offering *du jour.* Various kinds of communities of practice will be the epicenters of development.

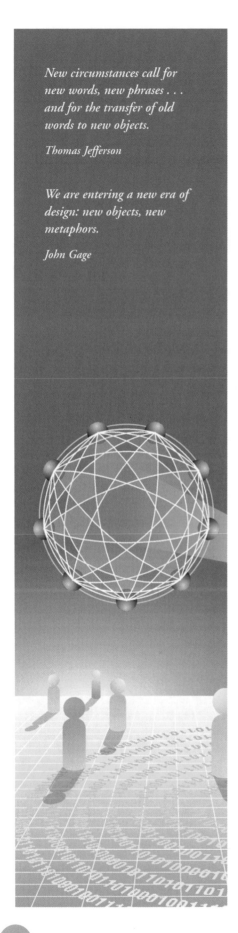

Beyond Existing Knowledge Concepts and Experiences

Today's pioneering examples are state-of-the-art practices. Our challenge is to move beyond these existing concepts and experiences to envision a world in which our knowledge experiences and competencies will be dramatically different from the here and now.

Moving Beyond Digitizing and Webifying Existing Practices

In applying the tools of ICT to any field of endeavor, the organization's first inclination is to digitize and Webify existing content, processes, and practices , as it has been with learning and knowledge management. But after digitizing course packs, texts, technical manuals, and organizational procedures, practitioners have begun to understand how to use ICT tools to create new forms, processes, and practices for learning and knowledge management. The early forms of new practices are being invented, but they need unifying and guiding principles.

Observing this process yields an important insight: individuals are the "heroes" of process transformation. Individual practitioners typically are the ones who see that merely digitizing existing practices does not reap the expected dividends. Organizational routines, principles, and practices have substantial inertia. Changes are typically originated by individuals—change-agents who are experienced practitioners, whose insights into practice enable them to understand how successful examples of innovation can be used to change the organization.

The Danger of Misappropriating Terms and Concepts

A common scene is repeated every day in virtually every knowledge-driven enterprise ranging from universities to corporations to professional societies. Leaders listen to discussions of transformational uses of knowledge networks, communities of practice, content marketplaces, and similar concepts and respond with the observation, *"Oh, that's just another term for what we've been doing for years."* Or, *"we've always had a community of practice."* Or, *"we wrote the book on knowledge networks."* These contentions are likely to be false. One of the greatest dangers facing knowledge enterprises is having the terms and concepts of knowledge transformation misappropriated and misused. But this is a predictable downside to the Knowledge Age brought about by our immersion in information-rich environments that can give rise to information overload and organizational knowledge *mis*-management.

To create a genuine e-knowledge revolution requires changes in our world view of knowledge and how it is experienced. It also requires new terminology and fresh metaphors to describe knowledge and the knowledge ecology of organizations.

e-Knowledge Has Much in Common with the Practices of e-Business

e-Business is more than e-commerce. It is the use of ICT to transform the way organizations conduct business. e-Business practices have transformed practices and processes in every industry they have touched. e-Business enables enterprises to fundamentally change their relationships with customers, members, learners, suppliers/partners, and/or other stakeholders. In the process, enterprises create new blends of physical and virtual resources and experiences that have never before been possible.

Like e-business, e-knowledge uses ICT to transform relationships, processes, and value propositions relating to the creation, management, and sharing of knowledge. This is a good place to begin: with the expectation that e-knowledge will dramatically transform processes and practices. But the upside of e-knowledge extends further to enhance our capacity to advance knowledge and even wisdom.

New Visions, New Terms, New Experiences, and New Behaviors

Transformation often requires a new vocabulary. Old words carry the baggage of established, implicit meanings. The same is true for existing disciplinary and topical constructs and familiar organizational structures. Learning and knowledge management have well understood meanings today. As they change into something quite different from today's practice, what new visions, terms, and practices will be necessary?

And what new experiences? How can we develop new knowledge patterns in the large segments of the workforce and learning force whose mental patterns and preferences are well established, even entrenched in a slow, sequential, patterned approach to learning and knowledge assimilation? How can we use our anticipation of these emerging conditions to accelerate and shape their development and prepare for a future for e-knowledge that improves ourselves, our institutions, and our society?

Transformation will require new competencies and behaviors from knowledge workers of all kinds. For example, we need to dramatically enhance our capacity to cultivate and share tacit knowledge, especially the tradecraft and bits of know-how relating to learning in context. The new patterns of behavior that evolve over the next few years—be they a supercharged version of swarming and klogging, conducted in peer networks and communities of practice, or something altogether different—are likely to surprise us. It's less important that we be able to precisely predict that new behavior. Rather, we need to be able to cultivate and nurture it.

Uses of Foresight About e-Knowledge

Transforming e-Knowledge aims to motivate reflective foresight on the future of e-knowledge. Richard A. Slaughter (2002) of the Australian Foresight Institute identifies three kinds of foresight:

- **Pragmatic foresight** is the most common, directed at simply carrying out today's business better. Foresight can be used to yield greater efficiency and productivity in a straightforward manner.
- **Progressive foresight** is different, containing an explicit commitment to systemic improvement. It is linked to efforts to reform business practices in view of wider social and environmental concerns. Reinventing processes, products, and services to achieve these goals is the essence of progressive foresight.
- **Civilizational foresight** takes yet another leap into the future, seeking to understand the characteristics of the next level of civilization, lying beyond the current configuration of technology/industrial/capitalistic interests and paradigms. It is based on the view that we are involved in long-term shifts towards a more sustainable world. Using the civilizational foresight lens forces us to question the worldviews and paradigms that will drive future society and its enterprises.

The chart on the following page compares and contrasts some of the changes that the future of transformative e-knowledge will hold.

Slaughter's framework below can serve as a guide to our foresight about e-knowledge in the following ways.

Pragmatic e-Knowledge Foresight	Progressive e-Knowledge Foresight	Civilizational e-Knowledge Foresight
Individuals and organizations can use foresight of e-knowledge to improve the efficiency and productivity of existing learning and knowledge management practices.	*Guided by progressive foresight, individuals and organizations can begin to reinvent and innovate processes and practices for learning and knowledge management.*	*In visioning our e-knowledge futures, a key consideration should be the capacity to use global e-knowledge to reach a higher plane of sustainable development and societal well-being.*
Individuals and enterprises can take immediate actions that will accelerate their readiness for e-knowledge and improve existing circumstances.	*Individuals and enterprises can build the perspectives and competencies that will lead to significant, progressive change.*	*Our visions of the e-knowledge future should engage a wide range of possibilities, including transformational change.*

The First Steps: Embryonic e-Knowledge Takes Root

- **Vision:** *In its infancy, e-knowledge is a digitized, Webified extension of today's practices.*

- **Digitize existing sources** *of data, information and knowledge, using existing concepts, definitions, and paradigms.*

- **Learning objects** *contain codified content.*

- **Learning object-based content** *for courses focuses on text and course pack-type materials.*

- **Explicit learning objects** *are the primary supporting element of emerging e-learning.*

- **Proprietary, vertical channels** *serve to aggregate content (publishers, disciplinary content repositories, learning management systems, and associations).*

- **Consumers are frustrated** *in their efforts to create personalized aggregations of e-knowledge.*

- **Publishers control** *the capacity of individual faculty, professionals, and practitioners to make e-knowledge available to the marketplace. Text book, trade book, university, and association publishers occupy dominant power positions.*

- **Most learning is tactical within organizations,** *focusing on filling specific knowledge gaps through learning experiences.*

- **Knowledge management practices develop in leading-edge organizations.** *Limited in scope and penetration of organizational decision making in most organizations.*

- **Knowledge is experienced through first generation prototype tools.** *Proof of concept applications exist today. Rapid, parallel access of knowledge from online sources is possible in most settings.*

- **Knowledge is treated as a strategic resource in leading-edge enterprises.** *Only a few leading-edge enterprises have the perspective and tools to use knowledge to establish competitive advantage.*

The Futures: Transformative e-Knowledge

- **Vision:** *e-Knowledge will enable new practices, including the transformation of relationships, processes, and practices relating to the creating, learning, management, and sharing of knowledge. e-Knowledge can change the foundation of society and organizations.*

- **Create new sources and practices,** *including new standards, structures, processes, best practices, business models, and strategies for creating and exchanging data, information and knowledge. Create genuinely new experiences for users of e-knowledge.*

- **e-Knowledge objects** *contain codified content, insight, context, and guides to effective use.*

- **e-Knowledge content** *for courses includes text and course pack-like materials, plus explicit knowledge, guides to effective use, and access to communities of practice where tacit knowledge resides. New ways emerge to comprehend and use both explicit and tacit knowledge.*

- **Explicit and tacit learning content** *are key to learning, especially for organizational and advanced tradecraft learning.*

- **Horizontal, open channels** *develop for accessing, aggregating, and determining value of content. Different levels of repositories and meta-marketplaces arise. Legal, technical, and financial standards for knowledge assets management emerge.*

- **Consumers are empowered** *to personalize aggregations of content and insight. Many consumers become producers of content as well (e.g., through weblogs, or "klogs" and participation in content marketplaces. Organizations use "klogs" among communities of practice to identify and share tacit knowledge).*

- **Individual faculty, professionals, and practitioners** *can create and exchange knowledge directly through institutional repositories and marketplaces. Individual producers are empowered. Demand aggregators also gain power.*

- **Strategic learning becomes the norm** *within organizations. Clear organizational goals and performance objects drive personalized, perpetual learning. Learning is closely associated with communities of practice.*

- **Knowledge management is practiced pervasively.** *Process and tradecraft knowledge is regularly captured and shared by all enterprises. Knowledge management tools enable organizational goals, strategies, and performance to be pervasively linked to individual, team, and organizational learning.*

- **Knowledge will be experienced in truly transformative ways, enabled by pervasive computing.** *Using plain language activation and interactivity, faster, reliance on intelligent agents, expert synthesis and evaluation, shorter shelf life, just-in-time analysis. Graphic and other modes of presentation.*

- **Knowledge is treated as a strategic resource in all successful enterprises.** *Higher standards are set for the strategic use of knowledge. Successful enterprises speed up their processes and change their dynamics and culture to use knowledge to compete effectively.*

Today

Tomorrow

CHAPTER 2

Vignettes from the e-Knowledge Future

- Tales from the Not-So-Distant Future
- Other Visions
- Understanding Our e-Knowledge Future

Storytelling is essential to having a conversation about change. It's a fundamental instrument in the knowledge navigator's toolkit. And it's easier to confront today's challenges by thinking from the future backward.

Vignettes from the e-knowledge future include snapshots from the everyday lives of denizens of the Knowledge Age. These vignettes are drawn from all over the globe. Perpetual learners engaged in formal and informal learning experiences. A manager of a pharmaceutical company dependent on continuously refreshed tacit knowledge. A faculty member at a successful distributed learning enterprise. The chief solutions officer at a major enterprise. An active member of a professional society that is indispensable to his practice. The chief learning officer at a government agency leading the way in strategic learning. A manager of a blended learning center. The relationship development officer at an e-content exchange.

Also included are snippets of vignettes created by other future voyagers with references to more complete information.

Planning from these futures backward provides the vision pull that enables the development of expeditionary e-knowledge initiatives and migration paths.

If you want understanding, you have to reenter the human world of stories. If you don't have a story, you don't have understanding.

David Weinberger

Terms & Concepts

Content Syndication: Digitizing e-content and making it available through knowledge exchanges.

Ubiquitous Technology: Environments in which cheap, low-power computers with convenient displays are embedded in everyday environments—home, work, schools, automobiles, and public places. Also called **ambient technology**, meaning completely surrounding, encompassing and available.

Mobile Technology: People carry mobile digital devices (PDAs, notebooks, organizers, smart cell phones and variations) that enable them to engage communication and information and reshape their activities.

Pervasive Technology: Surrounding, ubiquitous and mobile technology, operating together.

Supply Aggregators: Providers of content to e-knowledge marketplaces who aggregate content. Includes universities, associations and other enterprises.

Demand Aggregators: Users of e-content from marketplaces who aggregate demand from users. Includes universities, for-profit learning enterprises, associations and corporations.

Disintermediating: When the value chain is reinvented, middlepersons can be removed, or disintermediated. Over time, new opportunities to provide value appear in the value web, resulting in the appearing of new value-added providers. This is called re-intermediation.

Digital Natives: Persons who are at home in the digital environment and comfortable with the patterns and cadences of digital practices. **Digital Immigrants** are everybody else.

e-Knowledge Repositories: Places where the digital bits of e-knowledge are collected, aggregated and managed for use by a team, an enterprise, practitioners in a particular industry or academic discipline, or a consortium of organizations. Most early repositories are vertical channels, limited by proprietary software or ownership issues.

Interoperability: The ability of data, applications, and platforms to communicate with one another.

Open Source: Applications and devices whose source codes are known and operate according to open standards.

Indispensable Relationships: Knowledge is a key ingredient in enterprises forging relationships with learners, members or customers that are indispensable to their living, working, and learning.

Migration Paths: The emergent routes followed by enterprises in developing e-knowledge infrastructures and competencies.

Expeditionary: Describes an evolving, adaptive approach to strategy, product development, and competency acquisition that allows rapid response to change and emerging insight.

Mentats: Human experts who serve as synthesizers of what is important in particular areas of expertise.

Academic Enterprise Systems (AES): College and university systems which combine elements of course management, learning management, and content management, accessible through enterprise portals. Called learning and content management systems (LACMS) outside academe.

Tales From the Not-So-Distant Future

The emergence of e-knowledge will profoundly affect everyone. e-Knowledge users will develop new roles and functions. Existing knowledge management and learning processes will be reinvented. New practices will be developed and refined. Most persons in knowledge-rich enterprises will discover significant roles as both providers and consumers of e-knowledge. They will continue these roles throughout their careers.

People understand the future best through stories, anecdotes and tales. This is especially true when the future is a "jump shift" from the past. The following stories illustrate how the e-Knowledge Industry will affect the daily lives of learners, employees, customers, clients, and knowledge providers in the not-so-distant future. These individuals are all hypothetical, but their organizations and conditions are based on today's reality, extrapolated several years into the future.

Storytelling, when linked directly to a company's strategic and cultural context, is a powerful means of simultaneously building strategic competence and strengthening organizational character.

Douglas Ready, 2002

Vignette	Primary Focus
Michelle Bodine, USA Perpetual Learner, Wisconsin Department of Welfare	Reinvention of undergraduate and graduate learning provides a transition to a life of perpetual learning.
Graeme Jackson, Australia Faculty, University of Southern Queensland	A globally distributed learning enterprise for which content/knowledge management is a strategic advantage.
Masazumi Sato, Japan Manager, Nippon Roche Pharmaceuticals	Tacit knowledge is a key enterprise asset, understood, shared, and leveraged.
Conrad Elliott, USA Member, Computer Society of the IEEE	This professional society's body of knowledge transforms perpetual learning, professional meetings, and work.
Susan Dixon, USA Enterprise Solutions Officer, Virginia Tech	Enterprise application solutions create new value from technology investments.
Ynez Delgado, USA Chief Knowledge Officer, American Society for Training and Development (ASTD)	e-Knowledge and artificial intelligence establish "ambient e-intelligence" capabilities that members use to transform their enterprises.
Han Chou, China Manager, Blended Learning Centers	"Bricks and clicks" combination of physical and virtual resources are key for Third World learning.
Jurgen Schmidt, Germany Mobile Learner	Mobile work and learning changes the patterns and cadences of personal and professional practice.
Christine Haddad, United Kingdom Chief Relationship Officer, Knowledge Content Exchange	Knowledge marketplaces create new relationships for knowledge sharing.

In the not too distant future, e-learning will be a seamless and unscheduled activity.

Dale Spender

Michelle Bodine—
Perpetual Learner, Wisconsin Department of Welfare, USA

Michelle Bodine is undertaking a graduate program in psychiatric social work at the University of Wisconsin, Madison. She recently entered her program after completing her baccalaureate degree in social work at Ohio State University (OSU).

Exemplary Transformed Elements

- *Reinvented undergraduate learning— new forms of learning and assessment, choice, personalization*
- *Portal-centric graduate learning*
- *Lifelong access to a body of knowledge*
- *Greater involvement of professional societies in continuing graduate professional education*
- *Fusion of internship experiences with formal learning*

Reinvented Undergraduate Learning at OSU. While at OSU, Bodine sampled a wide range of learning experiences, from the traditional to the transformed. She especially liked OSU's "buffet" approach to many of its undergraduate courses, which had previously been handled in large lecture sections. This approach enabled her to select from a buffet of lectures, individual discovery laboratories (in-class and Web-based), team/group discovery laboratories, individual and group review (live and remote), small-group study sessions, videos, remedial/prerequisite/procedure training modules, contacts for study groups, oral and written presentations, active-large group problem solving, and individual and group projects. While at OSU, she never purchased a traditional textbook. Instead, she acquired a variety of article-rich course packs, online text and video materials and anthologies/syntheses of insights and new developments. Some of these materials were available as freeware, including some of the best materials.

Many faculty have redirected student resources under their influence from traditional texts into this variety of virtual contentware. As Bodine got into course-work associated with her major, she had the option of purchasing one-time versions of textual materials or subscribing to a perpetual subscription of materials that would be continually updated.

Portal-Centric Resources & Interactivity. At the University of Wisconsin, Bodine uses the UW enterprise portal to completely organize her daily life—academic events, her work activities, schedules, finances, cultural events—everything. She has personalized her portal to provide gateways to the full body of knowledge for psychiatric social work available through several sources. She personally prefers the portal services offered by the American Psychiatric Association (APA), which includes access to communities of practice for a variety of specialists, including psychiatric social workers. This portal provides either subscription or pay-for-use access to searchable repositories of all the latest theories and practice methods. It also accesses ongoing communities of practice where she can either seek guidance on particular issues or obtain syntheses of insight on new developments in the field. Bodine uses a number of other marketplaces that specialize in body-of-knowledge resources for medicine. She prefers those that offer three features: 1) expert reviews of content and its applicability in different settings; 2) syntheses of new developments by leading experts; and 3) databases of case histories, searchable by medical topic/issue, patient characteristics, and other variables.

Portal-based resources and interactivity are key to every aspect of Bodine's graduate education—access to a body of explicit and tacit knowledge, socialization into the profession and interaction with other learners, her advisor, other faculty, and experienced practitioners. To a greater extent than has ever been possible, the portal is Bodine's gateway through which she experiences her profession.

Bodine uses the knowledge management tools available through the portal to keep track of the topics she has covered and to maintain her notes, working papers, and portfolio of projects/cases. Her faculty mentors use these tools to access her materials and keep track of her progress. They often suggest new directions or additional resources. Bodine is maintaining an ongoing portfolio of her professional accomplishments and demonstrated competencies, including her internship and work activities.

Meetings Supported by Intelligent Agents and Knowledge Tools. Last week, Bodine had a meeting on campus with her mentor to discuss a new set of projects/cases. Bodine had her portal agent send working notes and descriptions before the meeting, which were arrayed on the conference room whiteboard when she and her mentor entered the room, as arranged. During the meeting, they reviewed the new cases, using the large display to array past statistics and graphics. Bodine verbally instructed her personal intelligent agent to search for related references, work-in-progress, and medical findings from APA's DSM. Key findings, agreements, and actions were entered into Bodine's knowledge base using a combination of plain language communication with the whiteboard's voice recognition capability and keyboarding with Bodine's notebook device. Bodine and her mentor instructed Bodine's portal agent to send e-mails or pages to key faculty and other stakeholders who would need to know the results of this meeting.

Personal Bodies of Knowledge Put to Use by the Enterprise. While serving her full-time internship at the Wisconsin Department of Welfare (WDW) this semester, Bodine has integrated access to the WDW portal into her UW portal. The WDW portal contains a set of work-support tools that enable Bodine to maintain her casework and reference appropriate support materials, clinical references, and legal materials. In addition, WDW staff engage in coordinated "klogging" through which each person Web logs notes, observations, and tacit knowledge about what is working in particular case contexts. These materials are searchable by knowledge management tools, maintaining confidentiality. Bodine's internship has been fully integrated into her degree program as a learning experience. She consults with her faculty mentors about issues relating to her internship assignment and interacts with work colleagues about practical application issues relating to her graduate study. She is working on several anonymous clinical case studies that will be submitted to the medical practices marketplace for inclusion and review. After graduation, Bodine plans work in a clinical setting. She plans to maintain the UW portal as her personal management tool after graduation and to continue a subscription to the APA practitioner portal after graduation.

Resources of Interest

Jarmon, Carolyn. 2002. Redesigning Learning Environments: Round 1 Final Results, Round II, Round III. *The Pew Learning and Technology Newsletter,* June.

Kvavik, Robert B. and Michael N. Handberg. 2000. Transforming Student Services. *EDUCAUSE Quarterly,* Number 2, 30–37.

Twigg, Carol. 2001. *Innovations in Online Learning: Moving Beyond No Significant Difference.* Pew Learning and Technology Program. www.center.rpi.edu/PewSym/Mono4.pdf

Knowledge is experience. All else is information.

Albert Einstein

Educators would do well to take to heart Esther Dyson's maxim to adopt the intellectual habit of treating proprietary on-line content as if it were free, focusing on ways to add value to it by offering related services.

Van B. Weigel

Graeme Jackson—
Faculty, University of Southern Queensland, Australia

The University of Southern Queensland (USQ) has been a recognized leader in e-learning practice and infrastructure for over a decade. Professor Graeme Jackson has been one of the leaders on campus in deploying distributed e-learning and defining new best practices in its application.

Exemplary Transformed Elements

- *Part of a distributed, global e-learning enterprise*
- *Portal-centric infrastructure has enabled reinvention of academic and administrative processes*
- *Enterprise infrastructure for knowledge management and customer relationship management*
- *Advanced content management and knowledge management, applied to learning are central to competitive advantage*
- *Faculty member as guide and mentor in aggregation of e-knowledge for learners*
- *Participation in community of reflective practice on e-pedagogy*
- *Faculty member as provider of e-knowledge through publishers and marketplaces*
- *e-Knowledge tools enable new approaches to learning object development*

Becoming a Global Distributed University. USQ has been a primary participant in the Virtual Colombo Plan (VCP), through which a comprehensive array of distributed e-learning programs has been crafted to serve the needs of the developing world. Over the past five years, hundreds of millions of dollars have been invested in this initiative. USQ's strategy has been to become a distributed global university, leveraging its virtual and physical resources to create high-quality, convenient, and efficient learning. At any time, USQ-developed learning programs are being offered on-site at USQ campuses in Australia, on-site at USQ satellite campuses or partner institutions/learning enterprises in Southeast Asia and China, or virtually to individuals and groups anywhere. All students—even those engaged as residential students at a campus location—use e-learning extensively. All campus academic and administrative processes have been reinvented through technology.

Over the years, USQ's continuous improvement and development as a global leader in distributed learning has been shaped by several interdependent forces: 1) a powerful, transformative vision of "fifth generation distance education;" 2) progressive development of enterprise applications infrastructures, processes, and cultural norms to support the vision; 3) building competencies of staff and faculty through practical experience in cutting-edge distributed learning; 4) operating in the highly competitive Australasian learning marketplace; 5) understanding and acting on the competitive advantage potential of content and knowledge management in learning; and 6) experimenting with tablet computers and other aspects of mobile computing.

Infrastructure to Support Intelligent, Flexible Learning. One of the keys to USQ's success is its portal-centric infrastructure, which is available to all learners and faculty engaged in USQ learning experiences. USQ calls its model "fifth generation distance education" or an "intelligent, flexible learning model."

As a case study, the USQ experience exemplifies the institution-wide corporate approach necessary for an organization to become 'fast, flexible and fluid' as it strives to develop the capacity to implement fifth generation distance education.

Professor James C. Taylor, 2001

The intelligence and flexibility come from a combination of several factors:

- using the campus portal to access and personalize institutional processes and resources for learners, faculty, and staff;
- technology-mediated communication, including automated response systems;
- knowledge and content management systems that facilitate competency development and tracking; and
- Internet-based access to Web resources and interactive multimedia (online).

In registering for learning experiences and sequences, learners can select a variety of options, ranging from traditional lecture and seminar formats to online cohorts of 35 learners. This semester, Professor Jackson is moderating two learner cohorts in advanced statistical methods and leading a team of ten tutors who are facilitating 20 learner cohorts in introductory statistics. He is also supervising five graduate students—three in China, one in Singapore, and one in Melbourne.

Learning Cohorts and Computer Mediated Communication.
All of these cohorts are guided through their studies by interactive navigational tools, setting broad parameters of subject content, and accessing hot-linked Web resources or elements drawn from USQ's content repository and/or other marketplace options. Interactivity is key to USQ's pedagogical model. Interactivity among learners and between learners, faculty, and other experts/tutors who serve as mentors is facilitated through USQ's Computer Mediated Communication (CMC). The

CMC enables asynchronous discussion groups formed around learner cohorts and specific content areas, as well as informal social interaction. The CMC is much more than a threaded discussion on steroids. It deploys advanced knowledge management and learner relationship management system tools. The CMC is an essential ingredient in USQs academic enterprise system (AES). The most thoughtful interactions from the AES are structured, synthesized, tagged, and stored in searchable databases. Eventually, the insights in these databases, including differences in the responses from students in different settings, form a rich pedagogical resource.

Content and Knowledge Management Are Central.
In 2002, USQ selected WebCT as a strategic partner for several reasons, including WebCT's strategic commitment to progressively introducing content and knowledge management tools and competencies into learning management systems solutions. Content/knowledge management capabilities have been used at USQ at several critical junctures in developing, experiencing, and supporting learning to:

- enable faculty to develop new learning objects, klogs of what works in particular learning settings and other learning-related knowledge bits;
- enable the interjection of just-in-time knowledge, reflecting new development, into existing learning objects;
- support learners during their learning experiences with AES-facilitated access to explicit and tacit knowledge resources; and
- keep track of knowledge that learners have experienced, competencies demonstrated, and patterns of interactivity with faculty, mentors, and other sources of expertise.

The following descriptions and supporting schematic illustrate how content/knowledge tools are used in developing learning objects and course materials.

1) USQ faculty, mentors, and other experts create:
   a) learning objects that are contained in learning object repositories and whose metatags are managed through associated content management systems; and
   b) knowledge bits containing insights on context and application, and on the skills and interests of individuals, which are available through knowledge management systems (KMS).

The KMS also contains syntheses from dialogues from past courses.

2) Knowledge editors organize this knowledge.

3) Instructional designers structure learning experiences embedded in courses.

4) Learners access all of these resources through the AES, learning explicit knowledge directly and using guides to tacit knowledge to contact faculty and other experts.

Focused Interactions with Learners.
Professor Jackson has few conversations with his students that are trivial, fundamental, or out-of-context. Student "reflections" are posted on the AES and result in discussions that are typically complex and energetic. Selectively using AES tools, Professor Jackson jumps into the flow of ongoing conversations, guiding the discussion through a AES-provided synthesis of past insights and his own insights. He also uses AES tools to prod and encourage individual learners and to intervene when automated records show learners have not been engaging in the interactivity.

Communities of Reflective Practice on e-Pedagogy.
USQ uses communities of reflective practice on e-pedagogy to link its faculty, tutors, mentors, and related experts in advancing their knowledge and the application of effective learning. Professor

Jackson is a key participant, supervising the two staff members that are assigned to support the community and synthesize insights and process improvements. These global communities use the knowledge management and learner relationship management tools of the AES to produce a continuous stream of information on the level of interactivity, engagement of learning resources, and demonstrated competencies of individuals and learner cohorts. They are reflective students of "what works" in intelligent, flexible learning. They are often asked to collaborate with other learning communities.

Mobile, Pervasive Computing. The University of Southern Queensland has been a leader in the development of wireless "tablet computers," which are cheap and easily carried by faculty and students. In due course, these devices have added new features, including voice recognition, greater bandwidth capabilities, and more sophisticated, readable displays. Dr. Jackson uses his tablet computer to interface with the USQ knowledge base wherever he may be. His tablet computer also interacts with the pervasive computing devices on the USQ campuses and other settings.

An Internationally-Recognized Resource and a Source of Revenues. Professor Jackson often hosts visitors from other institutions and has traveled extensively demonstrating this model. Variations on the USQ model (infrastructure, processes, and content/pedagogy) are being deployed by other universities in Asia, Europe, and North America. Some learning enterprises have entered into direct licensing agreements with USQ and their infrastructure providers. USQ's communities of practice have developed substan-tial repositories of e-knowledge content resources and related pedagogical insights, which are available for fee through several disciplinary repositories and market-places. This is a significant revenue stream for USQ. In addition, USQ has been able to improve its margins on learning through the efficiency and effectiveness enhancements made possible by its infrastructure, processes, and best practices.

Resources of Interest

Taylor, James C. 2001. *Fifth Generation Distance Education.* Australian Department of Education, Training and Youth Affairs, Higher Education Division, Higher Education Series, Report No. 40, June. www.dest.gov.au/highered/hes/hes40/hes40.pdf

Content/Knowledge Management Tools

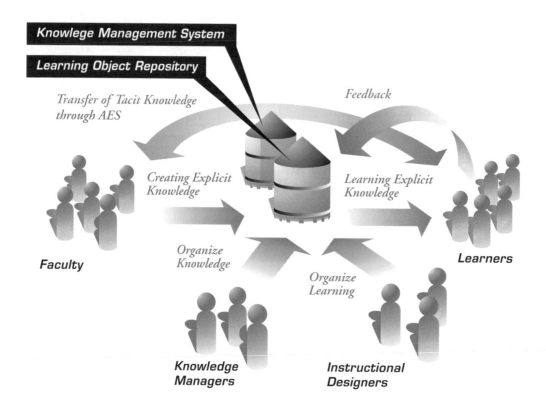

Masazumi Sato—
Manager, Nippon Roche Pharmaceuticals, Japan

Nippon Roche is a pharmaceutical division of the global Swiss healthcare company, Roche Group. Masazumi Sato has worked for them for the past 15 years, rising to the role of manager of a marketing and sales team. In the 1990s, Nippon Roche struggled in a difficult business climate, fighting fierce competition, stagnating market growth, and fundamental industry realignment. Understanding and meeting the needs of customers was seen as a critical element to establishing advantage in this environment. So Nippon Roche launched the Super Skill Transfer (SST) Project in 1998. This initiative focused on leveraging and integrating the tacit knowledge developed by the firm's front-line medical representatives (MR) in their engagement with medical doctors.

Exemplary Transformed Elements

- *Tacit knowledge captured and shared with every employee through stories*
- *Strategic learning to the desktop, laptop, PDA*
- *Strategic, enterprise learning driven by changes in corporate strategy, goals, new products*
- *Manager and employees as knowledge and learning activists*
- *Tacit knowledge insights collected across multinational divisions of Roche Group*
- *e-Knowledge for secondary marketplaces is a profit center*

Capturing Core Beliefs and Effective Practices.
Earlier efforts had failed to improve sales through training or capturing best practices. In observing high-performing MRs, leadership observed they learned by doing and by improvising to create solutions. So Nippon Roche brought 24 of its best performers together for a six-week process of exploring the fundamental questions of their mission and ideal roles. In the process, these high performers revealed their core beliefs and captured in stories and metaphors the tacit knowledge that was key to success. Management used satellite TV as part of an integrated platform to share explicit and tacit knowledge throughout the enterprise. The benefits have gone far beyond sales process innovation to continuous innovation throughout the organization.

Pervasive Knowledge Systems.
In the past five years, Nippon Roche has built upon the success of the SST initiative. It has created a pervasive knowledge management system that is used by employees at their desktop, laptop, PDA, or other interactivity platform. Employees can access, seamlessly and easily, a vast range of insight on their products and their application. Moreover, the customer relationship management (CRM) component of the portal provides each MR insight on the past history and preferences of individual medical doctors, information that is critical in problem-solving and solution-creating sessions with the client. Finally, the MR can use the system to interact with Sato or other experts to brainstorm solutions and possible approaches. The knowledge system captures syntheses of the best questions, discussions and insights, which can be searched and accessed by Sato or other MRs using intelligent agents.

Widely understood, internalized tacit knowledge is the key to Nippon Roche's success in the Japanese marketplace. Continuous, rapid changes in the marketplace require this knowledge to be synthesized, updated, and shared with far greater speed than in the past.

Guided and Energized by a Knowledge and Learning Activist.
Sato's role is that of knowledge and learning activist. He personally interacts with all of his MRs and encourages them to share progress and insights with the knowledge systems and one another. The importance of tacit knowledge is understood throughout the team. Sharing of insight is an indicator of personal performance that is evaluated and accounts for 20% of an individual's compensation.

Enterprise Learning for Everyone.
When Nippon Roche changes strategy or introduces a new product or service, Sato and his MRs have a personalized learning program "pushed" to them via the enterprise knowledge management system. In addition, MRs can elect a variety of personalized learning experiences to extend their skills. The MRs can engage these materials anywhere—in their offices/work area, conference and meeting settings at Nippon Roche, at home, or in other settings. They also can choose a variety of modes of presentation/engagement—text, graphics, and/or audio presentation. Many of the MRs choose to listen to materials using headphones during their long train rides in the morning and evening. The MRs can also engage Sato, other MRs, and other key resources to ask questions or suggest additional insights. New product launches typically are accompanied by group meetings or video conferences to build commitment and to discuss implications and implementation issues.

A strategic story that incorporates the language representing people's shared experience of the organization's core values is likely to be a story that is heard.

Janis Forman

Tacit Knowledge is Studied, Understood and Celebrated. Sato's team regularly meets to review and fine tune new elements of tacit insight. The knowledge management system also generates regular reports on performance, both individually and by teams, and sales efforts that include deductions and inductions about reasons for success. The tacit knowledge insights from Nippon Roche are regularly assembled by the corporation's enterprise-wide knowledge management system and compared with insights from other divisions of the multinational Roche Group. The meta-analysis of these different elements of tacit knowledge are very important in understanding how success factors vary from setting to setting and culture to culture.

Widely understood, internalized tacit knowledge is the key to Nippon Roche's success in the Japanese marketplace. Continuous, rapid changes in the marketplace require this knowledge to be synthesized, updated, and shared with far greater speed than in the past.

Secondary Income from Non-Proprietary Knowledge. Sato's team, like other groups within Nippon Roche, has generated a variety of syntheses of their insights on sales and problem solving in pharmaceutical settings. Most of these are treated as highly proprietary and are key to Nippon Roche's success. However, a subset of nonproprietary knowledge has been made available to several secondary marketplaces and has become a key element of the academic programs of several business schools and medical schools. This is a significant source of secondary income for Nippon Roche.

Resources of Interest

Deloitte & Touche Consulting. 2001.
From e-Learning to Enterprise Learning.
New York, Deloitte Research, 112–115.

Conrad Elliott—
Member, Computer Society
of the IEEE, USA

Conrad Elliott is an electrical engineer with Texas Instruments (TI) in Austin, Texas. He has an adjunct faculty appointment with the University of Texas at Austin. He is a member of the Computer Society of the Institute for Electrical and Electronics Engineers (CSIEEE), the world's premier professional society serving computer professionals. It serves well over 100,000 members and several hundred thousands of customers who acquire free and fee-based products, services, and experiences from the society's Web site and various portals accessible from the Web site. Of CSIEEE's $40 million (U.S.) budget, less than ten percent comes from dues—over 90 percent comes from consumer-based revenues.

A Powerhouse Body of Knowledge. For years, the CSIEEE has been a publishing powerhouse. In 2000, its publishing and meetings portfolio included 21 periodicals, major e-publishing ventures, 170 books annually, and 150 sponsored conferences annually, with associated tutorials on emerging topics and applications. Over the past five years, the society has been migrating this portfolio of resources into a defined body of knowledge accessible through its Web site. The body of knowledge has been made available to several other repositories and marketplaces, enabling the CSIEE to reach far broader markets of consumers for its e-knowledge.

Portal-Centric Experiences. Conrad Elliott uses the CSIEEE portal every day. He has created a personal portal as a gateway with links to his TI portal, the CSIEEE portal, the University of Texas portal, and the portal for the Round Rock Baptist Church. The TI portal provides Elliott with the company's own body of knowledge on corporate strategy and policies, products, market developments, competitive analysis, and personal employee issues. Changes in TI's market environment are continuously reflected in updates to the TI body of knowledge and in personalized learning assignments that are "pushed" to Elliott via company e-mail. Personalized learning assignments are tailored through the corporate knowledge management tools; general corporate learning is handled as portal postings for all employees. Elliott also receives learning assignments as part of three product development teams on which he is serving.

Exemplary Transformed Elements

- *Society's virtual body of knowledge feeds many e-knowledge marketplaces*
- *Blended learning is a major source of revenue*
- *Communities of practice are the primary organizational element*
- *Members/practitioners as creators of e-knowledge, not just consumers*
- *Society's resources are a key element of graduate and certificate programs in computer science, globally*
- *Ambient work and learning environments created for professional meetings around the globe*

Using Pervasive Computing Tools. Elliott willfully deploys his knowledge tools to increase the amount of knowledge he can process/manage and the number of tasks he can juggle. On the days when he makes the half-hour drive to work, he uses the pervasive computing devices in his automobile to communicate with his office workspace, arranging for materials to be assembled on his whiteboard when he arrives. He deploys agents to search for materials necessary for his day's activities and sends e-mails and copies of materials/references to knowledge repositories to others. While traveling, Elliott uses the same tools to move assignments forward in his absence.

The CSIEEE knowledge and learning resources are an essential element in Conrad Elliott's job performance and his continuing professional development and recognition of his standing and accomplishments within the profession. His levels of recognition from CSIEEE have become a de facto certification of professional competence.

Perpetual Knowledge Enhancement and Refreshment. While the TI portal provides for Elliott's learning needs directly related to his job, the CSIEEE portal is his source for knowledge enhancement relating to new developments in computer science and electrical engineering. He has personalized his CSIEE portal so he will receive push e-mails regarding new developments in five technology specialties that are essential for his TI product teams. He is currently participating in two emerging communities of practice, each of which was evolved by popular demand over the past two months to address several new cross-disciplinary topics. While he is very active in CSIEEE professional and technical activities, he is uninvolved in governance, standards, or other traditional professional society activities.

"Bricks and Clicks" Meetings & Tutorials. Elliott attends three or four CSIEEE special meetings a year, either in person or as a paid "lurker" at live or asynchronous video seminars of several sessions that catch his fancy. He also participates in five CSIEEE tutorials a year, each on emerging, highly specialized technical, or application topics. These half-day sessions are conducted live. About 25 participants are in the room with the speaker with hundreds or even thousands accessing virtually. For the virtual viewers, the split screen provides a view of the presenter and the audience along with the text of his/her remarks, accompanying slides, and

running comments from viewers in other locations. Following the tutorial, a two-week community of practice is formed around the topic, facilitated by either the faculty delivering the tutorial or another mentor from the field. Results of the dialogue are synthesized using knowledge management tools and provided virtually instantaneously as part of CSIEEE's body of knowledge.

Ambient Learning Environments. CSIEEE has utilized pervasive computing technologies to create what they have styled "the ambient learning experience" as a supplement to their annual meetings. The "ambient," as it is popularly called, is staged in cities around the world on a rolling basis. At any time, five or six cities are staging ambient meetings, which can last for three to five days at a particular site. CSIEE members or other practitioners interested in advanced computing issues come to the ambient setting (a hotel, conference center, academic center, or community center outfitted with pervasive computing technologies to create an ambient, sensing environment that can communicate with attendees). Elliott uses the ambient to immerse himself in contemplation on key issues for a set period of time, removed from the competing demands of the office and other environments.

Experiencing the Ambient. The last ambient that Elliott attended was scheduled to be open on Tuesday, October 23, between 07:00 and 23:00 hours. Elliott arrives at 10:00 and as he walks in the door and sits in a comfortable chair in a designated receiving area, is greeted with the salutation, "Hello, Conrad, I've reviewed your record, the assignment you did last night and the set of topics in which you are interested. Let me suggest the following schedule of time and energy today." On the ambient screens near his chair, Elliott sees a schedule of interactions with individuals (some face-to-face at the ambient and the others face-to-screen with people from around the world) and a list of online resources dealing with the two issues he had identified for the day's interactivity. Elliott reviews and synthesizes insights from the materials and directs that his syntheses be saved. He converses with the ambient and negotiates several changes in the schedule. He leaves the receiving area and proceeds to the first of several work sites he will visit this day.

Ambient environments have enabled associations and professional societies to enhance and extend their meetings, seminars, and workshops. Physical convening is still important to most society members. Ambient meetings can be held in smaller cities and used to augment programming of chapters and special interest groups. Even large national meetings have a variety of small ambient spaces scattered about that can be used to extend learning and networking opportunities.

From Site to Site, Topic to Topic. The first site consists of three comfortable leather chairs with several large ambient screens in proximity. Two other attendees at the ambient join him. They spend the next three hours engaging with virtual resources displayed on ambient screens, engaging in conversations with other interested participants in ambient settings around the globe. Elliott then spends an hour immersed in two on-site conversations with local participants who want his perspectives on several issues on which he is regarded as an expert. At 15:00 hours, Elliott asks the ambient to put him in touch with the most recent synthesized findings on the application of ambient environments to public policy decisions. After reviewing these materials, he instructs the ambient to direct them to his personal body of knowledge. The ambient asks

Elliott to create a three-page synthesis of ideas for posting to the ambient body of knowledge on these topics; Elliott agrees and completes the assignment that evening. His response is posted that evening and viewed by 2,000 colleagues over the next ten days. He also continues six conversations via e-mail with persons with whom he had interacted during the ambient day, following up on ideas that had been planted and required further exploration.

Reducing the Cost of Learning Materials. In teaching his students at UT Austin, Elliott creates a tailored virtual text from materials available through the CSIEEE or one of the content marketplaces that integrates CSIEEE materials into their offerings. These materials usually cost $50, far less than printed texts with comparable topical coverage, which are not nearly as current. Elliott liberally laces his coursework with new examples and developments gleaned from the CSIEE portal by him or his students, who access the portal through student memberships. Elliott captures insights from his students and practitioners through knowledge management tools, and shares syntheses of them with other practitioners.

Knowledge management tools are essential to learning experiences, capturing, and synthesizing tacit knowledge from learners, mentors, and practitioners.

Perpetual Learning Through CSIEE. Conrad Elliott has earned both a baccalaureate and master's degree in computer science from Virginia Tech. Rather than pursuing a doctorate, he is engaged in a program of perpetual learning through CSIEEE. This program is targeted to recognizing contributions and levels of accomplishment of advanced practitioners. It involves participation in topical meetings and tutorials; invited communities of practice that involve senior practitioners, academic experts, and researchers; and

contribution of peer-reviewed learning materials to the society's body of knowledge. The society has developed a formal professional recognition program tied to the participation of individuals in this range of activities. The various levels of recognition conveyed by participation have become *de facto* standards for excellence in the profession among senior practitioners.

Resources of Interest

Ducatel, K., M. Bogdanowicz, F. Scapolo, J. Leijten, and J-C. Burgelman. 2001. *Scenarios for Ambient Intelligence in 2010.* February, IPTS-Seville, 7.

Susan Dixon—
Enterprise Solutions Officer, Virginia Tech, USA

Susan Dixon is the Enterprise Solutions Officer at Virginia Tech, a major research university that has long been recognized as a leader in the use of technology to support academic and administrative services. Over the years, Dixon's position and responsibilities have changed to reflect the evolving state of technology applications and solutions at Virginia Tech. She reports to the CIO but typically works with solutions teams from academic and administrative units across the university.

Exemplary Transformed Elements

- *Enterprise Solutions Officer*
- *ERP, LMS, KM have fused into enterprise applications infrastructure and EAIS—fusion of academic and administrative applications*
- *e-Repositories and participation in knowledge marketplaces*
- *Value on investment drives ICT developments*
- *Enterprise portal-based lifelong relationships with students and alumni*
- *New relationships with technology partners, focusing on solutions and services*
- *Web based service applications*

Fusion of Portal, ERP, Learning Management System and Knowledge Management. Since the late 1990s, Virginia Tech has been a leader in using its enterprise portal to reinvent how students, faculty, staff, alumni, and other stakeholders experienced the university's services and knowledge resources. Ongoing, cross-departmental design teams progressively fused academic and administrative services through the enterprise portal, using SCT's Banner suite of products. Moreover, a solutions team used the portal to enable users to experience the campus learning management system, repositories of course support materials, and other academic support tools. This project stimulated a broader campus initiative on knowledge asset management, which brought together several vice provosts, the dean of libraries, the general counsel, executive director of the book store, and Dixon to develop the university infrastructure, policies, and protocols to digitize, repurpose, and share the university's digital assets. This repository included course materials and learning tradecraft, research, articles from refereed journals, and application assets from public service activities and the Extension Division. Midway through this project, Dixon was given the title of Enterprise Solutions Officer, and entrusted with convening enterprise solutions initiatives of this nature, which she has continued to the present.

New Relationships with Technology Solutions Providers. As the nature of Virginia Tech's technology infrastructure and solutions inventory have changed, so has its relationship with its technology providers. Tech's relationship with SCT, its ERP solution provider, evolved into more of a services and solution partnership. As proprietary software and applications were replaced by interoperable applications , the university came to rely on SCT to provide a broad selection of integration, implementation, and solution enhancement services. Over time, advances in Web services enabled Virginia Tech to seamlessly integrate Web-based services into its applica-

tions portfolio, furthering the solution provider relationship.

Web Services Extend Virginia Tech Services. Virginia Tech has used Web services to integrate "best-of-breed" solutions into its applications solutions portfolio. It uses Sallie Mae Solutions for billing and related functions. Moreover, under Susan Dixon's direction, Virginia Tech has developed several "best-of-breed" solutions, including an innovative search engine for e-knowledge repositories. These solutions are being used by hundreds of enterprises.

New Value from ICT Investment. As Enterprise Solutions Officer, Dixon is called on to justify new initiatives by a sophisticated review process that examines both return on investment (ROI) and value on investment (VOI), a set of metrics that examines the intangible, non-financial outcomes that are enabled by technology capabilities. At Virginia Tech, VOI has focused on the capacity to reinvent business processes and enhance relationships with students, faculty, staff, alumni, and other stakeholders; manage and leverage the university's knowledge assets and engage in external sharing; create vibrant communities of practice in a wide variety of areas, both academic and administrative; and develop the personal capabilities of individuals and the enterprise as a whole. The university has continued to realize significant value from its investment in technology and reinvention of processes and relationships.

A Continuing Relationship with Alumni. The enterprise portal-based experience has provided Virginia Tech with an instrument to forge an ongoing relationship with its alumni. President Charles Steger has offered alumni free continuing education experiences in order to engage them in a perpetual learning relationship. A wide variety of other experiences have been offered through the portal to engage alumni in the daily life of the university.

If you look at the Nobel Laureates, in case after case, the critical event was a surprise.

Herb Simon

We are a community of practice, but also a community of learners, trying to keep ahead of the waves of change.

Tina Sung

Resources of Interest

Hagel, John and John Seely Brown. 2001. Your Next IT Strategy. *Harvard Business Review,* October, 105–113.

Norris, Donald M. 2002. *Assuring Value from Your Technology Investment.* White Paper, October.

Ynez Delgado—
Chief Knowledge Officer, American Society for Training and Development, USA

Ynez Delgado is the chief knowledge officer at the American Society of Training and Development, the world's premier professional association and leading resource on workplace learning and performance issues. ASTD's membership includes nearly 70,000 people, working in the field of workplace performance in 100 countries worldwide ASTD provides information, research, analysis and practical information derived from its own research, the knowledge and experience of its members, its conferences, expositions, seminars, publications and the coalitions and partnerships it has built through research and policy work. Its members work in nearly 20,000 multinational corporations, small and medium sized businesses, government agencies, colleges and universities.

Since joining ASTD's staff five years ago in 2002, Delgado has presided over a transformation in the use of knowledge at ASTD, which has influenced best practices at thousands of enterprises in which its members work. This transformation has been shaped by ASTD's notion that "ambient" knowledge describes the emerging e-knowledge environment. Like oxygen, this pervasive, constantly available resource serves you on demand in whatever context is most effective.

Exemplary Transformed Elements

- *Ambient knowledge combined with artificial intelligence to create "ambient e-intelligence"*
- *"Input Once, Use Anywhere"*
- *Expeditionary development of applications platforms*
- *Cost accounting for the cost and price of knowledge*
- *Users Group became community of practice in ambient e-intelligence*

Ambient e-Intelligence. Delgado has engaged ASTD's senior leadership and member leaders in taking this principle to the next level. Specifically, they have merged e-knowledge with artificial intelligence, to create the next generation of collective intelligence. This so-called "ambient e-intelligence" has created a parallel consciousness that serves the organization by constantly learning, growing and gathering intelligence through the dynamic interactions of its members and sensors. In the emerging Knowledge Economy, this knowledge infrastructure among the most valuable organizational assets it enables measurable and radical increases in personal and organizational productivity.

Input Once, Use Anywhere. ASTD partnered with Knowledge Media, Inc. (KMI) to develop the knowledge infrastructure that would enable ambient e-intelligence. From the start, this infrastructure was based on the vision of just the right content, to just the right person(s), at just the right time, on just the right device, in just the right context, and for just the right environment. KMI's motto of "input once, use anywhere" was reflected in the development of reusable knowledge objects through manual, automated, and real-time indexing and tagging. These knowledge objects can be repurposed and reused in a wide range of ASTD products, services, and experiences.

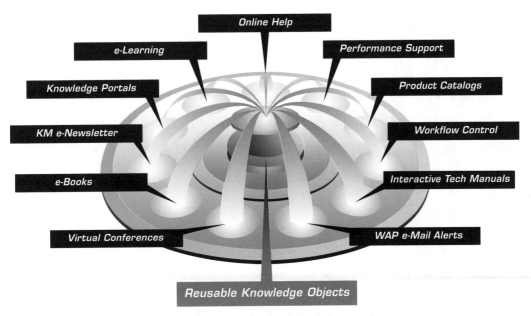

"Input Once, Use Anywhere"

Online Help
e-Learning
Performance Support
Knowledge Portals
Product Catalogs
KM e-Newsletter
Workflow Control
e-Books
Interactive Tech Manuals
Virtual Conferences
WAP e-Mail Alerts
Reusable Knowledge Objects

Manual, automated and real-time indexing and tagging of knowledge objects.

Expeditionary Development of the Applications Platform. ASTD did not reach this plateau of performance overnight. Rather, ASTD and KMI worked in an expeditionary manner to progressively incorporate new standards, technologies and practices into its enterprise applications infrastructure and solutions. Some of the accumulated milestones that enabled Delgado to discover the emerging practice of ambient e-intelligence included:

- ***Consolidation of Knowledge Standards.*** ASTD's platforms were initially compliant with SCORM 1.2 and have progressed through SCORM 4.0 as the core standards for knowledge reuse.
- ***Fusion of Learning and Knowledge Management.*** ASTD/KMI's platform has achieved interoperability, enabling the fusion of knowledge management and learning.
- ***Automated Knowledge Creation and Indexing.*** One of Delgado's fundamental reasons for selecting the KMI platform was its use of automated tagging, indexing, and taxonomy

generation. Over time, these tools have become even more robust, dramatically reducing the cost of knowledge reuse.
- ***Incorporation of Artificial Intelligence (AI) Tools.*** Artificial intelligence has combined with intelligent agents to interpret natural language queries and deliver knowledge as needed.
- ***Knowledge Reuse Architectures.*** Over time, ASTD has achieved its vision of reusing and repurposing knowledge objects in any setting and context.

Delgado has used these capabilities to fuse performance measurement, ASTD's distributed processes, and knowledge management.

Cost Accounting for the Cost and ROI of Knowledge. Over the past five years, Delgado has progressively implemented activity-based costing, allowing ASTD to benchmark and measure the improvement in its processes. These measurements have become a fundamental element in ASTD's enhancement of its relationship with members and non-member customers.

e-Knowledge systems are context neutral.

Bill Redeen

Users Group Becomes Community of Practice in Ambient e-Intelligence. Because of the leading-edge capabilities made possible through the KMI applications platform, its users group has become a recognized community of practice in ambient e-knowledge. Through participating in this community, Ynez Delgado has gained fresh insights on the use of ambient e-intelligence by leaders in different industry sectors such as: Defense Technical Information Center, repository of research and development for US Department of Defense (DoD); Defense Acquisition University, winner of distinguished distance learning program of the year; Cable & Wireless, a leader in ambient e-intelligence applications, and others.

Instructional programs that are experienced out of context are becoming too numerous and too long for employees or customers who are time-limited and urgent.

Gloria Gerry

Resources of Interest

National Press Club Breakfast Seminar and Webcast. 2002. Integrating E-learning, Learning Management and Knowledge Management, Joint Knowledge Media, Inc. and Autonomy. June 13. www.knowledge-media.com.

Redeen, Bill. 2002. SCORM 1.2/1.3: Knowledge Reuse, Constraints and Recent Case Studies. *ADL Plugfest 6 Presentation and Webcast.* Defense Acquisition University. August 3. www.adlnet.org/index.cfm?fuseaction=Plugfest6Schedule

Han Chou—
Manager, Blended Learning Centers, Guandong Province, China

Han Chou manages a regional network of "blended learning centers" in the Guandong Province of China. These centers were originated in the late 1990s by an international education and training infrastructure company, which used its multiple, on-site delivery mechanisms to serve students throughout the Pan-Asian territory, including Japan, China, Korea, the Philippines, Indonesia, Southeast Asia, Australia, New Zealand, India, and Pakistan.

Meeting the Needs of Pan Asia. These centers arose in response to the particular needs of learners in remote areas of Pan Asia. Lacking sufficient ICT infrastructure in homes and businesses to support distance learning, distance learning center companies worked with communities to establish locally owned, sophisticated learning labs, with Internet, video-conferencing capabilities, and anywhere from 20 to 120 computer work stations. Subsequently, other smart classroom features were added. Other companies like India-based NIIT and educational providers like Informatics in Singapore, the STI Educational Network

in the Philippines, the Australian Centre for Language (ACL), RMIT University in Australia and INTI College in Malaysia were early players in establishing learning centers in various parts of Asia.

Exemplary Transformed Elements

- *Initially based on need for ICT-rich physical places for blended learning in Third World*
- *"Bricks and clicks" combination is key*
- *Pervasive ICT and knowledge management infrastructure is key*
- *On-the-ground relationship with learners is strategic ; CRM is a critical discipline*
- *Relationships with a range of universities and other learning providers, using consistent infrastructures and processes*
- *Dramatic reduction in the cost/price of the elements of learning—content, interactivity, space, assessment, certification*
- *Leverage of infrastructure, best practices, and business models— establish centers in U.S., Europe, other developed centers*
- *Evolution into fused-use physical space for work, learning, and other activities*
- *Place remains a critical ingredient in the equation*

Han Chou's responsibilities focus on several key issues:
- working with locales to develop and enhance learning center facilities and attract learners through relationships with government ministries, businesses, and local organizations;
- assuring the successful integration of learning and other support services into the local blended learning centers; and
- providing feedback on satisfaction, continuous improvement, and new services and/or offerings required.

Blending Learning Solutions. From the start, learning center companies provided a mixture of the infrastructures, services, and relationships with learning providers necessary to support blended learning. Its core infrastructure included:

- a global server network that took bandwidth to the local learning centers and users;
- a content object repository (COR) that made course content perpetually available;
- a student information system (SIS) functioning in a multi-point, multilingual mode to integrate all the learning and administrative functions;
- a CRM system for analyzing customer/ learner data, assessing learner satisfaction, and conducting marketing, sales and service interactions for potential students;
- continuous publishing systems (CPS) enabling authors to write, edit, approve, and deliver documents/learning content from their computers via the Internet to a common database that generated both hardcopy and electronic materials for serving an online Learning Management System (LMS); and
- a browser-based LMS linking with the SIS to provide trainers, lecturers, and students with advanced instructional, learning, and community-building tools.

Local Learning Centers as Gateways. Accessed from local learning centers, these infrastructures and services provided the gateway to learning offerings from accredited learning providers. Local learning centers forged relationships with internationally-known educational providers, who offered learning using enterprise infrastructure, processes, protocols, and relationships with local learning centers. By 2002, the learning center company had forged a strategic relationship with a variety of colleges, centers, polytechnics, and universities in Australia and New Zealand and with the Global University Alliance, founded by Athabasca University (Canada), Auckland University of Technology (New Zealand), George Washington University (USA), Hogeschool Brabant International Business

School (Netherlands), Royal Melbourne Institute of Technology (Australia), University of South Australia, University of Glamorgan (UK), University of Derby (UK), and the University of Wisconsin, Milwaukee (USA).

The "bricks and clicks" combination offered by blended learning centers proved decisive in introducing distributed learning into the Pan-Asian marketplace. The "on-the ground" relationship with learners and local leaders proved essential in attracting and serving learners. Initially, the blended learning centers focused on non-degree and associate-level offerings. Baccalaureate-level and degree programs were added progressively as the model spread.

Finding Lower-Cost Solutions to Fit the Needs of the Marketplace. In the course of time, the learning center model progressively refined its approach to create a highly scalable model for learning that yielded significant cost savings in either a blended or virtual learning application. While different learning providers were utilized, the learning center company's infrastructures and services were used to reduce the cost of content, interactivity, space, assessment, and certification. Content cost was reduced using the content object repository (COR) and continuous publishing systems (CPS) to create, reuse, update, leverage, and scale basic course content. Using local mentors and learner-to-learner interactivity to replace faculty-to-learner engagement for basic issues reduced the cost of faculty interactivity. Physical space costs were borne by local learning centers. Assessment and certification of competency were built into the learning process in a highly efficient, technology-supported mechanism. These cost reductions enabled the learning center company to compete

effectively with other providers in the Pan Asian marketplace.

Physical space for learning can still be attractive and necessary in the Knowledge Age. Indeed, most great, good public places in the twenty-first century will have physical places where people can go to fuse work, learning, recreation, contemplation, and personal development. Food and drink will be part of the mix as well.

Deploying a New Model to Markets in Europe and the Americas. Over time, the learning center company was able to leverage its infrastructure, best practices, and business models to introduce the blended learning center model to the U.S., Europe, and other developed countries. Forging alliances with a variety of partners—small business development centers, office incubators, and community associations—the learning center company provides non-credit and degree programs from accredited institutions at a lower price than is available through traditional distance learning offerings.

Meanwhile, the blended learning centers in Pan-Asia have taken a different evolutionary step as well. In many communities, they have evolved into centers for a wider variety of community-based functions beyond learning and job training, including small business research and incubation, cultural, and entertainment centers and work and learning centers for emerging businesses. This model has expanded to metropolitan areas that were not served by previous generations of blended learning centers.

Resources of Interest

Australian Government/World Bank. 2002. The Virtual Colombo Plan. www.developmentgateway.com.au/vcp.html

Education systems are communication systems and therefore they are networks which can exist at different fractal levels.

John Tiffin and Lalita Rajasingham

Jurgen Schmidt— Mobile Learner, Germany

Jurgen Schmidt is business development manager for his local chamber of commerce, and is also registered on an executive MBA course. Most of his fellow students use their lunch period to work on the joint assignments that are a feature of the course and then share ideas using email. But in his job, he is usually travelling back to the office at that time. This is because every morning he is sent to the premises of members or prospective members of the chamber of commerce.

On those visits, he often spots business opportunities for the people he is visiting, and knows he has a good chance of quickly turning those opportunities into real projects, if he is able to have immediate access to all the information held in his office. Every afternoon, there is a meeting of all the departmental managers, and he has to attend just in case they want his advice on business development, although most of the discussion is on issues that have nothing to do with him so in general he just sits at the back and gets on with reading his in-tray. When that meeting finishes, he has to write reports on his visits. The chamber of commerce has a clear-desk policy, meaning that every day's reports and other administration must be completed before staff can go home.

Exemplary Transformed Elements

- *Mobile work and learning environments*
- *Ability to compete on time much enhanced by using mobile communications in a secure way to ensure anywhere, anytime access to other people and to knowledge repositories*

Schmidt used to work long hours, but then he discovered mobile computing and ambient intelligence. Now, he is connected whenever he wants, to whatever and whomever he wants. Both while he is travelling to clients, and during his visits, he has immediate access to all of the facilities available in his office. He also subscribes to various instant alert services; they send messages to his phone via SMS (for text) and MMS (for pictures). His phone passes the messages to his laptop, which is connected to it using Bluetooth. His laptop connects automatically to the nearest wireless network, using open standard protocols such as 802.11a or b. Special security protocols, arranged previously, are observed to ensure that the transactions are private. He gets details of calls for tenders (requests for proposals) that are relevant to the people he is visiting. During his visits, he can join in 'ad hoc' workgroups, using 802.11a or b wireless cards to link his laptop to their office network, to share information. At any time he can check his office files, set up a conference call with colleagues back at the office, send emails and many other tasks that were previously only possible when he got back to the office. Previously 'dead' time, spent travelling or sitting passively in meetings, becomes available. At noon, he can join in discussions with his fellow students, even though he is sitting in the train, returning from visits.

During his sometimes boring afternoon meetings, he can write his visit reports and send them as emails to the office administrator. Life is less stressed. He now has time to look at ways to become even more productive. He sets aside some of his free time to undertake some benchmarking of other chambers of commerce and to check out their ways of managing knowledge. And he sends off his MBA assignment, which these days he is able to submit well before the deadline.

Resources of Interest

- Mobilearn Project www.mobilearn.org

Christine Haddad—
Chief Relationship Officer,
Knowledge Content Exchange
(An e-Knowledge Marketplace),
United Kingdom

Christine Haddad is the chief relationship officer for the Knowledge Content Exchange (KCE), an e-knowledge repository that has set itself up as a meta marketplace for e-knowledge from all sources—colleges and universities, textbook and trade publishers, professional and trade associations, corporations, individual faculty, researchers, and practitioners. The marketplace is built on an open standards architecture that enables the collection, management, updating, repurposing, metering, and exchange of content from all sources and of all types, including explicit and tacit knowledge. The KCE rewards both providers and users of learning content. It rationalizes the distribution of shares of the intellectual property revenues that result when learning objects and other materials are used.

Exemplary Transformed Elements

- *Marketplace works with organizations to establish intellectual property rules, rights, and exchanges*
- *Individual and organizational providers are empowered to aggregate supply and leverage their ability to aggregate demand*
- *Marketplace aggregates supply of content from many sources—publishers, universities, professional societies, and trade associations, learning management system companies, others*
- *Marketplace pool explicit and tacit knowledge plus performances and experiences*
- *Value added through a variety of services—content assessment and review, aggregations of knowledge recommended by experts, assessment, use search engines, and other user support tools*
- *Micropayments for content and insight of various kinds*

- *Most users do not want to build content aggregations from scratch—rely on recommendations*
- *Changing definition of expertise—many more experts can provide content and insight; other experts evaluate and recommend; networks of expert content and insight develop.*
- *Unit price for explicit content declines dramatically, higher prices for performances and experiences*
- *Relationships and capacity to aggregate supply and demand are highly strategic; content becomes commoditized.*
- *Wide range of pricing options and levels of granularity*

Setting Organizational Protocols and Processes for Knowledge Sharing. The KCE is much more than a technology engine. Working with individual organizations, professional societies, and trade association leaders, it has developed the basic elements of knowledge asset management:

- sets of relationships with aggregators of supply and aggregators of demand;
- protocols, property rights processes, and legal agreements for organizations, specifying the intellectual property shares for organizations and their employees; and
- benchmarks on the technical, operational, and cultural needs of knowledge asset management and sharing.

For example, when a university or corporate university aggregates and uses a collection of content for a course, intellectual property shares are distributed to the author of the content (and her employer, if appropriate) and to the university using the content. These processes have become the *de facto* standard and save organizations millions in the process costs of digitizing and metering content. Haddad forges the relationships with organizations that participate in the KSCE, negotiating exchange rates and protocols and facilitating the organization's participation in both the supply and demand side of the equation.

Knowledge repositories can help reinforce an organization's cultural rituals and routines.

Thomas Davenport and Laurence Prusak

Content marketplaces enfranchise many new providers of content. They also empower consumers. They enable the combination and exchange of digitized, contextualized content from different publishers and in many different forms. These marketplaces enable the crystallization of complex networks of expertise and access to communities of practice. Performances, experiences, and other high value products are made available as well.

A New Approach to Content Aggregation.

The KCE makes it possible to combine content from different publishers and to aggregate collections of knowledge in different levels of granularity—entire texts, chapters, sections/topics, and paragraphs plus individual simulations, graphics, and videos. Some faculty and other users prefer to search, evaluate, and combine at the topic level. However, most prefer to aggregate content at the chapter level or to select competing content on the recommendations of distinguished peer evaluators. The KCE aggregates content from providers like MERLOT who employ their own content reviewers. Some reviewer relationships are negotiated by Haddad who has attracted a wide spectrum of expert evaluators, ranging from recognized practitioners and content experts to distinguished critical thinkers who provide periodic assessments of the best new ideas or learning objects they have discovered, on a monthly basis. Professional societies and trade associations create a "preferred selection" of the best new content in their body of knowledge, which commands a premium price. Experts are paid a small share when their recommendations result in a purchase.

Horizontal Marketplaces.

Marketplaces such as the KCE have dramatically changed the marketplace for digital content. The vertical silos of traditional content providers are broken up by the horizontal structure of marketplace exchanges. The intellectual property value of publishers' content is driven down by competition from new, individual authors who are engaged in the marketplace through their universities, associations, and other organizations. The exchange does not just contain textual content; graphics, simulations, and videos of performances and interactive experiences are also available. The exchange contains evaluations of and linkages to communities of practice, providing access to the ongoing creation of insights.

Insights from Experts.

The marketplace redefines the meaning of "experts." Today, publishers establish the experts through selection, development, and publication of text. In the future, a far broader selection of professionals and practitioners will be enfranchised to provide content expertise through these marketplaces. Exchanges will also contain references to networks of experts in a vast variety of hybridized fields of expertise. Even in an era of powerful search engines, human expertise and judgment is relied upon to identify what is really significant in most fields of endeavor. Communities of practice have arisen around the influence of key experts. As chief relationship officer, Haddad follows both an architectural and a biological model; he specifically enlists the services of recognizes experts in some areas and provides the frameworks and protocols that enable natural experts to emerge in these new disciplines.

Making Partners Smarter—and Richer.

One of Haddad's key roles is working with organizational partners to provide guidance in preparing their knowledge and metadata in ways that it can be repurposed in other fields and disciplines.

Many professional societies and trade associations have found that their sales of learning objects and access to communities of practice have increased by a factor of ten to new consumers outside their usual industry markets. The American Association of Pharmaceutical Scientists and the CSIEEE have been especially successful in driving sales of their learning objects and access to tacit knowledge in new, secondary marketplaces.

Resources of Interest

Crow, Raym. 2002. *The Case for Institutional Repositories.* White Paper, Release 1.0. Washington: SPARC. www.arl.org/sparc

McElroy, Patrick. 2002. *A New Paradigm for Acquiring, Managing, and Distributing Content in Higher Education Institutions.* White Paper. July.

Young, Jeffrey R. 2002. Superarchives Could Hold All Scholarly Output. *Chronicle of Higher Education,* July 5.

Other Visions

Other writers have crafted vignettes of the e-knowledge future.
Sample the following and complete your journey on-line.

Scenario
Augmented Reality through Ubiquitous Computing

By Chris Dede

"Alec and Arielle strolled through Harvard Yard on the way to the museum to collect data for their class assignment. Each carried a handheld device that pulsed every time they walked past a building. This signaled that the building would share information about its architecture, history, purpose, and inhabitants using interactive wireless data transfer. Alec usually stopped to use his handheld to ask questions about an interesting looking location. Today, he was in a hurry and ignored the pulses."

"Inside the museum, they split up to work on their individual assignments. When Alec typed his research topic into the museum computer, it loaded a building map into his handheld device, with flashing icons showing exhibits on that subject. At each exhibit, Alec could capture a digital image on his handheld device, download data about the artifacts and links to related Web sites, and access alternative interpretations about the exhibit. To ensure that the server sends him information tailored to his native language, reading level, and learning style, his handheld device automatically supplies information about Alec's age and background."

Complete viewing this vignette, and find others, at Cite Challenges Grand Web page:
www.citejournal.org/grandchallenges

Scenario
'Dimitrios' and the Digital Me (D-Me)

"It is four o'clock in the afternoon, Dimitrios, a 32 year-old employee of a major food-multinational, is taking a coffee at his office's cafeteria, together with his boss and some colleagues. He doesn't want to be excessively bothered during this pause. Nevertheless, all the time he is receiving and dealing with incoming calls and mails."

"He is proud of 'being in communication with mankind': as are many of his friends and some colleagues. Dimitrios is wearing, embedded in his clothes (or in his own body), a voice activated 'gateway' or digital avatar of himself, familiarly known as 'D-Me' or 'Digital Me'. A D-Me is both a learning device, learning about Dimitrios from his interactions with his environment, and an acting device offering communication, processing and decision-making functionality. Dimitrios has partly 'programmed' it himself, at a very initial stage. At the time, he thought he would 'upgrade' this initial data periodically. But he didn't. He feels quite confident with his D-Me and relies upon its 'intelligent' reactions."

Complete viewing this vignette,
and find others at:
www.cordis.lu/ist/istag.htm
Scenarios for Ambient Intelligence in 2010.

Here's to the future! The only limits are the limits of the imagination. Dream up the kind of world you want to live in, dream out loud, at high volume.

Bono

Today

Tomorrow

Through narrative, we construct, reconstruct, in some ways reinvent yesterday and tomorrow.

Jerome Bruner

Understanding Our e-Knowledge Future

These vignettes from our e-knowledge future represent a true "jump shift" in how people in many professional and academic settings experience knowledge. They capture the essence of how all kinds of people will use the pervasive atmosphere of e-knowledge to change the ways they live, work, learn, and enrich their personal development. Yet in many ways, these vignettes are familiar. They contain elements that we all recognize from leading-edge practitioners in today's developing e-knowledge environment. However, they are quite different from today in an important way: the seamless, personalized, and transformative use of e-knowledge that will be possible in the future, but is not fully possible today, even in demonstration settings.

Even leading-edge enterprises cannot live the future portrayed in these vignettes— yet. The development of numerous, necessary elements of the e-knowledge telecosm are still in our future:

- truly pervasive, interoperable, and scalable standards and e-knowledge infrastructures and marketplaces;
- seamless integration of the structures and techniques of e-knowledge in enterprises;
- well-developed competencies in the use of e-knowledge for individuals, teams, communities, and enterprises; and
- proven capacity to reinvent processes and reward new patterns of behavior.

Some of the elements of this future will be developed externally and/or by groups of individuals or enterprises. Others are within the grasp of individuals and each organization. Our e-knowledge vision can and must vault into the future. However, our actual progress is more methodical, evolutionary, and exploratory. It is about charting migration paths that are *expeditionary*.

Expeditionary e-knowledge initiatives enable individuals and enterprises to chart migration paths to their e-knowledge future. Through these initiatives, enterprises will develop ICT infrastructures to support e-learning and knowledge management, reinvent processes, and build competencies, discover what works in the use of e-knowledge and reinvent best practices, business models and strategy. Such initiatives are our probes into the future of e-knowledge.

Particular migration paths vary by industry, enterprise, and setting. Migration paths are built on two elements: revolutionary vision and expeditionary action. The essential animating element of migration paths is a keen understanding of the transformative power of e-knowledge. A clearly articulated vision of the e-knowledge future provides *vision pull* that enables enterprises to use evolutionary, expeditionary initiatives to eventually achieve truly transformative outcomes.

CHAPTER 3

Paths to the e-Knowledge Future

- Revolutionary Vision, Expeditionary Strategy
- The e-Knowledge Imperative
- Paths to the e-Knowledge Future
- Tracking the Indicators of e-Knowledge Economy

The Knowledge Economy requires learning to be tied directly, immediately and explicitly to the performance of individuals, teams, communities of practice and the enterprise. e-Knowledge will change how learners experience knowledge, especially just-in-time knowledge and tradecraft-rich knowledge. In the process e-learning and knowledge management will both grow and become fused.

Knowledge Age learning will focus on the strategic needs of the enterprise, not just filling competency gaps or developing human capital for future use. Strategic, enterprise learning will balance between structured/directed learning and unstructured/autonomic learning. Directed learning will be launched by enterprises to communicate and change their strategy, culture and/or products and services. It will involve individuals, teams or the entire enterprise. Autonomic learning will originate within the enterprise, initiated by individuals and communities of practice at grassroots level. It relies on enterprise infrastructures but will not be explicitly directed by enterprise-level leadership.

Expeditionary migration paths to the e-knowledge future will be enabled by changes in Web technologies, standards, and marketplaces for e-knowledge. A second driver will be developments in enterprise knowledge ecologies —infrastructures, processes, capabilities and cultures. These two forces will enable cascading cycles of reinvention in enterprise best practices, business models and strategies for both e-learning and knowledge management.

Terms & Concepts

Distance Learning: Providing learning experiences when faculty and learners are separated by distance. Most distance learning uses a program delivery metaphor.

Distributed Learning: Faculty, mentors, learners, and resources are distributed across physical and virtual settings, linked by networked technology.

e-Learning: The use of networked ICT to enhance, extend, and enrich learning experiences, changing access to knowledge and revolutionizing the patterns, cadences, and depth of interactivity. e-Learning uses an interactivity metaphor.

Deep Learning: Promotes the development of conditionalized and contextualized knowledge and metacognition (the ability to think about one's level of understanding) through communities of inquiry and/or communities of practice.

Blended Learning: Learning that combines physical and virtual resources and interactions. Also called "bricks and clicks" learning or "clicks and mortar" learning.

Tactical Learning: Learning that accomplishes short-term objectives and/or fills specific skills gaps (training).

Strategic Learning: Learning that is designed to align individual objectives with the enterprise's overarching strategies and objectives. It can be customized to fit each individual, teams, or working groups. Strategic learning uses knowledge management systems to "push" personalized, directed learning to employees on a perpetual basis. It also develops the infrastructures necessary to support autonomic learning.

Directed Learning: Learning directed and designed by the enterprise for individuals, teams or the entire enterprise, in response to changes in strategy, culture, new products, or market conditions.

Autonomic Learning: Learning that originates within the enterprise, as determined and shaped at the grassroots level by communities of practice.

Portals: Enterprise portals are the secure gateway through which learners, faculty, customers, staff and other stakeholders experience the enterprise's products, services, and knowledge. Portals are key to process reinvention.

ERP: Enterprise Resource Planning systems are the fully integrated software suites that support the organization's finance, human resources, back-office business and customer relationship processes.

CMS: Course Management Systems support online management of course content, registration, grading, and other supports.

LMS: Learning Management Systems support online and blended learning. **Learning Content Management Systems (LCMS)** provide substantially more robust content management capabilities designed to support the creation, storage, assembly, and delivery of modular, re-usable learning content.

CRM: Customer Relationship Management capabilities enable enterprises to personalize and enhance their relationships with learners, faculty, staff, customers, and other stakeholders. The end game is creating **indispensable** relationships.

Revolutionary Vision, Expeditionary Strategy

Leading-edge enterprises have seen the future of e-knowledge, and they have jump shifted their vision and strategies as a result. Their targeted future is not a simple extrapolation of the past. But to get to their future, they had to start by building on and changing existing infrastructures, processes, competencies, and culture. Consider how the following leaders are building migration paths to the e-knowledge future:

- *The University of Southern Queensland's* vision is to be a global leader in fifth generation distance learning, based on best practices in using powerful e-knowledge infrastructures that combine e-learning support and knowledge management tools. USQ is is developing the e-knowledge infrastructure and tools to support blended learning involving three modes: on-campus, off-campus, and online.
- *The U.S. Department of Defense's* e-knowledge vision calls for every soldier accessing a seamless atmosphere of knowledge and learning to support current operations, problem-solving, and personal growth. DOD is investing hundreds of millions of dollars in e-learning and knowledge management infrastructures and practices, digitizing and repurposing content, and new kinds of relationships with technology partners.

- *The Association of Pharmaceutical Scientists* is guided and energized by a vision of a readily available body of knowledge and communities of practice for pharmaceutical scientists in academic, research, and practice settings through which learning and knowledge seeking will be fused. Due to the rapid velocity of change in pharmaceutical knowledge, these materials must be continually updated and repurposed.
- *The Monterrey Tech System (ITESM)* aims to be the leading learning provider in Latin America. Currently, it utilizes 30 interconnected campuses and 1,000 virtual classrooms, leveraging the efforts of 7,100 faculty exchanging syllabi, digital library, standardized courses, and evaluation. ITESM reaches ten different countries in Latin America.
- *e-University* in the United Kingdom attracts up to 50 participating universities to create online learning resources. e-University's vision is to help each of these universities discover their individual migration paths to the deployment of e-learning and other e-knowledge tools.

Understanding future migration paths requires an understanding of three things: 1) how the Knowledge Economy's imperatives will fuse learning and knowledge management and dramatically enhance their capabilities; 2) the manner in which expeditionary migration paths can be used to discover the precise combination of elements necessary for success in the e-knowledge future; and 3) the ability to track the primary elements of the emerging e-knowledge practice, both in one's own enterprise and generally, in order to position for success.

Theory is knowledge that doesn't work. Practice is when everything works and you don't know why.

Hermann Hesse

The e-Knowledge Imperative

The Knowledge Economy requires a new relationship between e-learning and knowledge management. They must not just be integrated, but fused, losing their distinct identities. In the process, their capabilities must improve dramatically.

e-Learning in the Knowledge Economy

e-Learning is the use of networked ICT to extend, enhance and enrich *every* learning activity. In the process, both access to knowledge and patterns of interactivity can be revolutionized.

In the future, the term e-learning will describe a part of every learning activity. The "e" will be redundant. The "e" in e-knowledge management, e-knowledge and e-business will also be redundant.

The potential enrichment provided by e-learning occurs in several ways, including:

- access to searchable repositories of online resources—text, simulations, syntheses of great questions and answers, important elements of tradecraft, and insights from communities of practice;
- new, richer means and patterns of inter-activity between and among learners, faculty, mentors and other experts; the metaphor for distance learning is program *delivery*, while the metaphor for e-learning is *interactivity*;
- genuinely new learning experiences based on the combination of physical and virtual resources and interactivity (so-called "blended learning");
- *deep learning* experiences that develop conditionalized and contextualized knowledge and the ability to reflect on one's level of understanding, through communities of inquiry and/or communities of practice; and

- use of knowledge management tools to capture explicit and tacit knowledge, bring just-in-time knowledge into learning experiences, add value to learning experiences, and increase the efficiency/reduce the cost of learning content.

Put simply, tomorrow's successful learning enterprises will use e-knowledge to add value to learning activities, create new experiences for learners, enhance the efficiency of learning and content aggregation, and reduce the unit costs of learning content and interactivity.

As Van B. Weigel points out, e-learning uses the unique capability of the Internet to extend the reach (number of learners reached) and the richness (quality, depth, and scope) of learning.

Technology should enrich the experience of learning. e-Learning technologies may save some costs and add a measure of convenience, but if they do not deepen the learning experiences of students, they are not worth much.

Van B. Weigel, 2002

e-Learning will create a new range of learning experiences that will be fused with work, discovery, recreation, commerce, contemplation, and other activities. The new e-learning enterprise will develop (and require) new practices and standards for learning content, scalable models for learningware, and reinvention of traditional models for classroom and distance learning. The first wave of these reinventions is underway today.

e-Knowledge will Change All Learning Experiences

Will e-learning change everything? No, not literally. Some of the patterns and cadences of traditional learning experi-

ences will continue in some settings, although with greater efficiency and with some new experiences for traditional learners. But e-knowledge will enable truly new experiences in deploying and repurposing information and knowledge resources in learning, application, and enterprise decision making. It will also facilitate new kinds of interactivity through which personalized knowledge and insight can be shared and developed.

e-Learning will lose its identity as a distinct, take-time-out-for-it activity. As it does, e-learning and e-knowledge management infrastructures and activities will be more closely linked. Ultimately, they will be fused. All e-learning and e-knowledge management activities will become fast, fluid, flexible, and fused.

Changing the Elements of Learning. The imperatives of the Knowledge and Service Economy are changing all of the elements of learning. The core change in learning in the Knowledge and Service Economy is that learning is tied directly, immediately, and explicitly to the performance of individuals, teams, communities of practice, and the enterprise. Knowledge Age learning is driven by performance enhancement and immediate contribution to the organization's bottom line. This is a profound change from the traditional vision of learning as a developer of human capital.

Enterprise learning in the Knowledge Economy is a balance between two forces: structured learning and autonomic learning. *Structured or directed learning* is launched by enterprises when they are communicating and changing strategy and culture, launching new products, providing market research, or other important information. Directed learning is personal-

Enterprise Learning Elements

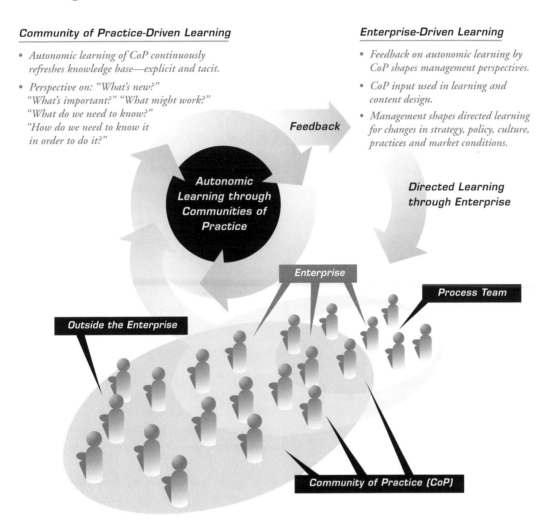

Community of Practice-Driven Learning

- *Autonomic learning of CoP continuously refreshes knowledge base—explicit and tacit.*
- *Perspective on: "What's new?" "What's important?" "What might work?" "What do we need to know?" "How do we need to know it in order to do it?"*

Enterprise-Driven Learning

- *Feedback on autonomic learning by CoP shapes management perspectives.*
- *CoP input used in learning and content design.*
- *Management shapes directed learning for changes in strategy, policy, culture, practices and market conditions.*

ized to individual needs, but directed from management levels. ***Autonomic learning*** originates within the enterprise by individuals and communities of practice that are perpetually confronting learning needs and fashioning learning experiences as part of the community of practice. Autonomic learning relies on enterprise infrastructures, but is not directly managed by the enterprise-level leadership. It may be provoked or stimulated by actions taken by management, but autonomic learning charts its own course.

Autonomic learning is like breathing, the beating of the heart, and the other autonomic responses of the human body. It happens automatically, using enterprise infrastructures, processes, relationships, and culture. The existence of vibrant communities of practice, taking responsibility for learning and the stewardship of knowledge, are the crucial facilitating element of the autonomic learning environment. Autonomic learning is more than autonomous or self-paced learning, and is a better metaphor for learning in community of practice environments. The existence of structured and autonomic aspects of infrastructures, processes, and activities is a signature characteristic of the e-knowledge enterprise. Pervasive e-knowledge enables autonomic behavior, not only in learning, but in other production and management functions as well. Achieving the optimal balance between the structured/directed and autonomic will be a continuing challenge along each enterprise's migration path.

Leading-edge organizations have discovered the importance of integrating knowledge management and learning. Integration occurs when systems are interfaced or develop common infrastructures and distinct practices are enabled to work together. Fusion occurs over time, as different systems, processes, and practices are merged so fundamentally that the natures of the original elements are altered and their distinct identity fades.

The Changing Role of Learning in the Knowledge Economy

Traditional Learning	Learning in the Knowledge and Service Economy
Learning's Value Proposition and Organizational Context. Learning builds long-term human capital (education) for eventual use or is targeted at specific skills gaps (training).	**Learning's Value Proposition and Organizational Context.** Some learning develops human capital or specific skills. Most learning yields immediate value, solves problems, and builds tangible competitive advantage.
The Driving Forces for Learning. Learning is driven by long-term human development needs or by the necessity to fill specific knowledge gaps.	**The Driving Forces for Learning.** Learning is driven directly by ongoing changes in the business environment, which are immediately translated into changes in organizational strategy, programs, competencies, and processes. These changes are immediately reflected in tailored learning programs and personalized interventions.
Infrastructures for Learning. Separate learning silos exist in different parts of the organization. Some integration of learning infrastructure occurs across the enterprise.	**Infrastructures for Learning.** Infrastructures for learning and knowledge management are fully integrated. No silos; same infrastructure serves for the entire enterprise.
Patterns and Cadences of Learning. Intermittent learning, formal courses, and classes. A delivery metaphor characterizes learning.	**Patterns and Cadences of Learning.** Perpetual learning that can be engaged in wherever learners might be. Some formal courses and classes remain, complemented by highly granular learning experiences and modules. Interactivity replaces delivery as the driving metaphor.
Relation of Learning to Other Activities. Learning is a distinct activity. One takes time out for learning.	**Relation of Learning to Other Activities.** Learning is fused with work and many other activities. Just-in-time learning becomes pervasive.
Customization and Personalization. Learning experiences are seldom customized or personalized. When they are, the process is time-consuming, expensive, and limited by technology systems and organizational competencies.	**Customization and Personalization.** By design, every learning activity is rapidly and seamlessly customized to emerging needs. Learning is personalized to fit the learning preferences and requirements of individuals. Much learning is autonomic, engaged in by communities of practice to meet emergent needs.
Response Time for Learning Design and Delivery. Learning is based on off-the-shelf curriculum or time-consuming tailoring to meet emerging needs.	**Response Time for Learning Design and Delivery.** Environmental changes are rapidly translated into changing organizational requirements, strategies and tailored learning.
Balance Between Structured and Autonomic Learning. Learning is primarily structured or self-paced. Autonomic learning by the individual and community of practice is impossible with traditional knowledge tools.	**Balance Between Structured and Autonomic Learning.** Both are essential. e-Knowledge enables the explosion of community practice-based, autonomic learning.

The Fusion of Knowledge Management and Learning

Typically, knowledge management and learning have been treated as distinct topics and practices, developing in different parts of the enterprise. Further, knowledge management has flourished in corporate and business enterprises and has been slow to develop in learning enterprises. Leading-edge organizations are ending this separation. Three elements are driving this fusion.

Development of Standards, Repositories, and Marketplaces for e-Knowledge. The e-knowledge standards movement has surfaced the need for the integration of learning and knowledge management. After all, both require interoperable repositories and marketplaces for e-knowledge if they are to be successful. Moreover, standards developers have discovered—albeit somewhat serendipitously—that integrating knowledge management and learning professionals and practices has created a greater critical mass that has proven helpful in gaining attention and support for standards efforts. A key trigger for this taking place is the emerging comprehension of the requirement for managing *content* and *process* together. This is both a service to the learner and an enhancement to organizational capability

Acquisition of Infrastructures, Processes and Competencies. At some stage in their evolutionary development, organizations practicing knowledge management and learning discover the need to integrate infrastructures, processes, and capabilities for each. This awakening is different for each organization. As organizations proceed with the integration of infrastructure, they progressively reinvent learning and knowledge management processes and develop competencies in how to create, manage, update, and share e-knowledge. Experience yields these insights in different ways.

Strategic, Enterprise-wide Learning Requires Fusion. Confronted with the challenges of competition in the global marketplace, organizational leadership comes to the realization that strategic, enterprise-wide learning is critical to its competitive advantage (Deloitte and Touche, 2001). And that strategic learning can only be achieved when the organization's infrastructures, processes, and practices for learning and knowledge management are truly fused. For corporations, strategic learning means the ability to translate organizational goals, performance objectives, and strategies into personalized learning experiences that can be pushed to employees, customers, suppliers, and partners at any time. It also means the ability to use communities of practice to serve as essential learning venues. For learning enterprises, for which learning is their primary service, strategic learning translates into five abilities:

- fusion of knowledge management tools into its dominant learning infrastructures to enrich learning experiences and manage their costs;
- integration with the strategic learning systems of other organizations so it can function as a learning provider;
- engaging management/administration, faculty, and staff in learning to advance the strategies and goals of the enterprise and to share their knowledge and further develop their competencies;
- supporting vibrant variations of both structured and autonomic learning; and
- nurturing the development of communities of practice to shape both the creation of knowledge and the nature of learning experiences.

Strategic, enterprise-wide learning will be the new gold standard in the Knowledge Economy.

Fusion Is Not Inevitable

Desirable, closer merging of knowledge management and learning is far from inevitable. Brandon Hall (2001) identifies four obstacles to merging learning and knowledge management in business enterprises:

- *Organizational and functional barriers.* Learning and knowledge management professionals are separated, organizationally and functionally. Training/learning tends to be in Human Resources, while knowledge management typically resides in a special place in each organization, directly below the executive level.
- *Complex and ambiguous concepts.* Knowledge management, in particular, is either unknown or misunderstood.
- *Divergent communities of practice.* While this is changing, learning and knowledge management professionals attend different professional meetings. They identify with different communities of thought and practice.
- *Divergent technologies.* Knowledge management and e-learning software represent two different industries with few firms serving both markets.

To this list, a fifth barrier may be added: learning enterprises such as colleges and universities have barely discovered the principles and practices of knowledge management, let alone integrated them with e-learning. This is a major deficiency that leading-edge institutions are working to overcome.

New terminology is necessary to reflect the fusion of the theory and practice of knowledge management and e-learning and to leave behind the baggage of past usage carried by both terms.

Stages of Learning Development

Tactical Learning	Integrated Learning	Strategic, Enterprise-wide Learning
Learning is a practical response to specific needs.	Departmental training is shared across the organization.	Learning is a consistent, enterprise-wide tool for rapid response to organizational challenges.
Learning fills specific skills gaps.	Learners take responsibility for developing essential knowledge.	Individual learning strategies are tied to performance and compensation.
Islands of disparate training approaches exist throughout the enterprise.	Holistic learning, standard systems, and processes emerge.	Fused infrastructures and processes develop for knowledge management and learning.
Content is the same for all participants, no consistent processes exist for content update.	Content is modular, linked to learning architecture and knowledge management tools.	Content is modular and personalized, based on individual learning styles, skills and knowledge levels.
Few linkages occur between learning and learner development, knowledge management, and organizational performance.	Linkages emerge between learning and organizational performance.	Organizational goals and performance factors are linked to and drive learning directly, immediately, and perpetually.
Alliances and partnerships serve specific learning requirements: they merely need to interface with enterprise systems.	Alliances and external relationships become more critical to integration of LM and KM.	To create an enterprise-centric, strategic learning capability requires a net of alliances and external relationships that must fuse with enterprise systems.
Limited tools are available for autonomic learning.	Limited tools are available for autonomic learning.	Enterprise-wide learning relies on a combination of structured and autonomic learning, supported by new tools.

Adapted from: "From e-Learning to Enterprise Learning,"
e-view by Deloitte Consulting and Deloitte and Touche, 2001, 10–11.

The Power of the Value Net

So the basic idea of a value chain for e-knowledge must be expanded to the notion of a *value net*. Some refer to this as a *value web*, a *value stream,* or a *value constellation.* This value net will be non-linear and orthogonal. It will accommodate the many new sources of value that will result from the new services required to create e-knowledge aggregations, repositories, and marketplaces. The value net will deconstruct and reconstruct the basic value propositions and cost/price structures for e-knowledge of all kinds.

To a great extent, much e-content will become a commodity, and its unit price will drop—particularly where it is already purposed for modularity and interoperability. We know from experience that existing Internet-based accessibility to knowledge resources has reduced unit prices, slashing the profitability of content providers serving their traditional customers. Finding new markets for their e-knowledge and creating new, value-added knowledge products is a critical challenge for traditional knowledge providers confronting the e-Knowledge Economy.

Reaching, Attracting and Serving New Markets. The communication capacity of the Internet to reach new markets is not enough to assure success. In order to truly attract new markets (and hold onto old markets) e-knowledge providers must add genuine value to e-knowledge resources. They must create versions of knowledge resources that are especially suited to online media and create new, compelling experiences for the user. Online versions of news media demonstrate this principle, as they are tailored for the online environment and create new experiences that enable the customer to engage news coverage more effectively.

In networks we find self reinforced, virtuous cycles. Each additional member increases the network's value, which in turn attracts new members, which in turn increases value, in a spiral of benefits.

Kevin Kelly, 1997

Learning is not so much about content any more—it's about services.

Dale Spender

Our business organizations are extremely effective at hiding the performance crisis—from themselves as well as everybody else.

Gloria Gerry

Other Changes in the Knowledge Value Net

A wider range of content producers will be empowered—individuals (faculty, researchers, practitioners), universities, learning management system providers, publishers, media companies, professional societies and associations.

The kinds of content available for learning will expand—recontextualized content from rich repositories such as digital libraries, news archives, and museums.

Communities of practice will provide extracted tacit knowledge and insights—syntheses of insight from communities of practice may command a premium price.

Much of the content of proprietary knowledge management systems will remain proprietary—however, much tacit and explicit knowledge will find its way into marketplaces and communities of reflective practice for industries and professions.

Just as e-knowledge providers can reach new markets, new competitors can reach markets that have been semi-protected—competition will be keen.

Some learners and practitioners may be willing to pay premium prices—for collections of insight certified by leading universities, professional societies, and/or other trusted organizations, individuals may be willing to pay premium prices, but the quality must be worth it.

Tell me and I'll forget.
Show me and I'll remember.
Involve me and I'll understand.

Confucius

Networked relationships—collaborative expert networks, communities of practice, teams, working groups—also demonstrate value added and the creation of unique experiences particularly suited to the issues that are the subject of the collaboration. The power of the network grows in relation to the number of engaged participants who have insights to contribute. A network with global reach and rich connections has the potential for high latent value. In the networking game, answers to questions such as "*Whom do you know who . . . ?*" are often easier to find within an online community of practice.

Adding Value in an Atmosphere of "Less is More." The economics of abundance also is at play in the Knowledge Economy: abundance of connections, information, and choices. Time and the attention of busy consumers has become the one scarce resource; timeliness and ease of use are recognized as keys to economic advantage. Unlike the economics of scarcity of the Industrial Age, where physical resources are in short supply, the Knowledge Age operates in a context of abundant information supply. But in this new scenario the processes of value added are even more critical, adding new choices and criteria for selecting among choices. Consumers of e-knowledge desire seamless expedited processes of search and acquisition. Consider the following current examples of new value-add mechanisms.

- *Crafting metadata to describe information resources adds value to those information resources.* But the value doesn't stop there. In the Knowledge Economy, one person's data is another's information is another's knowledge. In other words, one person's metadata is another's data. Metadata repositories will be developed and managed as services.
- *Search capabilities and strategies must be developed.* Web technologies now make it very easy to store search strings or "strategies" for later use. The search

queries may be used across multiple, distributed repositories of content. These search strategies can be viewed as codified knowledge acquisition methodologies. When well crafted, they have high value.

- *Content syndication is a useful, value-add service.* Through aggregating digital copies of journal articles within a primary portal (e.g., Emerald Full Text), researchers can easily locate and compile collections of specific articles. Another example is MeansBusiness where the content used is more granular than an article; this company successfully aggregates composite texts based on key search concepts, aggregating summaries, and abstracts that deal with these concepts. It is an adaptation of an earlier publishing approach used by Executive Book Summaries.

Syndication of e-knowledge promises to be an integral tool in making knowledge content available to new and broader marketplaces.

- *Portals provide efficient access, interactivity and delivery.* Educational portals are a multi-directional value web involving an institution, the learner, and a multitude of information services. Institutional portals integrate institutional information services and processes and provide personalization. Sophisticated portals are more than mega-directories. They utilize client usage to inform and enhance future services. They provide for personalized access to a select range of information services (directories, news, courses, communities of practice).
- *Aggregators facilitate search & access.* As use of the Web develops, repositories and registries of aggregated information in targeted areas have also developed. Examples include: Achieve Inc. (a US-based repository of state competency standards mappings). www.achieve.org/

- *Engaging communities of practice in feedback loops adds value.* Amazon has been doing this successfully with its system of book reviews. MERLOT does this with its approach to collecting metadata on course materials in the academic community, giving emphasis and easy expression to the age-old academic tradition of "peer review."

- *Communities of practice create, capture and, share tacit knowledge.* The World Bank is sometimes now known as "the Knowledge Bank" in recognition of a successful restructure during the 1990s to become a knowledge-based institution, involving stakeholders, staff, and clients from all over the world in knowledge sharing aimed at new efficiencies.

- *Harvesting the judgment of experts.* In his book, *World Without Secrets*, Richard Hunter uses the term "Mentat," originally coined by Frank Herbert in *Dune*, to describe human experts who serve as synthesizers of what is important in particular areas of expertise. Over the next five to ten years, Hunter reckons that the limitations of search engines will create a valuable niche for such synthesizing sages. Typically, communities of practice are where Mentats can be found.

In a World Without Secrets . . . *Mentats will increasingly be measured not by their ability to provide more information, but by their ability to make accurate predictions, give concise data, and reduce the amount of information their clients must handle. Of course, this increases the hidden power of the Mentat . . . (who) do what computers can't and won't do for the next ten years: make decisions and predictions based on qualitative figures like judgment, benefits, values and emotions.*

Mentats fill a number of increasingly important rolls in the World Without Secrets:

- *Mentats tell us what matters and how. They provide the frameworks we use to interpret the world or a piece of it.*
- *A framework is based on values, so it's one of the things that defines a community. In other words, a Mentat leads a community.*
- *Like other leaders, Mentats make decisions or assist us in doing so.*
- *Mentats filter out as much information as possible, so what remains is the good stuff.*
- *Mentats inform us when something important has changed that requires us to reconsider our ideas and frameworks.*
- *Mentats provide a basis for personal trust to resolve the claims of competing information.*

Richard Hunter

So the e-knowledge imperative is impelling leading-edge enterprises to develop new approaches to their acquisition, managing, and sharing of knowledge. Let us consider the migration paths they are charting.

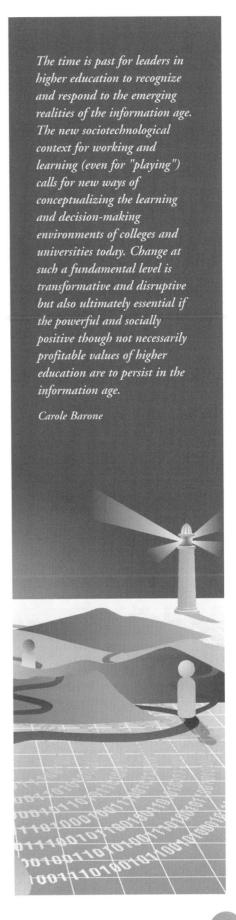

The time is past for leaders in higher education to recognize and respond to the emerging realities of the information age. The new sociotechnological context for working and learning (even for "playing") calls for new ways of conceptualizing the learning and decision-making environments of colleges and universities today. Change at such a fundamental level is transformative and disruptive but also ultimately essential if the powerful and socially positive though not necessarily profitable values of higher education are to persist in the information age.

Carole Barone

Paths to the e-Knowledge Future

Expeditionary initiatives are low-cost probes into the future.

Donald Norris

One of the most important tools for an IT leader is a mental road map of the future.

Douglas Van Houweling

Enterprises that have crafted a "jump shift" vision of the e-knowledge future understand that many aspects of the future are cloudy or unknowable. Standards, repositories, and marketplaces are still in the proof-of-concept or development stage. New generations of enterprise infrastructure applications and e-knowledge solutions are emergent, not fully developed. The solution is to progressively take actions that can develop infrastructures and competencies and increase readiness for e-knowledge. Leading-edge e-knowledge enterprises like USQ, the World Bank, and AAPS are taking an expeditionary approach to achieving their e-knowledge vision.

The Other "e"—Expeditionary

The emergence of an e-Knowledge Industry represents the collision of exponential technological adoption—the digitization and interconnection of knowledge—with systems and practices that prefer incremental change, traditional learning, and knowledge development. The emergence of the e-Knowledge Industry is likely to be disruptive and to create the opportunity for the emergence of "killer applications" (killer apps)—new ways of creating, managing, and sharing knowledge that are genuinely fresh and compelling experiences.

Killer apps are the collisions between exponential technology adoption and systems that prefer to change in even, incremental ways. How disruptive they are depends on where in the technology curve they are introduced.

Downes and Mui, 1998

The forces shaping killer apps can be forecast, and changes in the value chain projected. However, the nature of the killer app itself cannot be predicted with elegant precision. Experience has shown that the best way to invent killer apps is through an iterative process of rapid prototyping, feedback, and continuous adaptation. For e-knowledge this process consists of:

- rapid prototyping of new e-knowledge processes and experiences;
- using learners and other knowledge users as perpetual focus groups, creating feedback loops; and
- continuously adapting and changing the new processes and experiences, based on user feedback and responses to marketplace developments.

Over time, the new killer app emerges. The term that best describes these sorts of e-knowledge initiatives is "expeditionary."

Expeditionary development of products, services, and experiences requires enterprise leaders to be open both to new opportunities and to genuine surprises. As Jame Brian Quinn (2002) suggests, "Today's world calls for less hypothesis testing and more systematic observation." In an expeditionary world, the advantage is seldom won by the enterprise with the best ideas, alone. Rather, advantage goes to those that are best able to introduce and continuously, progressively refine a new product and experience so that the killer app is discovered and emerges.

Building e-Knowledge Infrastructures and Capabilities. Through expeditionary initiatives, organizations can develop the infrastructures, build the competencies, reinvent the processes, and recalibrate their best practices for learning and knowledge management in the face of emerging developments in e-knowledge standards, processes, and marketplaces. Every organization's expeditionary initiatives and distinctive migration path will change in the face of developments in these different elements and the organization's adaptations. As they reshape their expeditionary e-knowledge initiatives, it will be necessary for organizations to monitor and consider the impact of all of these factors.

Cascading Reinvention of Processes and Practices

Ultimately, all of the processes and practices of knowledge management and learning will be substantially changed, even transformed. Progressively, organizations will use ICT to reinvent all organizational processes, including learning, learning support services, administrative support, and knowledge management. So at the very time that the e-Knowledge Industry is emerging, its processes and practices will be reinvented. The scope and nature of reinvention will expand as new tools, infrastructures, and best practices become available. Cascading cycles of reinvention will continue over some time as the killer apps of e-knowledge practice emerge and are refined.

In the future, organizational e-knowledge processes, knowledge ecologies, and best practices are likely to be very different than those of today. A cascading series of reinventions will lead to new strategies, business models, and best practices for e-learning and e-knowledge management.

Tracking the Indicators of the e-Knowledge Economy

Given the cascading reinvention of e-knowledge, how can one chart its development? The answer is simple if not easy: by tracking snapshots of three families of indicators, which capture the major, interacting developments in the field.

Technologies, Standards, and Marketplaces for e-Content

A cornerstone of e-knowledge is the creation of modules of content that can be stored, repurposed, and combined, and the use of which can be metered and charged to a customer where appropriate. These modules will be available in a range of forms: highly granular (paragraphs, individual images, video clips), to chapters and topics, to full texts and anthologies. Such modular content is typically referred to as "learning objects."

Repositories and responsive marketplaces for e-content are being developed today. For this to happen, standards must be developed that enable true interoperability for learning objects and practices. In the education sector, groups like MERLOT, Open Knowledge Initiative (OKI), and the Learning Federation are developing shareable repositories of content. The Learning Objects Network is working with Sun and Artesia to develop repository capabilities for the Advanced Distributed

Learning (ADL) initiative for the U.S. Department of Defense. In the association industry, specific trade and professional groups are developing repositories that define the body of knowledge for the profession or industry and provide access to digitized resources through the portals of the American Association of Pharmaceutical Scientists, American Health Information Management Association and others.

Repositories, bodies of knowledge, exchanges and marketplaces will all serve as alternative channels for providers and consumers of learning objects and tacit knowledge. Over time, "meta-marketplaces" may develop to aggregate and repurpose the resources available to consumers by creating horizontal channels that cut across vertical knowledge silos.

Standards, processes, and marketplaces for e-content are emerging from the efforts of:

- working groups and organizations dealing with the arcane world of standards aimed at developing specifications for fluid, flexible, interoperable "learning objects;" and

Tracking the Indicators of the e-Knowledge Economy

Technologies, Standards and Marketplaces for e-Knowledge

Best Practices, Business Models and Strategies

Infrastructures, Processes, Capabilities and Cultures

When the intellect is tightly coupled to the world, decision making and action can take place within the context established by the physical environment, where the structures can often act as a distributed intelligence, taking some of the memory and computational burden off the human.

Donald Norman

• consortia and corporations establishing processes, clearinghouses, and marketplaces for exchanging learning content.

Standards, processes, and marketplaces for e-content are essential, but they will be incomplete without advances in public and private infrastructures for exchanging and deploying content.

Infrastructures, Processes, Capabilities and Cultures for e-Knowledge

The developments in Internet2 and the so-called "Semantic Web" are creating the environment conducive to e-knowledge exchange. Equally important, organizations have been developing their internal infrastructures, processes, capabilities and cultures when creating new experiences in learning and knowledge application. While significant progress has been made over the past decade, truly transformative changes will occur over the next five to ten years. These infrastructures, processes, capabilities and cultures cover a wide range of technologies.

Most colleges and universities, corporations, professional societies and associations, and government agencies have been enhancing their infrastructure to deal with e-knowledge capabilities. All are extensively deploying enterprise portals, ERP, Web services, and communities of practice, distinctively tailored to the needs of learners, members, customers, suppliers, and other stakeholders. The CRM, learning management systems (LMS), course management systems (CMS), and learning content management systems (LCMS) applications vary substantially from sector to sector. Corporate enterprises, government agencies, and consultancies are typically more advanced in knowledge management applications using these infrastructures.

The dimensions and textures of organizational infrastructure in higher education

were demonstrated at EDUCAUSE 2001 and reiterated at EDUCAUSE 2002. Carl Jacobsen of the University of Delaware, Carl Berger from the University of Michigan, and Robert Kvavik of the University of Minnesota described how the combination of portalization, Web-based interactivity, ERP systems, learning management system platforms, networks, communities of practice, and expert service providers were creating flexible platforms for creating new learning and knowledge deployment experiences. Berger described the next killer application for higher education— the capacity to create a new breed of powerful, personalized, learning and professional development experiences far exceeding the traditional capabilities of colleges and universities.

We are on the threshold of these infrastructure capabilities today. The developments in standards and marketplaces for e-knowledge will combine with these infrastructure capabilities to supercharge a new wave of best practices and new business models and strategies for e-knowledge.

Hardware and Networking Infrastructures. The Internet and World Wide Web are developing into substantially more robust platforms to support learning and knowledge management. Internet2 and other initiatives are expanding the Internet's bandwidth potential. Moreover, the focus is shifting from "hard" to "soft" infrastructure issues. Processes, standards, and interoperability are becoming major issues. The Semantic Web is about the richness of exchange of semantics in data structures, especially those associated with domains of practice. That is, electronic agents resident on the Internet will be able to interpret metadata to understand the content and context of the packets the Internet is transporting. These developments are an essential predicate to the development of dependable, seamless and cost-effective infrastructures for the e-Knowledge Industry.

Portalization and Personalization. Learning enterprises are dramatically enhancing their capacity to interact effectively with learners through the creation of portals. Enterprise portals are gateways that can be personalized to fit the information and communications requirements of individual learners. Institutions like the University of Minnesota, Virginia Tech, Weber State University, Monash University, and the University of British Columbia are using their portals to establish active, intimate relations with alumni and learners for a lifetime of better relationships with learners. At EDUCAUSE 2002, Kenneth C. Green reported that roughly half the institutions reporting on his survey had developed or were planning enterprise portals. (Green, 2002) Other learning enterprises are using the tools of CRM to add value to and streamline their managed learning and/or knowledge environments. Some university teaching and learning departments, such as University of Wisconsin's Learning Innovations Department are turning their LMS into a Relationship Management System (RMS) through building administrative relationship support to students.

The portal movement is powerful in other sectors. Corporations have used organization intranets to develop powerful, flexible platforms for organizational, team, and individual learning and business development. Association portals are creating powerful communities of practice constructed around the body of knowledge for the industry, profession, or craft represented by the association. Today, many individuals are using portal capabilities from their employers, associations, and universities. Tomorrow, even more powerful portal-based experiences will be available.

In the future, individuals will use personal portals to manage daily interactions with enterprise portals from their employer, university, associations, civic organizations, and other sources of information, insight, and interactivity. Portals will be selected based on their value and ease of use.

New Generations of ERP and CRM. Companies like Oracle, PeopleSoft, SAP, SCT, Datatel, and Jenzabar are enhancing their existing ERP offerings in a variety of ways to accommodate portalization, communities of practice, and LMS interaction. In addition, some are incorporating customer relationship management tools. Future ERP will need to integrate with LCMS and other knowledge management tools. The next generations of Student Information Systems (SIS) developed by software companies such as Oracle, PeopleSoft, and SCT are likely to have more of the characteristics of CRM systems, focusing on relationships in addition to transactions. Consortia involving universities and software companies, such as Uportal, are also collaborating to deliver extra-institutional portal technology that is positioned for longevity and (open systems) interoperability. From the individual user's perspective, these trends in portal development

More advanced knowledge management techniques applied in the higher education arena have the potential to improve the way we plan, teach, and learn.

Pamela K. Stewart

One of the most important tenets of e-learning is that it bridges work and learning. While the best classroom experiences bring work into the learning environment, the best e-learning brings learning into the work environment.

Marc J. Rosenberg

also complement the growth in nomadic computing technology (laptops, palm tops, wireless devices) that will provide for true device independence where personal information services will follow the person not the device.

Learning Management Systems (LMS) and Learning Content Management Systems (LCMS). A new group of companies are developing sophisticated learning content management tools that enable enterprises not just to create and access flexible repositories of content, but to understand the interaction of employees and others with that content. These tools are essential to enterprises managing the content and context of learning and application. Companies developing LCMS include Centra, Docent, ePath Learning, Generation21, Global Knowledge, IBM Mindspan, WebMCQ, Knowledge Mechanics, Leading Way Knowledge Systems, Giunti, HarvestRoad, and others.

Across the world, learning management companies, institutions, and other learning enterprises are creating new breeds of learning management systems—sometimes also referred to as Managed Learning Environments (MLE). These systems provide a means for organizations to manage online learning experiences and integrate them with traditional learning offerings. The most advanced LMS track student progress and competencies. Many create communities of reflective practice. Some of these systems are proprietary, others feature open architecture compliant with emerging standards for learning content. There are over 150 proprietary LMSs currently at large in the world of learning. Many of these offerings are integrating the LMSs with enterprise portals. Companies like WebCT, Blackboard, TopClass, e-college, Granada, Prometheus, Saba, Docent, click2learn, IBM learning Space, Oracle (iLearn), and institutions like the Macquarie University, Monterrey Tech, and the Open University of the Netherlands are leaders in these ventures.

In practice, LCMS and LMS are complementary. Over time, they must be interoperable and seamlessly share metadata. They must integrate with institutional ERP and legacy systems. They must interoperate with repositories of content not initially purposed for learning (such as news archives and digital libraries). As enterprises develop easily integrateable, interoperable applications solutions, the current distinctions between types of systems will disappear.

Learning Content Management Systems will increase in importance with the increase in e-knowledge traffic. At the same time, they will lose their distinct identity as they become a seamless part of the portalized capabilities of an organization's infrastructure. New generations of LCMS capabilities will need to deal with the integration of just-in-time knowledge into learning, performance, and decision support.

Expert Networks and Communities of Practice. The tacit knowledge that is critical to most organizations resides in formal and informal networks. Internal enterprise networks have been greatly enhanced by the development of organizational intranets in recent years. Some have spawned genuine communities of practice. Most expert networks reside within single corporate enterprises and are strictly proprietary. On the other hand, a substantial number of formal and informal networks are affiliated with professional societies, trade associations, philanthropies, and other non-profits. They span an entire profession, industry, trade, or philanthropy, and are the foundations for emerging communities of practice offering access to a formal body of knowledge consisting of content, context, process, and tacit knowledge. The proliferation of strategic alliances, joint ventures, and other partnerships within the business world also underscores the configuring power of networks and networked know-how.

Reinventing Best Practices, Business Models and Strategies in e-Learning and Knowledge Management

Over the course of the next decade, we can expect a cascading cycle of reinvention in the practice of e-learning and knowledge management. These reinventions will build on what we have learned about the early generations of e-learning and knowledge management, as summarized below:

- In colleges and universities across the globe, most of the participants in online or blended learning have been the institution's own core students, not new students reached through distance learning.

- Most distance learning and online learning have merely digitized existing processes and practices, thereby failing to yield cost savings, enhancements in the learner experience, or competitive advantage.

- In *Deep Learning for a Digital Age*, Van B. Weigel presents a compelling vision of how traditional colleges and universities can create **blended learning** environments to create communities of inquiry that lead to deep learning experiences. Weigel emphasizes that the Internet can be used to create richer learning experiences, not just to reach remote learners.

- The Pew Grant Program in Course Redesign has used e-learning to reinvent and enhance learning experiences in US colleges and universities. Carol Twigg (2001) chronicles how this approach yields a combination of cost savings, enhanced performance, great flexibility and personalization, and accelerated learner progress.

- Institutional infrastructures and processes supporting e-learning are a critical success factor for leading e-learning providers such as University of Maryland University College (UMUC), University of Wisconsin Learning Innovations (UWLI), and British Open University (OU). These infrastructures and processes

enable several competitive advantages:
  - the ability to leverage a single pool of world-class learning materials across multiple courses (OU);
  - the capacity to manage and add value to the institution's relationship with the learner, beyond individual courses (UWLI);
  - the ability to offer and flexibly adjust a variety of physical, virtual, and blended learning versions of courses (UMUC);
  - the capacity to roll out cohort-based learning (UMUC) where online cohorts of 25, lead by a mentor, are the model; and
  - the infrastructure and capabilities to create communities of inquiry through "knowledge rooms" such as the eCafe at the Wharton School at the University of Pennsylvania.

- USQ has created a powerful vision of the "fifth generation learning environment" as described by Taylor (2001). This model blends e-learning and knowledge management tools. Eventually, USQ's infrastructures will dramatically reduce the costs of learning materials and organizational processes in addition to enhancing all aspects of the learner's experiences.

- The COLIS (Collaborative Online Learning and Information Systems) project led by Macquarie University, in partnership with four other Australian universities and industry partners, has successfully developed an integrated approach learning management and information services provision.

- Many for-profit e-learning ventures have failed. NYUonline (New York University's for-profit venture) and Virtual Temple (Temple University's for-profit) recently closed as did UMUConline. Unproven business models and strategies are the central reason for failure.

- e-Learning in non-university settings (corporations, associations, other non-profits, government agencies) is growing, not as a standalone function, but as a fundamental element of performance enhancement and communities of practice.

The idea that both quality and accessibility can be improved simultaneously has come to be the hallmark of Internet technologies.

Van B. Weigel

e-Learning allows learning and performance professionals to do things we have always wanted to do: to deliver learning and information immediately; to deliver everywhere; to coach; to empower individuals; to collect and distribute best practices; to increase dialogue; to bust through the classroom walls; to increase community; and to know who is learning, referring to source materials, and contributing.

Allison Rossett

- Many corporations regard knowledge management as a strategic function and have placed it high in the executive structure. However, while many have invested substantially in knowledge management they are yet to reap significant returns on that investment.
- Many practitioners in corporate settings hold high hopes for the merging of learning with knowledge management. They see this merging as a potential means for making learning more strategic and for giving knowledge manage-

ment a means for interacting more effectively with employees and suppliers.

Using these lenses, one can follow the progress of e-knowledge in theory and practice. These lenses enable us to understand current practice and anticipate future processes. These efforts will accelerate over the next few years. As standards, processes, and marketplaces develop for e-content while organizational infrastructures and competencies advance, so will the state of reflective practice.

CHAPTER 4

Technologies, Standards, and Marketplaces for e-Knowledge

- Internet Culture Drives the e-Knowledge Industry
- Internet Infrastructures and Technologies
- Application Integration Through Web services
- Standards Incorporate Consensus and Create Value
- Repositories and Emerging e-Knowledge Marketplaces

Advancements in e-knowledge technologies are happening in three main areas: Web Infrastructure, Applications Integration and e-Knowledge Standards.

Web Infrastructure:
The development of the Semantic Web, Grid computing and Internet2 are enhancing the capacities of the World Wide Web and Internet. Technical standards and protocols are essential to mainstreaming these next generation capacities.

Applications Integration:
Web services related technologies (XML, SOAP, UDDI and WSDL) will enable disparate applications and platforms to communicate and engage data easily and seamlessly.

e-Knowledge Standards:
Emerging standards will enable e-knowledge to be captured, understood and re-applied in new contexts. This includes standards for metadata, learning management, content modularization, knowledge management, workflow and performance support.

These developments will enable the development of enterprise repositories for collecting, maintaining and exchanging e-content, context and narrative for learning, research and other forms of scholarship.

Cross-enterprise marketplaces for e-content will become major factors in most industries. Such marketplaces will open previously unattainable secondary markets for e-content.

Terms & Concepts

Learning Objects: Modules of re-usable learning content that are available in a full spectrum of forms and characteristics, ranging from paragraphs, individual images, and video clips, to chapters, full texts and anthologies.

Metadata: Data about data; information about information. Metadata is used to describe information resources and learning objects. Typically, it reveals the contents of the learning object so enabling discovery, management, and exchange. It sometimes exists as a 'wrapper,' directly attached to a learning object; other times, it exists separately in searchable repositories.

Standards: Formally or informally agreed-upon models that signal consensus. e-Knowledge standards will enable networks, computation and communication devices, applications, and data to interact with one another.

The Grid: Grid computing involves harnessing the latent power of distributed computing systems to create massive grid arrays that can be used by scientists for research or by companies like IBM, Sun, and HP/Compaq to create distributed platforms for delivering services to their clients.

Internet2: The next generation of the Internet, providing great bandwidth and capability to its subscribers.

Web Services: XML, SOAP, UDDI, and WSDL enable disparate applications on varying platforms to communicate, opening the door for Web services that provide the promise of seamless interoperability between applications and platforms.

XML: eXtensible Markup Language.

SOAP: Simple Object Access Protocol.

UDDI: Universal Description, Discovery and Integration.

WSDL: Web Services Description Language.

Internet Culture: there are four sub-cultures that shape the Internet as we know it. 1) techno-meritocratic, 2) hacker, 3) virtual communitarian and 4) entrepreneurial cultures.

Orthogonal Relationships: The e-knowledge environment enables multi-directional sharing of knowledge. The resulting value web incorporates relationships that can be expressed in dimensions that are wholly independent of each other. For example, cost and satisfaction.

Ontologies: descriptions of concept domains that bring together controlled vocabularies and taxonomies with a high degree of relational specificity.

Parasitic Computing: Networked servers are made to unwittingly perform computation on behalf of a remote node.

Augmented Reality: Use of networked technology to provide knowledge and tools that enhance the capacity of people to perform tasks.

Resource Description Framework (RDF): A language specifically designed to support the sharing of metadata and information enriched by it.

Ambient e-Intelligence: Combining of artificial intelligence with e-knowledge to create collaborative intelligence for use by communities of practice.

Internet Culture Drives the e-Knowledge Industry

Individuals and organizations must discover new ways of conducting the business of e-knowledge if they are to achieve order-of-magnitude leaps in the capacity to share knowledge. The essence of these new approaches is embodied in the sub-cultures, capabilities, and dynamics of the Internet. Broadly speaking, most of us can identify two key cultural elements that contribute to the development of the Internet:

- A transactional, financially-driven culture of business and commerce; and
- A freewheeling, informal, individual- and community-driven culture.

In the world of software development and distribution, this culture expresses itself in polarities such as proprietary versus 'open source' systems. This tension will not find an easy resolution and will likely continue. In addition to the need to satisfy cultures, there is a bottom-line technical requirement for the e-Knowledge Industry to flourish: the user must be able to share data and applications must work across technology platforms. In a word, what is needed is interoperability.

From a more scholarly analysis, Manuel Castells identifies *four* key Internet sub-cultures: "the techno-meritocratic culture, the

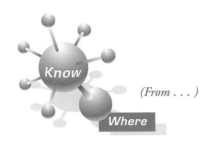

(From . . .)

hacker culture, the virtual communitarian culture, and the entrepreneurial culture. Together they contribute to an ideology of freedom that is widespread in the Internet world." (Castells, 2001). This analysis is important because it also places emphasis on *culture* as a driver of change. Furthermore, Castells makes the point that the cultural roots of the Internet are deep and will shape commercial use.

The Internet was born at the unlikely intersection of big science, military research, and libertarian culture . . . all the key technological developments that led to the Internet were built around government institutions, major universities, and research centers. The Internet did not originate in the business world. It was too daring a technology, too expensive a project, and too risky an initiative to be assumed by profit-oriented organizations . . . the culture of the Internet is rooted in the scholarly tradition of the shared pursuit of science, of reputation by academic excellence, of peer review, and of openness in all research findings, with due credit to the authors of each discovery. Historically, the Internet was produced in academic circles, and in their ancillary research units, both in the heights of professional ranks and in the trenches of graduate student work, from where the values, the habits, and the knowledge diffused into the hacker culture.

Manuel Castells

The Internet is an invention on the scale of Gutenberg's; it blows up the existing trade-off between richness and reach with the same bundle of economic resources.

Philip Evans and Thomas Wurster

Many dot.com ventures failed to understand the implications of the Internet culture for e-business—among many other factors. It comes as no surprise that some of the most promising initiatives regarding learning object exchanges and e-knowledge marketplaces are following the values of Internet culture that Castells describes. There are three primary vectors of technological development that are enabling the development of an interoperable global infrastructure:

- **Infrastructure Development of the Semantic Web, the Grid, and Internet2.** These technologies deal with emerging infrastructure capabilities, or capacities, of the World Wide Web and Internet. They are relevant to all organizational infrastructures and users of Internet technology, even if they are connected to local area networks rather than the Internet. This future will not be mainstreamed without technical standards and protocols.
- **Integration through Web services-related Technologies** (e.g., XML, SOAP, UDDI, WSDL) that will enable disparate applications and platforms to communicate and exchange data easily and seamlessly. These developments will enable seamless integration of enterprise and Web-based applications.
- **Standards.** e-Knowledge-related standards (metadata, learning management, content modularization, knowledge management, workflow, and performance support) enable e-knowledge to be captured, understood, shared, and re-applied in new contexts.

This chapter describes the nature of these technological developments; how to understand key emerging standards and the Internet culture that pervades their development; the emergence of enterprise repositories and e-knowledge marketplaces, building on these technologies and standards, and some of the policy implications for organizations and managers.

Internet Culture Trumps Enterprise Prerogatives

Many enterprise leaders are accustomed to treating knowledge resources like a centralized computing resource in the early days of computing. Setting local rules for allocating access to knowledge resources and restricting who has access to what is treated as a local prerogative. But in the world of the Semantic Web, grid computing, Web services, peer-to-peer sharing, and interoperability, the rules are set by the Internet culture. As Richard Hunter points out in *World Without Secrets*, even information that organizations want to keep secret gets shared (e.g. in communities of practice and other channels of secondary access). One implication is that the competitive advantage gained from any single innovatory product or service (e.g., a new course) is now short-lived, because the know-how that was used to create that product or service will leak out.

Enterprises must play as part of a global knowledge structure if they are to compete in the e-Knowledge Industry. Enterprise leadership, infrastructures, processes, and cultures must reflect that reality.

Applying the Lenses of Knowing

The technologies, standards, and marketplaces for e-knowledge are best viewed through the primary "lenses of knowing." The lenses of "what," "who," "when," "where," "how," "why," and "if" are deployed through the remainder of this book.

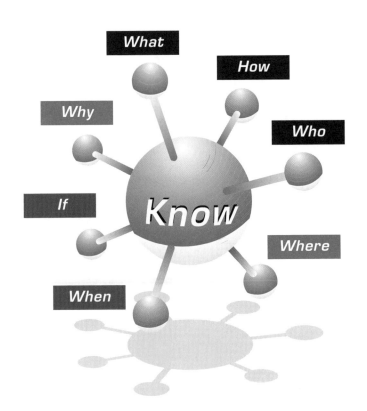

Know What . . .
(keywords = KM, KM systems, information structure, semantics, ontologies, choose your topic . . .)

Know How . . .
(keywords = networking, consulting, collaborating, sharing, researching, reflecting, developing, testing, maintaining, doing, innovating, managing, learning, navigating . . .)

Know Who . . .
(keywords = networks, authorities, institutions, individuals, collaborators, practitioners . . .)

Know Where . . .
(keywords = where-to, where-from, strategic positioning, planning, reflecting . . .)

Know Why . . .
(keywords = context, business planning, strategy, reasons . . .)

Know When . . .
(keywords = timing, pacing, planning, just-in-time scheduling, context, the past, the future . . .)

Know If . . .
(keywords = scenarios, scenario development, foresight, futures, contingency, just-in-case . . .)

Internet Infrastructures and Technologies

In many ways *all* the standards efforts profiled in this chapter can be seen as providing a foundation for the next jump-shift in the Knowledge Economy, enabled by enhanced Internet capabilities, in which far more can be done to exploit past and future knowledge. In terms of key technology developments, there are three large-scale R&D efforts underway: the Semantic Web, the Grid and Internet2.

The Semantic Web

Tim Berners-Lee provided the original vision and follow-through to invent the Web as we know it. Together with other members of the World Wide Web Consortium (W3C), he is also providing the vision for extending it to new capability (Berners-Lee, Tim, James Hendler, and Ora Lassila. *Scientific American*,

2001). Known as the Semantic Web, this extended capability will deliver better access to richer content, as well as mechanisms to extend automation and ensure trust. The term "semantic" is used to indicate the importance assigning contextual meaning to information to enable effective knowledge exchange.

The Semantic Web will rely upon encoded *meaning* in its information structures and the *relationships* between information. The key technology supporting this initiative is the Resource Description Framework (RDF), a "language" specifically designed to support the sharing of metadata and information enriched by it. The widespread implementation of RDF will therefore facilitate the growth of new value chains in both information and knowledge.

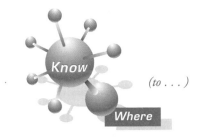

The Semantic Web Improves Productivity of People and Networks. Why is this important? Most of the uses of intelligent agents and knowledge searching described in the vignettes in Chapter 2 are enabled by the Semantic Web. This can make knowledge workers far more productive than today. Consider the following extension of one of our vignettes:

"Conrad Elliott wishes to enrich a seminar he is giving next week on applications of ambient technology to professional association meetings. Working at his desk, he verbally instructs his intelligent agent, a creation of software, to gather all the latest information on the use of distributed, ambient meeting environments among professional societies. He specifically asks for information on meetings of scientific societies, focusing on the topics of the session, the number of participants in different settings, length and nature of the interactions, learning outcomes, and relation to ongoing communities of practice on these topics. The agent accesses the digital library to refresh its knowledge of the semantics relating to ambient meetings and professional societies, then explores the Semantic Web, searching "tags" for the concepts it needs. The agent culls through the thousands of potentially useful examples, based on the explicit instructions from Elliott and implicit instructions drawn from past experience and searches by him and by other members of his community of practice. The agent reports its findings to Elliott, arrayed in preferred formats that have evolved from past searches."

Making the Semantic Web Possible. For the Semantic Web to become transparent and ubiquitous in our lives in relation to e-knowledge, several things will need to happen. The standards and protocols supporting such exchanges will need to develop and achieve widespread acceptance. Repositories and marketplaces abiding by these standards and protocols will need to make bodies of knowledge available for exchange, repurposing, metering, and updating. Because of its richly interconnected semantic structures (such as embedding expertise with information), the Semantic Web provides the means to manage the ever-growing glut of information. Moreover, this capacity to use semantic structure to deal with content, context, and narrative will elevate the amount of expertise and learning tradecraft that can be communicated in exchanges involving learning objects. But with this new infrastructure, new interfaces engaging users

and the Web will need to achieve amenity and enable an entire community of users to be more efficient. And finally, users will need to develop both skills and habits of mind that enable them to seek and process knowledge much more effectively and more rapidly than today. They will need to be able to hone new skills in processing information *about* knowledge they are seeking and in *experiencing* the knowledge they have acquired. Their knowledge quests will likely involve far richer patterns of interactivity with other individuals and communities of practice, both in acquiring knowledge, communicating insights, and refining those insights.

The Grid

For some time, the research community has been looking at ways to link computers together, regardless of the distance between them, to create the equivalent of a single more powerful computer. This has progressed to the point where huge levels of computing power can be made available. For example, the US-based National Science Foundation (NSF) is developing a supercomputing grid that is scheduled for completion in 2003. It will be capable of performing 11.6 trillion calculations per second, all with a guaranteed quality of service.

A related development is the availability of software that enables groups of personal computers to tackle tasks that used to be restricted to supercomputers. Each personal computer works on just a small part of the overall task. The overall effect is to build an aggregated capacity that is equivalent in terms of raw computing power to a single, much larger computer but without a guaranteed quality of service.

Tapping an Underutilized Resource. Although the bulk of that work continues to focus on challenging research problems in science and engineering, the approaches

and software developed by those researchers are of increasing relevance to the rest of us. For example, the NSF and the European Commission are collaborating in studies of how a Learning Grid might be established for widespread use. This offers the possibility of providing teachers and students with access to advanced computer simulations, of the kind that historically required a supercomputer, but at little or no cost to their institution. What makes this possible? The necessary high levels of raw computing power are available today but are not being used. They reside in over a billion personal computers in use globally. Over the course of a day, it is likely that each of those computers is on but not doing useful work (for example, its user may leave it unattended for a few minutes). At a global level, this represents a huge waste of resources, which can be overcome by linking computers via the Internet. As yet, few organizations have recognized or anticipated this in their administrative procedures, and through a lack of understanding of the possibilities and a fear of what might result if they allow linking of computers in this way, they are resistant to sharing their organization's "untapped" computer power.

Harnessing the latent power of distributed, interconnected computing systems and building the aggregated capacity of "virtual organizations" is the vision of scientists and researchers of so-called Grid technologies. It is also the vision of less community-minded individuals and organizations, which periodically look for ways to exploit the trust that underlies the willingness of individuals and organizations to link their computers to the Internet. For example, in 2001, the US Internet service provider Juno offered free Internet access to its four million subscribers. How many of them would have checked the small print that entitled Juno to free use of their unused processor power? Juno proposed to rent out that processor power to biotech companies. (www.biotech.about.com/library/weekly/aa_juno.htm) And in 2002, users of peer-to-peer file swapping were offered a new program, Kazaa, free. In the terms of use, which not all potential users read carefully, was a clause granting the right to make use without compensation of unused processor power and also unused storage space. As with Juno, the aggregated power was to be rented out. Many of us access the Internet from home and from work. In the latter case, by agreeing to such clauses, we may be allowing free use of all the processors and storage on our organization's network. Few network managers would be happy with this.

The Threat of Parasitic Computing. Even more controversially, ways now exist to gain access to your processor power without telling you. An example is known as parasitic computing, in which "servers unwittingly perform computation on behalf of a remote node. In this model, one machine forces target computers to solve a piece of a complex computational problem merely by engaging them in standard communication." (Vincent Freeh, University of Notre Dame. www.nd.edu/~parasite). This works by ingenious use of the standard set of protocols that ensures reliable communication on the Internet and in most private networks. Current implementations of parasitic computing are not efficient, so at present we need not worry. But this has the potential to transform the Internet. While Professor Freeh and his colleagues have developed ways to spot parasitic computing, he points out that "its existence raises important questions about the ownership of the resources connected to the Inter- net and challenges current computing paradigms."

It should be stated up front that while "the Grid" is handy common terminology for the ultimate supercomputer spanning the entire globe, there are actually many lesser grids being developed, some of which are targeted at e-knowledge and e-learning. In a way, the same can be said of the Web.

TeraGrid is a cooperative effort "to build and deploy the world's largest, fastest, most comprehensive, distributed infrastructure for open scientific research. When completed, the TeraGrid will include 13.6 teraflops of Linux Cluster computing power distributed at the four TeraGrid sites, facilities capable of managing and storing more than 450 terabytes of data, high-resolution visualization environments, and toolkits for grid computing. These components will be tightly integrated and connected through a network that will initially operate at 40 gigabits per second and later be upgraded to 50-80 gigabits/second— 16 times faster than today's fastest research network."

www.teragrid.org

A number of important initiatives aimed at standardizing Grid efforts include the Globus Toolkit™, an open-source suite of standard protocols that serves as reference implementation architecture (that is, best practice guidelines) for a variety of e-science initiatives, and the Global Grid Forum.

Close to a decade of focused R&D and experimentation has produced considerable consensus on the requirements and architecture of Grid technology.

Ian Foster

Examples of Grid Computing Projects. A number of ambitious Grid projects, largely scientific in conception, have been implemented in recent years that require large amounts of data crunching. Most prominent among the early projects have been Compute Against Cancer and the SETI@Home project. The latter of these projects now harnesses the previously unused CPU time of over half a million personal computers and delivers the equivalent of 1,000 CPU years per day to the task of analyzing radio data from outer space. Likewise, networking brings the possibility of linking people in ways that magnify their knowledge and the contribution they can make to an organization.

"In a future in which computing, storage, and software are no longer objects we possess, but utilities to which we subscribe, the most successful scientific communities are likely to be those that succeed in assembling and making effective use of Grid infrastructures and thus accelerating the development and adoption of new problem-solving methods within their discipline."

Ian Foster, February 2002

Grid computing is not limited to scientific applications. Major hardware providers such as Sun, IBM, and HP/Compaq are pursuing the use of massive grid computing to create new generation of networked computing and powerful applications solutions that they will make available to their customers over the Web.

Internet2

Similar in spirit to the partnerships that created the Internet as we know it today, the Internet2 initiative is primarily a US-based consortium led by around 200 universities working with industry and government to develop and deploy advanced network applications and technologies. Its goals are to:

- create leading edge network capability for the research community;
- enable development of revolutionary Internet applications; and
- ensure rapid transfer of new network services and applications to the broader Internet community.

Internet2 Applications. Within formal education settings, there are already applications of Internet2 capability being developed, many of which make use of the high bandwidth and digital video processing potential. For example, the Laboratory for Computational Science and Engineering at the University of Minnesota has developed Internet2 tools to enhance its distributed learning capability. Its researchers are pursuing collaborative scientific visualization techniques that utilize high performance computing across distributed networks. . In principle, the Internet2 could be used to make the results of such computations available to groups of learners and to provide those groups with some form of video conferencing without requiring old-style ISDN (telephone-company) video conferencing equipment.

As a collaborative effort on a much larger scale, the Internet2 K20 initiative brings together Internet2 member institutions, primary and secondary schools, colleges and universities, libraries, and museums to apply advanced networking tools, applications, and e-content in the pursuit of early innovation.

As with Grid projects, Internet2 also builds on the distributed architecture and collaborative potential of the Internet. The Internet2 "Commons" is a framework for collaboration established for large-scale research within the education community based upon collaborative tools. Initially, these tools have primarily been enabled to work within a video-conferencing platform but it is planned to develop the framework to focus on other interactive services as well.

While there is a small degree of international collaboration, at present the Internet2 project is still largely driven by and for a United States constituency. (ref: Internet2 K20. www.internet2.edu/k20)

Complementary Visions for Network Computing

Semantic Web	The Grid
Distributed networks model	Supercomputing model
Symbolic, heuristic	Numeric, algorithmic
Extension of current web	Scientific computing
Rich meaning, based on representations of context and relationship; machine processible	Resource sharing
Semantic search—find, share, combine (not just documents)	Coordinated problem solving
	Multi-institutional virtual organizations
See: www.w3.org/2001/sw/	Programs and computations as community resources
	See: www-fp.mcs.anl.gov/~foster/grid-projects/

Application Integration through Web Services

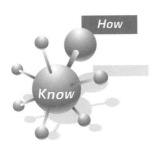

If your application has an interface described in WSDL, and interacts with clients by exchanging XML messages encapsulated into SOAP envelopes, then it is a Web Service.

Fabio Casati

A little over 30 years ago, the development of TCP/IP provided the technical foundation for the Internet. A scant 10 years ago, HTTP and HTML were developed as foundations for the Web. At the turn of the twenty-first century, XML had heralded new frontiers for e-business, promising robust new layers of middleware. The *de facto* standardization of XML made this possible, spawning thousands of new niche applications. And just as HTML delivered publishing tools to all who have access to the Web, the XML-based standards and protocols underlying the development of Web services will deliver comparative expansion in service provision. "Web services" will extend the notion of who may become a service provider.

With advances in computer networks and programming—driven by the increasingly collaborative and distributed nature of business, research, and learning—the next generation of the Web is being built to accommodate integrated, dynamic, and transactional processes that assist in supporting peer collaboration and automating workflow. Importantly, Web services standards and protocols are being developed upon the foundations already in place. Moreover, Web services provide a "future-proofed" means for scalable Internet applications and capability.

Key technologies enabling this layer of infrastructure development include:

- XML (eXtensible Markup Language);
- SOAP (Simple Object Access Protocol);
- UDDI (Universal Description, Discovery and Integration); and
- WSDL (Web Services Description Language).

While Web services can be deployed in a variety of both proprietary and non-proprietary ways, the essential capability is platform-neutral. During 2002, the W3C established a number of working groups to develop abstract models and formal definitions of Web services. The Web Services Description Language (WSDL) has been one of the ongoing outputs of this work and is a means for exposing and discovering services, applications, and data in a standard XML description, thereby enabling dynamic interactions between distributed applications.

What sorts of Web services applications could be developed for learning settings? Gleason (2002) and Jacobson (2002) offer the following examples:

- a class roster services that provides class rosters to online grade books and enterprise-wide learning management systems;
- a clearinghouse function that validates the immigration status of international students;
- a credit card service that accepts credit card and payment information and returns bank authorization;
- an interface service that permits students, faculty, and researchers to use an online art collection on their own terms; and
- a student loan tracking service that allows students to monitor the status of guaranteed student loans.

Over the next five years, Web services-based applications will enable many enterprises to integrate "best of breed applications" into their existing enterprise applications infrastructures.

Standards Incorporate Consensus and Create Value

If the (enterprise's) application creates a trust with the user and a trust with the provider of the Web Service, then a trust arrangement—referred to as transitive trust—is created.

Bernard Gleason

It's this simple. Research and development produces the promise and proof of concept but the new generations of e-knowledge-related standards will be the enduring foundations of the emerging e-Knowledge Industries. Standards signal consensus and marketplace maturity whether they exist formally as *de jure* or informally as *de facto* standards. These standards will enable networks, computation and communication devices, applications, and data to communicate with one another and interoperate in ways that have not been previously possible. Whether standards arise through extensive collaboration among standards bodies or through *de facto* acceptance by the marketplace, their endgame is to foster commonly accepted ways for networked devices to communicate and share data.

Standardization as a valued human activity achieved its first documented milestones in the field of engineering where it helped drive the industrial economies of the nineteenth century. By comparison, standardization in the area of ICT to support e-knowledge is in its infancy. It is just over a decade since small groups of aviation industry specialists began laboring in relative obscurity to develop the first generation of standards for "computer-based training." Following their lead, a broader base of stakeholders (computer engineers, software vendors, the military, educationists, publishers, and government agencies) have in more recent times laid robust foundations for the evolution of infrastructure that will support and promote e-learning. Meanwhile, other spe-

cialists have toiled on defining standards pertinent to knowledge management, electronic commerce, and other e-activities. Over the past five years, these standards development efforts have grown in intensity, importance, and visibility. In a *de facto* manner, these previously disparate collaborations are discovering synergies in their efforts for standardizing e-learning, knowledge management, and e-business.

Example: National Health Services University

Many institutions and learning enterprises are adopting the emerging e-knowledge standards and engaging their communities in a dialogue on their strategic significance. For example, the National Health Services University (NHSU) in the UK has recognized the importance of standards in establishing consensus and a clear vision about the direction of e-learning and e-knowledge. The NHSU Project Management Group developed a white paper suggesting that adopting e-learning standards would enable NHSU to:

- mix and match content from multiple sources;
- develop interchangeable content that can be assembled, disassembled, and reused quickly and easily;
- ensure that NHSU is not "trapped" by proprietary learning technology;
- increase the effectiveness of learning by enabling greater personalization and targeting of the right content to the right person at the right time;
- improve the efficiency and return of investment of learning content development and management; and
- increase the quality and quantity of e-learning content.

The white paper goes on to proclaim that by following these standards, NHSU will be able to achieve the five "abilities" of interoperability, re-usability, manageability, accessibility, and durability. (NHSU, 2002, p.2). Other institutions and learning enterprises are creating similar expressions of support and intent that are useful in raising the consciousness of learning enterprises to these developments.

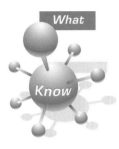

Standards and the Creation of Value

The word "standard" is commonly used in a wide variety of ways. It can mean a social convention, a dress code, a skill level, or a video format. In French, the words "norme" and "normalisation" are used as translations for "standard" and "standardization." In the context of formal organizations such as ISO (the International Organization for Standardization), a "standard" has a very precise meaning.

> *A standard is a published document which sets out specifications and procedures designed to ensure that a material, product, method, or service is fit for its purpose and consistently performs the way it was intended to.*
>
> *Standards Australia*

Standardization of everything from bolt and screw specifications to railroad gauges turned the Industrial Revolution from localized and national phenomena to an international movement. The Internet Revolution would have been impossible without *de facto* standards such as TCP/IP, HTTP, HTML, XML, and more yet to come. And the e-knowledge revolution will not occur without standards in modular content management, vocabularies and meta-data, portable IDs, security, and enterprise system architecture integration.

A Global Investment. Standardization amounts to a huge investment globally. This investment makes good economic sense on many different levels. Standards help grow markets and facilitate trade. The e-Knowledge Industry is no different in this respect from the domestic lighting or cellular phone industries. Standardization of key components enables interoperability while stimulating diversity and innovation.

Economic value chains are fueled by two contrasting activities—the appropriation of value and the creation of value. Standardization is focused almost entirely on the creation of value. While it often delivers new efficiencies to a given market it is not focused on best utilization of resources—that is the concern of an enterprise's management.

With standards now emerging that support the growth of e-learning and knowledge management, value can be assigned or discovered depending on who you are. For example, a CEO of a company developing learning content will see value in routine processes that deliver standards-compliant, quality products and, potentially, greater market share. One employee of the same company may see value in the optimization of assembly processes while another may see the opportunity for innovation; while another, who may be concerned about professional development issues of learning content designers, may see a clearer career path.

Key Standards Areas Facilitating e-Knowledge

Standards developments in a variety of interconnected areas are essential to the achievement of a global, interoperable e-knowledge infrastructure.

History shows that revolutionary changes, tipping points, do not take off without widespread adoption of common standards. Common standards for metadata, learning objects, and learning architecture are mandatory for similar success of the Knowledge Economy.

Wayne Hodgins

The web is a serious commitment to common meanings.

Tim Berners-Lee

Metadata. This is a fundamental digital building block of the Knowledge Economy. Metadata describes knowledge objects, and is used to support the indexing, search, discovery, retrieval, and use of those objects. If one thinks of the analogy of a web-based store, the metadata is analogous to the online catalog of products and the knowledge objects are analogous to the products themselves.

Metadata adds descriptive, technical, administrative, and structural value to data and information. Metadata assists in clustering related information resources and in providing the capacity for "chunking" information for easy reuse, interoperability, transaction, archiving, and preservation. A digital object that is not enriched with metadata cannot be used effectively in contexts for which it was not designed.

High-value digital repositories require well-described and organized metadata throughout the collection. Print collections can rely on a single front-cover or catalogue descriptions of content and context. Digital collections require extensive tagging that enables an e-book or journal article to be segmented into modular, durable, and independent chunks. The tradecraft of achieving metadata chunking in a cost-effective manner will be one of the critical emerging competencies of the e-Knowledge Industry.

Metadata is about both "how" and "what." The initial focus of working groups defining metadata standards such as the IMS Dublin Core was *how* to describe characteristics of information through metadata fields and related subcategories. The *what* of metadata is twofold—deciding what fields among the dozens defined by these metadata standards are necessary for a particular market or application (e.g. Dublin Core), and how to specifically identify the subcategories within the identified metadata fields

to make sense in different markets (e.g. postsecondary education, K-12, corporate training). This involves a narrowing of options and providing a sort of "pull down" menu for many categories (particularly those related to subject area) so users can understand easily what the descriptors mean and objects can be more easily tagged. For example, the community of practice for physics could determine the subcategories appropriate for learning objects in the discipline. These would differ subtly from subcategories used in nearby disciplines and sub disciplines. Descriptions of concept domains, like physics, with controlled and specified vocabularies, meanings and relationships are called ontologies.

The early focus of metadata description has focused on technical, administrative and content-fixated description of information. A key challenge in the development of the Knowledge Economy will be to develop metadata standards to enable the flexible economic exchange of information objects. Knowledge objects will become substantially more complex, combining content, context, and best practices and requiring complex mechanisms for recognizing value. A sort of "matrix of economic value statements" will emerge as an essential component of metadata. This will enable the value webs that will develop for each market. But the most difficult economic challenge is to drive down the cost and price of metadata through dynamically generated knowledge objects, autotagging, and sophisticated tradecraft. Routinely and economically creating ontologies and metadata will be an important capability for the Knowledge Economy.

.

Content Management. It is now over a decade since the first standards began to emerge in the field of computer-supported learning. The Aviation Industry delivered the first such specifications; what's more, they're referenced today in an updated form within the SCORM (Sharable

Content Object Reference Model), developed by the US Department of Defense Advanced Distributed Learning (ADL) initiative. Why are standards for content management necessary? The essential reason is that digital information by its very nature is portable; it can be constituted and re-constituted, chunked-down and aggregated, and, when modularized into standard bits, is easily assembled. Without standard content formats and methods of management content, marketplaces cannot mature.

It will also be important to consider how to maintain the value of content over the longer term. One problem here is the existence of well-meant initiatives to reduce the importance of consistency and the dominance of particular languages and spellings. As an example, the Web site freespeling.com (with only one "l" in spelling) argues for freedom to choose new spellings; its surveys indicate a preference for FREND rather than friend, HITE for height, and KAOS for chaos. And kaos is what would result for content management if we experienced significant linguistic drift.

Learner Information. Standards associated with learner information involve technologies that support unique identification and authentication, and thereby provide performance support and portability of student information within e-learning courseware and between institutions. Standard formats for learner information enable different system components to share information about learners.

Security. Remember the days not so long ago when online banking was still just a possibility because adequate security infrastructures were not yet developed? The single reason why online banking services, and e-business more broadly, is now widely accepted is because the security systems are in place. Trusted mechanisms that protect data and networks from un-

authorized access are, of course, not specific to e-knowledge but they're critical if the e-Knowledge Industries are to flourish. There are many standards already developed in this area and many under development—they range from enterprise firewall systems to digital signatures and unique ID and password combinations. Without well-developed security technologies (including standards and protocols), the "Web of Trust" that is envisioned by the World Wide Web Consortium as a pinnacle of development will not be achieved.

Enterprise Systems Integration. From an enterprise (including institutional or organizational) perspective, a key area of standardization is to do with systems integration. Without systems integration and interoperability, full service implementation cannot take place. Technologies such as Web services (mentioned earlier) will be important here. Integration needs to span a wide range of systems that include networking and communications, learning platforms, content management, knowledge management, human resource development, customer relationship management, enterprise resource planning, rights management, directory services, and repositories of various other kinds.

Organizational Workflow. Related closely to enterprise systems integration, organizational workflow standards are critical to developing robust mechanisms for knowledge management. However, with workflow and knowledge management standards, the emphasis is upon the flow of information and how to automate it where appropriate. It is about automating proven procedure and enhancing organizational efficiency and professional productivity.

The above synopsis is in no way intended to be exhaustive. The very nature of innovation within the digital world is that new technologies and, hence, standards will continue to develop as a result of previous practice.

The very purpose of science is to help us understand the complex world around us through simple explanations. The purpose of technology is to make new artifacts fulfill the needs of humans, not to make their lives more complicated.

Michael Dertouzos

Examples of e-Knowledge Standards

As the international standards movement has gained momentum, a broad range of activities have come under scrutiny.

Area of Standards	What It Is	Key Players and Developments
Vocabularies and Metadata	Metadata standards provide frameworks for the description, discovery, and management of knowledge resources. Controlled vocabularies enhance effectiveness. Learning objects use metadata to manage content and context. Learning objects are a key building block for marketplaces and repositories.	• OCLC (Online Computer Library Center Inc.) has facilitated the Dublin Core Metadata Initiative as a forum for the development and internationalization of interoperable cross-domain metadata standards. OCLC is a nonprofit membership organization that serves over 41,000 libraries in 82 countries. • IEEE has accredited a Learning Object Metadata (LOM) Standard. • IMS Global Learning Consortium, ADL initiatives, ARIADNE, and other initiatives have adopted or adapted LOM. • Educational Modeling Languages (e.g., EML) are emerging as a means to describe and manage pedagogical usage of learning objects. IMS is working to situate this effort. These languages will assist in developing dynamic e-learning environments. • The Global Knowledge Economics Council is leading efforts toward international standardization of knowledge management. It has made significant progress on the production of terminology and vocabularies to support this. • The Digital Library Federation has developed METS, the Metadata Encoding Transmission Standard, as a generalized model for encoding descriptive, administrative, and structural metadata for digital library objects. • The PRISM Working Group is developing a metadata standard for "syndicating, aggregating, post-processing, and multi-purposing content from magazines, news, catalogs, books, and mainstream journals." • ISO/IEC JTC1 SC36 is developing a common vocabulary for usage in the standardization of IT for learning, education, and training. • HR-XML develops specifications aimed at producing industry standard vocabularies relevant to Human Resources (e.g., recruitment, staffing, competencies). • XTM is advancing the Topic Maps Paradigm by leveraging XML to describe the associations between topics in heterogeneous collections of information.
Modular Content Packaging and Management	Allows streamlined communication between a content repository and an LMS. Courses and learning objects can be transferred from one CMS/LMS to another, re-purposed, and combined.	• IMS Content Packaging specification (commercialized as LRN by Microsoft). IMS Simple Sequencing specification (under development). • AICC guidelines and recommendations. • ADL SCORM based in part on Aviation Industry work. • IEEE LTSC is in the process of creating accredited standards based on two parts of SCORM that were derived from AICC specifications. • MPEG has developed content standards for handling digital video and is in process of extending content management to include standards for managing intellectual property rights.

Examples of e-Knowledge Standards (continued)

Area of Standards	What It Is	Key Players and Developments
Learner Records	Enables different system components to share information about learners. Provides a key for performance- and decision-support systems.	• IMS Learner Information Package (LIP) specification. • Personal and Private Information (PAPI) drafted by IEEE and now being examined by ISO/IEC.
Security	Provides trusted mechanisms that protect data and networks from un-authorized access.	• Security issues are complex and continually requiring resolve—the primary groups working in the technology infrastructure domain are the IETF and W3C. Specific topics include network security, user authentication, computer system security, and cryptography. • The IETF and W3C are jointly developing standards for digital signatures. • The Open Knowledge Initiative (OKI) has developed authorization and authentication systems for access to data, e.g., NT Domains, LDAP Servers, Kerberos, etc.
Enterprise Systems Integration	Focuses primarily on interoperability of administrative systems.	• SIF is "creating a technology standard that will revolutionize the business of [k-12] education" through specifying protocols that enable, e.g., student information systems to interoperate with human resources, financial management, and voice telephony systems both within and between schools. • IMS has developed specifications for enterprise systems and is in process of developing these further. Also related to the issue of integration are the IMS specifications on Digital repositories Interoperability. • OKI is developing a suite of APIs that define and implement access between learning technology and common services.
Organizational workflow	Supports processes critical to knowledge management and e-business.	• WfMC has been promoting and developing workflow standards for about a decade. • OASIS is developing a suite of protocols and languages associated with ebXML aimed at specifying the public interfaces required for e-business. • The Business Process Management Initiative (BPMI) is complementing the work of OASIS through development of standard private interfaces. • The GKEC has established a standard process and scoped out areas of activity associated with knowledge economics standardization.

Adapted from: Geoff Collier and Robby Robson, Elearning Interoperability Standards, January 2002, 2–4.
A truly global collection of organizations is engaged in the development of standards and specifications.
Individuals and organizations should follow the developments emanating from these groups.

e-Knowledge Standards and Specifications Organizations (indicative list)

Acronym	Name	Focus
ADL	Advanced Distributed Learning initiative www.adlnet.org	Development of distributed learning architecture that services US online instructional requirements, particularly for military and paramilitary stakeholders. Key output has been the collection of specifications known as SCORM (Sharable Content Object Reference Model).
AICC	Aviation Industry CBT Committee www.aicc.org	Aviation industry technology-based training professionals. Develops guidelines in the development, delivery, and evaluation of Computer Based Training (also, 'Computer Managed Instruction') and related training technologies.
ALIC	Advanced Learning Infrastructure Consortium www.alic.gr.jp/eng/	Consortium of public and private organizations focused on the development and promotion of e-learning infrastructure in Japan.
CEN/ISSS WS-LT	Comité Européen de Normalization/Information Society Standardization System Workshop—Learning Technology www.cenorm.be/ISSS	"Learning Technology" standardization in Europe. Its early focus was primarily on the developing and promoting standards for metadata, taxonomies, vocabularies, and copyright.
DCMI	Dublin Core Metadata Initiative dublincore.org	Promoting the widespread (international) adoption of interoperable metadata standards and developing specialized metadata vocabularies for describing resources that enable more intelligent information discovery systems.
DLF	Digital Library Federation www.diglib.org	A consortium of (primarily university) libraries and related agencies formed for the purpose of extending their services and collections through the application of information technologies. Identifies standards and best practices for managing networked access to diverse digital resource collections. Also defines and develops prototype systems and components.
GGF	Global Grid Forum www.gridforum.org	Community of scientific researchers and practitioners developing open-source distributed computing ("grid") architectures, applications, guidelines, and standards.
GKEC	Global Knowledge Economics Council www.gkec.org	A broad consortium including representatives from various governments, academic institutions, and many of the Fortune 500 industrial firms. It focuses on issues concerning knowledge management and the growth of knowledge markets. GKEC also aims to develop knowledge economics policies, programs, and funds to assist developing countries close the knowledge divide.
HR-XML	HR-XML Consortium www.hr-xml.org	Develops specifications aimed at producing industry (XML-based) standard vocabularies relevant to human resources (e.g., recruitment, staffing, competencies).

e-Knowledge Standards and Specifications Organizations *(indicative list)*

Acronym	Name	Focus
IEEE LTSC	**Institute for Electronic & Electrical Engineers Learning Technology Standards Committee** *ltsc.ieee.org*	Chartered by the IEEE Computer Society Standards Activity Board "to develop accredited technical standards, recommended practices and guides for learning technology. The LTSC coordinates formally and informally with other organizations that produce specifications and standards for similar purposes."
IMS	**IMS Global Learning Consortium, Inc.** *www.imsglobal.org*	Develops and promotes open specifications for facilitating online distributed learning activities (e.g., managing modular educational content, tracking learner progress, reporting learner performance, and exchanging student records between administrative systems). Its key overall focus is the specification of interoperable systems that support e-learning.
ISO/IEC JTC1-SC36	**International Standards Organization/ International Electrotechnical Committee Joint Technical Committee 1 (Information Technology), Subcommittee 36: Standards for Learning, Education, and Training** *jtc1sc36.org*	JTC1-SC36 serves as the pre-eminent formal international forum for standards development in information technology for learning, education, and training to support individuals, groups, or organizations, and to enable interoperability and reusability of resources and tools.
OASIS	**Organization for the Advancement of Structured Information Standards** *www.oasis-open.org*	Non-profit global consortium developing and promoting adoption of interoperable e-business standards covering areas such as security, Web services, business transactions, electronic publishing, and topic maps. Over 400 corporate and individual members in 100 countries around the world. OASIS and the United Nations jointly sponsor ebXML, a global framework for e-business data exchange.
OKI	**Open Knowledge Initiative** *web.mit.edu/oki*	A consortium of higher education institutions developing an architecture which identifies points of interoperability.
OeBF	**Open eBook Forum** *www.openebook.org*	International consortium of publishers developing a suite of specifications for electronic publishing that will assist particularly in the management of publisher property rights for electronic books.
SIF	**Schools Interoperability Framework** *www.sifinfo.org*	A broad consortium of vendors formed under the auspices of the (US) Software and Information Industry Association. Its focus is in the specification of enterprise software systems that manage student, staff, and class information, resource planning, and records portability, including financial and library services.
W3C	**World Wide Web Consortium** *www.w3.org*	The W3C "develops interoperable technologies (specifications, guidelines, software, and tools) to lead the Web to its full potential." Its goals include universal access, trust, interoperability, scalability, decentralization, and development of the next generation Semantic Web.
WfMC	**Workflow Management Coalition** *www.wfmc.org*	The WfMC is an international coalition of vendors, users, and researchers with a mission to promote and develop interoperable workflow software systems and products.

Repositories and Emerging e-Knowledge Marketplaces

One of the fundamental capabilities for e-knowledge regards the storage and retrieval of modules of content, context, and narrative that can be stored, repurposed, and combined and whose use can be metered and charged to a customer where appropriate. These modules will be available in a range of forms: highly granular (paragraphs, individual images, video clips), to chapters and topics, to full texts and anthologies. In learning contexts, such modular content is typically referred to as "learning objects."

A Diversity of Repositories

Repositories of learning objects are a recent phenomenon. However, enterprises and institutions have been developing repositories of digital content for much longer—this is particularly so for the research and scientific communities. The first key to unlocking such archives for application in learning contexts and marketplace usage lies with the development of interoperability specifications, standards, and protocols, whether the repositories exist as centralized databases or as virtual, distributed collections. The second key is to refine enterprise practices and routines so that the cost of establishing, refreshing, maintaining, and using these repositories is driven downward toward economic viability.

Enterprise Repositories. Across all industries, enterprises have maintained various kinds of repositories of digital content for internal, proprietary use. Leading-edge enterprises that have recognized the jump-shift potentials of sharing knowledge are developing first-generation prototypes of enterprise repositories for sharing and exchanging e-knowledge with external parties. Without such repositories, knowledge management is difficult to cultivate. Companies such as Artesia Technologies, Knowledge Media, Inc., and the Scottish-based Dynamic Knowledge Corporation are creating tools that facilitate enterprise knowledge repositories.

Challenging Business Models for e-Publishing. The Internet culture is challenging the current publishing culture. It comes as no surprise that a significant groundswell has developed across a number of communities of practice that are challenging the traditional models of publishing and distribution. This is particularly so in the case of online scholarly journals, where the processes of peer review, editorial compilation, publication, and dissemination are all unbundled.

Pet food stores weren't the killer app for the Web . . . but peer-reviewed scholarly journals might be.

Sarah Milstein, 2002

As reported in *The New York Times,* there are about 25,000 peer-reviewed journals in science, technical, and medical fields. This means they are vetted by two or three specialists plus the journals' editors. For example, the *Journal of the American College of Cardiology,* for one, has trimmed its submission and review cycle to five weeks, down from six to eight, since it adopted an electronic peer-review system in January 2002. Glenn Collins, the journal's managing editor, expects to eliminate 80 percent of his mailing costs, which had typically run between $60,000 and $70,000 US. Even when the cost savings are minimal, though, publishers often install electronic systems for convenience. "The reason you do it is so that the authors can track the status of their manuscripts," says Catherine D. DeAngelis, editor in chief of the *Journal of the American Medical Association,* which plans to have an electronic peer-review system in place by January 2003. Once the Web-based system is installed, authors will be able to track the progress of a review in much the way as UPS and FedEx customers can track packages online (Milstein, 2002.).

Jeffrey Young (2002) and Raym Crow (2002*)* have both provided a compelling rationale that institutional repositories will build "superarchives" or collections of intellectual output. Such collections (or repositories) could stimulate new practice and new market conditions. Some of this new practice will foster growth in "publicly owned" knowledge through greater willingness to share intellectual output among institutions. Conversely, some new practice will focus on creating new syntheses, combinations, or extensions of existing forms of knowledge. These new offerings will command new premiums and drive new markets. Significant benefits could be experienced by authors, consumers, and institutions. Publishers will need to remain agile in discerning their roles in these new markets.

Institutional Repositories. In discussing the development of institutional repositories, Crow observes that the technical effort is dwarfed by the effort and organizational costs of addressing repository policy, content management, and faculty marketing: "These tasks include:

- developing content accession policies;
- deciding on what metadata to store and present;
- creating digital object identifiers (DOIs);
- crafting author permission and licensing agreements to disseminate work indefinitely;
- developing content creation and input guidelines suitable to long term archiving and proper presentation;
- training staff and authors in using the software to submit content;
- creating document submission instructions; and
- marketing the repository concept to respective depositors." (Crow, 2002)

We conclude that the Information Marketplace will touch essentially all human activity.

Michael Dertouzos

The three key digital content distribution issues are authentication, authorization, and access. These are difficult challenges that are best addressed by a shared, neutral resource.

Patrick McElroy

These expenses can be extensive at larger institutions and enterprises. The institutional repositories established to date have been at major research institutions. Does this solution scale down to less complex institutions? Indeed, it is unlikely that institutional repositories will be affordable by any institutions until the costs of entry are driven down substantially. This can be accomplished by providing model practices, policies, protocols, routines, and guidance on how to manage the cost of knowledge asset management. Professional societies serving the higher education industry should accept this challenge. In North America, the energies of the National Association of College and University Business Officers (NACUBO), EDUCAUSE, Association of Research Libraries (ARL), the National Association of College and University Attorneys (NACUA), and the American Society for Training and Development (ASTD) would be most welcome in this effort.

Institutional repositories, by capturing, preserving, and disseminating a university's collective intellectual capital, serve as meaningful indicators of an institution's academic quality. Under the traditional system of scholarly communication, much of the intellectual output and value of an institution's intellectual property is diffused through thousands of scholarly journals. An institutional repository concentrates the intellectual product created by a university's researcher, making it easier to demonstrate its social and financial value . . . While institutional repositories centralize, preserve, and make accessible an institution's intellectual capital, at the same time they form part of a global system of decentralized, distributed repositories. This attribute is central to the role repositories can play in a disaggregated model of scholarly publishing."

Raym Crow. SPARC, 2002

Multi-enterprise Repositories

A searchable and responsive marketplace that draws content, context, and narrative from many sources and repositories is one of the fundamental elements of an e-Knowledge Industry. For this to happen, technologies and standards must be developed that enable true interoperability for learning objects and practices. Groups like the Learning Objects Network, MERLOT, SMETE, and the Australian Le@rning Federation are developing shareable repositories of learning content. The MIT-created Open Knowledge Initiative (OKI) is building a scalable, sustainable open-source reference framework for all the online processes that support e-learning. This framework will help streamline the processes for assembling, delivering, and accessing educational resources. Such initiatives are the precursors of ***meta-marketplaces*** that will span industry verticals —education, publishing, learning management providers, associations, and professional societies—to create broad-based exchange of e-content and tacit knowledge through communities of practice.

Standards, processes, and marketplaces for e-content are essential, but they will be incomplete without advances in public and private infrastructures for exchanging and deploying content.

Association of Research Libraries— Scholar's Portal. Announced in mid-2002, this three-year project aims to deliver software tools that provide integrated Web access to "open," high quality (library-based) information services. It brings together a group of ARL members (University of Southern California, University of California-San Diego, Dartmouth College, University of Arizona, Arizona State University, Iowa State University, and the University of Utah) with Fretwell-Downing, Inc.

www.arl.org/access/scholarsportal/

Australian Le@rning Federation—Learning Object Exchange. Funded by State and Federal governments of Australia and New Zealand, the Le@rning Federation is developing an online exchange of high quality, reusable, and curriculum content that will support teachers in improving educational outcomes for K-12 students.

www.thelearningfederation.edu.au

Campus Alberta Repository of Educational Objects (CAREO). An educational object repository of multidisciplinary teaching materials jointly developed by the Universities of Alberta and Calgary in cooperation with the Canadian BELLE (Broadband Enabled Lifelong Learning Environment) project and CANARIE (Canadian Network for the Advancement of Research in Industry and Education).

careo.netera.ca

Distributed National Electronic Resource (DNER). A UK-based initiative that provides access to quality assured information resources on the Internet, including collections of scholarly journals, abstracts, manuscripts, maps, music scores, images, moving pictures, and sounds.

www.dner.ac.uk

EducaNext. A consortium of European universities, has developed a 'universal' brokerage platform enabling the creation and sharing of knowledge for higher education in Europe.

www.educanext.org

Educational Object Economy (EOE) Foundation. Positioned as a research and development "learning-community," the EOE builds standards-based tools that promote the use and testing of shared educational objects and open-source components-based software. It has a significant collection of java-based learning objects.

www.eoe.org

Health Education Assets Library (HEAL). Initiated by the University of California (Los Angeles), HEAL is now a collaboration involving the Association of American Medical Colleges and the (US) National Library of Medicine. Through developing a standards-based framework, it provides educators with free access to distributed collections of high-quality multimedia materials (such as images and videos) to augment health science education.

www.healcentral.org

> *The publisher's dilemma lies in determining just how digital the company should be right now, and how fully digital the company is envisioned to be in the future.*
>
> *Gordon Freedman*

Scholarly, Cultural, and Scientific Repositories

- **JSTOR**—an archive of scholarly journal www.jstor.com

- **DSpace**—an MIT superarchive aimed at "capturing, distributing, and preserving the intellectual output of MIT" web.mit.edu/dspace/live/home.html

- **PictureAustralia**—a distributed repository of cultural significance contributed to by galleries and libraries in Australia and New Zealand www.pictureaustralia.org

- **GEODISE** (Grid-Enabled Optimization and Design Search for Engineering)—grid based access to a knowledge repository www.geodise.org/

- **eScholarship at the University of California Digital Library** repositories.cdlib.org/escholarship/

- **OSU Knowledge Bank**—Ohio State University scholarly repository www.lib.ohio-state.edu/Lib Info/scholarcom/Kbproposal.html

ICONEX. Funded by the UK-based Joint Information Systems Council with the aim of facilitating the development and brokerage of interactive, interoperable, learning objects through establishing a standards-based repository.

www.iconex.hull.ac.uk

Learning Objects Network (LON). An Internet infrastructure company established to service the needs of a broad range of stakeholders engaged in standards-based development and packaging of learning objects. Stakeholders include publishers, corporations, the military, medical information providers, and training and education providers.

www.learningobjectsnetwork.com

Multimedia Educational Resource for Learning & Online Teaching (MERLOT). Initiated in the United States, MERLOT is now an international cooperative with a primary aim of providing a free and open repository of high-quality learning resources suitable for faculty and students in higher education. It achieves this through a subscription-based membership and through leveraging the academic tradition of peer review.

www.merlot.org

Resource Discovery Network (RDN). A collaboration of over sixty UK-based educational and research organizations, including the Natural History Museum and the British Library. It provides free resource discovery services that access a wide range of quality online resource collections organized according to academic discipline areas.

www.rdn.ac.uk

Scholarly Publishing and Academic Resources Coalition (SPARC). An alliance of universities, research libraries, and organizations focused on facilitating the optimum dissemination of scholarly output in the networked digital environment. It achieves this through incubation of innovative and cost-effective mechanisms of distribution and ongoing public advocacy for changes in the culture of scholarly communication and the systems that support it.

www.arl.org/sparc

Science Museums of China (SMC). The Science Museums of China (SMC) has been established with support from the Chinese Academy of Sciences to be a comprehensive Web site for "cherishing the goals of spreading scientific knowledge, advocating scientific methodology, and carrying forward scientific spirit." SMC is made up of a cluster of virtual science museums covering a range of disciplines.

www.kepu.com.cn/english/index.html

Horizontal e-Knowledge Marketplaces

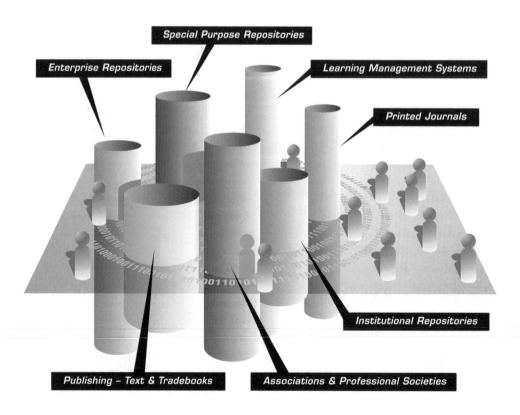

SMETE.ORG (Science, Mathematics, Engineering, and Technology Education). A digital library and portal of services for teachers and students developed by the SMETE Open Federation. It provides access to online teaching and learning materials and communities engaged in the disciplines of science, math, engineering, and technology.

www.smete.org

XanEdu. This company specializes in the production and delivery of *CoursePacks*, customized premium content and services including research tools that are designed to assist higher education faculty in development of online courseware and students engaged in research. It holds large collections of copyright-cleared materials, including key business and public policy documents as well as digitized archived materials, some dating back to the fifteenth century.

xanedu.com/

The Future of Marketplaces for e-Knowledge

The vignette of the Knowledge Content Exchange marketplace for e-knowledge is not far fetched. Similar ventures are undergoing trials today. Others are in development in Europe and North America. The unbundling of scholarly publishing, trade publishing, and other knowledge resources has the potential to free tens of billions of dollars in resources, reducing the cost of content. Equally important, this reinvention will empower individual providers of content, context, and narrative and the aggregators of demand, such as colleges, universities, other learning enterprises, corporations, and such like. Power relationships will never be the same.

An example is Learning Content eXchange (LCX), an emerging venture that endeavors to establish a meta-market for digital resources in the higher education space by meeting the needs of the consumers of digital goods—institutions, faculty, and students.

www.lcxcorp.com

This unbundling will occur through horizontal marketplaces that slice through the vertical silos of traditional publishers, universities, enterprise repositories, associations, government agencies, and other repositories of e-content.

Leadership in Innovation Comes from New Competitors. When it comes to creating genuine, paradigm-busting innovations, current market leaders seldom discover the breakthrough. As Clayton Christensen demonstrated in *The Innovator's Dilemma*, disruptive innovation generally sneak in from below while the dominant players are focusing on satisfying existing customers and making incremental improvements. The new, technology supported innovations come from the low-end of the market, either domestically or in global settings. Over time, the innovative offerings get better, attracting new customers based on lower costs, convenience, and improved quality.

Clayton Christensen writes in The Innovator's Dilemma that a successful value chain becomes, over time, increasingly focused on the needs of its established market . . . when a disruptive technology appears and begins to serve new markets with a new value proposition, the entire value chain is blindsided to the point of extinction. This tendency is exacerbated by the World Without Secrets. *The effort involved in keeping up with enormous volumes of information in established markets pushes aside ideas and information about new opportunities and markets. This is true of individuals and institutions alike.*

Richard Hunter, 2002

Embedded knowledge initiatives should only be undertaken for critical work processes.

Thomas H. Davenport and John Glaser

Trust cannot be built from bandwidth alone. Trust is not just about bits and bytes. It's about social relationships, and about building networks that deliver what they promise, be it a product, a collaboration, or simply reliable information.

Francis Fukuyama

These conditions are very much at play in the e-knowledge industry. Just scan the participant list of the multi-enterprise repositories cited above. While traditional market leaders are participating in ventures, they are not dominating the field. The leadership that will lead to the emergence of innovative, horizontal content marketplaces is coming from ventures and competitors outside the traditional publishing communities. e-Knowledge marketplaces of various kinds are likely to be one of the killer applications of the e-Knowledge Industry.

The emergent horizontal marketplaces are likely to support exchange of a wide range of highly granular learning objects and other knowledge offerings, including syntheses of new insights compiled by respected experts (mentats), marketplaces of knowledge, and services available from government and non-profit agencies; directories to communities of practice and access to distilled insights or participation privileges (ranging from lurking to full membership); recommended aggregations of content by industry/professional leaders, and such like. Indeed, the mechanisms for knowledge marketplaces can be applied to a wide variety of knowledge needs.

An immense and ever-increasing wealth of knowledge is scattered about the world today; knowledge that would probably suffice to solve all the mighty difficulties of our age, but it is dispersed and unorganized. We need a sort of mental clearing house: a depot where knowledge and ideas are received, sorted, summarized, digested, clarified, and compared.

H.G. Wells, 1940

Trust: The Tie That Binds

e-Knowledge as we describe it is impossible without the existence of trust. Trust is what enables the processes of knowledge sharing and consensus building. These processes drive two outputs: 1) the development of technology that works and 2) conformance testing with agreed upon standards. Trust that e-knowledge will be accessed, metered, and exchanged in conformance with agreed upon terms and conditions is fundamental to e-knowledge repositories and marketplaces. And trust is essential to developing enterprise infrastructures, processes, capabilities and cultures that will enable individuals and enterprises to achieve order-of-magnitude enhancements in their abilities to acquire, assimilate and share knowledge.

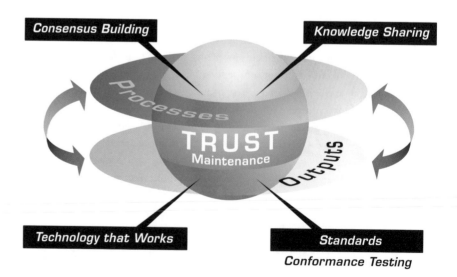

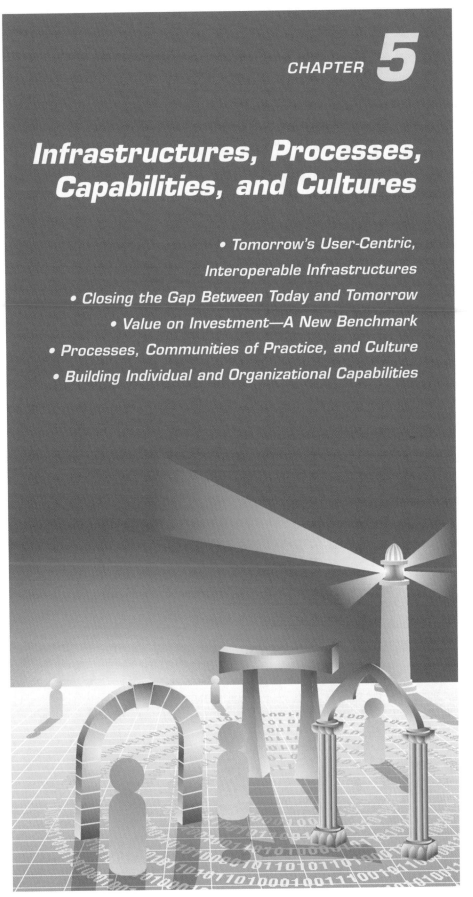

Infrastructures, Processes, Capabilities, and Cultures

- Tomorrow's User-Centric, Interoperable Infrastructures
- Closing the Gap Between Today and Tomorrow
- Value on Investment—A New Benchmark
- Processes, Communities of Practice, and Culture
- Building Individual and Organizational Capabilities

Over the past decade, enterprises have enhanced their capabilities for processing knowledge. Most have been tinkering with aspects of their knowledge ecosystem, not truly transforming their capacity to share knowledge. But over the next few years, new enterprise infrastructures, portals, Web services, Learning Content Management Systems, and community-building technologies will support a seamless web of interoperable applications that will support altering the enterprise knowledge ecology. These user-centric infrastructures will feature a personalized experience gateway through which users will engage products, services, and knowledge utilities of great power and amenity.

These new infrastructures provide more than a return on investment (ROI). They will yield a strong value on investment (VOI) based on their capacity to yield "soft benefits" such as supporting process reinvention and innovation, knowledge management, communities of practice, individual and organizational capabilities, and new leadership. These strategic benefits are essential to changing the enterprise's knowledge ecology.

Enterprises will focus on the strategic use of knowledge. They will change the dynamics of their operations through productivity enhancements, increased collaboration and innovation. Communities of practice will become recognized as the predominant organizational form in the e-Knowledge Economy. They will be the epicenter of autonomic learning and the development of individual and organizational capabilities.

A culture truly changes only when a new way of operating has been shown to succeed over some minimum period of time. Trying to shift the norms and values before you have created the new way of operating does not work. The vision can talk of a new culture. You can create new behaviors that reflect a desired culture. But these new behaviors will not become norms, will not take hold, until the very end of the process.

John P. Kotter and Dan S. Cohen

Terms & Concepts

Process Reinvention:
Using technology to reinvent business processes. Process reinvention is the heart of e-business—using technology to change the way organizations conduct their business. It changes the dynamics of organizations and their relationships with customers and stakeholders.

Enterprise Application Integration (EAI): Integration of disparate systems, typically using a "bus" architecture, where every system plugs into a common infrastructure and the bus handles the transactions for the systems. Today's EAI solutions are typically proprietary and are characterized by a high Total Cost of Ownership (TCO) and long timeframes.

Enterprise Applications Infrastructures and Solutions (EAIS): Tomorrow's technology-based "applications array" will consist of fully integrated combinations of Web site and portal, legacy systems, next generation ERP, CRM, Web services, learning management systems, content management systems and other specialty applications.

Return on Investment (ROI): ROI is the measure of the hard tangible benefits from technology initiatives, compared to the investment needed to produce them.

Value on Investment (VOI): VOI is the measure of the value of "soft" or "intangible" benefits derived from technology initiatives, compared to the investment needed to produce them. ROI is a subset of VOI.

WINWINI: The new metaphor for the user's experience—"What I Need, When I Need It." The EAIS will provide the next killer app—a ubiquitous system for students, faculty and support staff to carry out learning, instruction, and research.

Communities of Practice: Formal or informal groups linked by a common domain of practice and sometimes shared interests, which interact to advance and share explicit and tacit knowledge. When self-organized they can also be described as networks.

Knowledge Ecology: The combination of processes, culture, and capabilities, both internal and external, through which enterprises handle knowledge. Also **knowledge ecosystem.**

Changing Enterprise Dynamics: Organizational dynamics are changed by productivity enhancements, increased collaboration, and innovation. Changing what is done and how it is done by enterprises of all kinds is the key to changing the knowledge ecology.

Domain of Issues: The topical scope of a community of practice.

Shared Practice: The knowledge developed, shared and stewarded by a community of practice.

Double-Knit Structure: The weaving together of communities of practice and process teams.

Operational/Process Teams: A group with membership assigned by management, each member having clear boundaries of responsibility. The group is driven by project goals and milestones.

Tomorrow's User-Centric, Interoperable Infrastructures

To achieve order-of-magnitude leaps in their capacity to share and use knowledge, enterprises must transform their technology, infrastructures, processes, and cultures. These changes will be shaped by attitudinal differences between individuals who find Internet culture congenial versus those who are uncomfortable with it.

"The story of the creation and development of the Internet is one of an extraordinary human adventure. It highlights people's capacity to transcend institutional goals, overcome bureaucratic barriers, and subvert established values in the process of ushering in a new world. It also lends support to the view that cooperation and freedom of information may be more conducive to innovation than competition and proprietary rights."

Manuel Castells, The Internet Galaxy

This transformation should begin with an appraisal of the ways in which new and old knowledge competes in an organization; and with an assessment of the processes and participants (individuals and groups) that sustain knowledge flow and knowledge use in that organization. Such appraisals are guided by a powerful metaphor: each organization is a knowledge ecosystem supported by technology infrastructures, business processes, formal organizational structures, communities of practice, the beliefs and practices that define the organization's knowledge culture, and the capabilities and perspectives of staff, customers, suppliers, and other stakeholders. To prepare for success in the Knowledge Age, enterprises of all kinds must ensure that they make it easy for useful knowledge to be recognized and utilized constructively. Critically examin-

ing every aspect of their knowledge ecosystems as part of every planning process is essential to achieving that goal.

Tinkering Rather than Transforming

Over the past decade, enterprises have been tinkering with technical aspects of their knowledge ecosystem. They have not yet focused on making it easier to handle knowledge. They have been using their ICT infrastructures to enhance productivity and to change some of the processes through which they have conducted their businesses. This has enabled some leading-edge users to experience the first generation of Web-based applications, processes for sharing digital knowledge, and technology-enabled reinvention of organizational processes. Even these proof-of-concept applications have generated excitement about the future. Farsighted users have sensed the potential for creating genuinely user-centric experiences, sharing all kinds of knowledge and engaging the products and services offered by colleges and universities, corporations, associations, and other non-profit organizations.

On the Verge of Major Infrastructure Advances. Over the next few years, many enterprises continue to develop their infrastructures but with some significant differences. Advances in technologies and standards are facilitating the revolutionizing of organizational infrastructures. Proprietary applications software products —enterprise portals, Enterprise Resource Planning (ERP) systems, Customer Relationship Management (CRM), Learning Management Systems (LMS), community

Disruptive technologies and world-wide competition are driving a global business transformation. The very nature of work for many people in hi-tech and knowledge-based organizations has already fundamentally changed.

David Gurteen

software, and Knowledge Management Systems (KMS)—are being succeeded by open system architectures and protocols, albeit at a judicious pace. Web services promise to enable the easy seamless integration of disparate applications—ERP, legacy systems, best-of-breed specialty applications, and knowledge applications of all kinds. A seamless web of interoperable applications will succeed today's distinct proprietary applications suites. These capabilities will enable organizations to reshape their business processes, support emergent communities of practice in new ways, and reshape their enterprise knowledge cultures. With each such reshaping, they become progressively better placed to spot barriers to innovation and ways to bridge the gap between "knowing" and "doing."

Enterprises need to take a systemic view in reviewing and refashioning every aspect of their knowledge ecosystems, preparing for the new knowledge sharing capabilities and experiences that will be expected by learners, *employees, suppliers, partners, and other stakeholders. Future customer expectations should shape the vision and development of enterprise applications and solutions.*

Planning from the Future Backward

Today's infrastructures are the foundations for the enterprise infrastructures of the future. But rather than extrapolating from today's reality forward, it is preferable to use foresight planning to craft a vision of how we will experience e-knowledge in the future and the infrastructures and applications necessary to support those experiences. From that vision, we can "plan from the future backward," identifying the gap between today's environments and those required to meet the vision of tomorrow. Charting migration paths to the envisioned e-knowledge future will require progressive and systemic transformation of all of the aspects of organizational knowledge ecosystems.

Pervasive Technology Environments

Chapter 1 described the pervasive technology environments of the future, in which individuals will use mobile and ambient technology to communicate and experience e-knowledge at home, school, university, work, automobiles, and in a variety of public places.

Those environments profoundly change the availability of knowledge and the paths it follows, the speed with which it flows and the ways in which it is recognized, valued or found wanting. Knowledge ecosystems will change dramatically.

Put simply, these ambient and mobile environments constitute the gateway through which knowledge users will engage infrastructures and applications associated with the Internet/Web and with the variety of enterprises with which they associate. For any individual, these enterprises include various permutations of employer, school, college and university, other learning enter-

e-Knowledge Experiences and the Infrastructures and Knowledge Ecology to Support Them

- *Vision*
- *Infrastructures*
- *Processes*

GAPS

- *Communities of Practice*
- *Capabilities (individual & organizational)*
- *Culture*

Today's Infrastructure and Knowledge Ecology

prises, professional societies and trade associations, government agencies, and other entities. The level of transitive trust that each individual places in these entities and the relative importance of their resources will shape the relative role they play in each individual's constellation of relationships. Individuals will use personal portals or other means to manage their relationships with the interactivity and resources available through Web and the significant enterprises, like colleges and universities, with which they have trusted relationships.

Enterprise Applications and Solutions Are Critical

To participate successfully in this e-knowledge environment, each enterprise must create robust enterprise infrastructures and applications, accessed though their Web site and enterprise portal, using a variety of wireless and wired devices. These infrastructures and solutions require interoperability and scalability, meaning that applications and knowledge can be shared across different enterprises and technology platforms and scaled to enterprises of different sizes. These solutions also require powerful security, authentication, and verification capabilities.

User-Centric, Interoperable Infrastructures

Tomorrow's infrastructures will not just be user-friendly; they will be user-centric. A wide range of stakeholders will engage an enterprise's products, services, and knowledge resources using powerful knowledge tools. They will be able to shape the content, context, and nature of their experience.

Toward the Experience Gateway. Users will experience an enterprise's offerings through personalized interfaces that constitute a sort of "experience gateway." Individuals will engage the gateway and experience different "levels" or "degrees" of intimacy, personalization, and cus-

tomization. The least intimate degree of engagement will be provided by the enterprise Web site, which will provide public access to anyone. A range of portal capabilities that will serve "insiders"—members, learners, customers, suppliers, alumni, donors, sponsors, exhibitors, or partners—will furnish a richer level of engagement. As the degree of "customer intimacy" progressively advances, the experience gateway will also afford "amenity," a level of ease of use that makes the gateway recede into the background and makes the experience of using it seem natural and familiar.

The enterprise ICT infrastructures of the future will support pervasive interactivity through which users will personalize their interactions with all of the services and applications provided by the enterprise; knowledge resources of all kinds; and interactions with humans, knowledge agents, and other entities.

The Enterprise Applications Array. Instead of distinct, proprietary applications, such as traditional ERP, LMS, LCMS, and community-building software, users will experience a fully integrated array of seamless, interoperable, and integrated capabilities. Powerful personalization tools will be integral parts of these applications. In a very real sense, enterprise applications will be fused, not just integrated. This will bring all of the components into a single, unitary service as far as the user is concerned. The user will address needs and solve problems, unaware of which application she is using or which enterprise unit is serving her needs.

Web services, Shared Services, Co-sourcing. Easy-to-combine Web services will be made possible by innovations in standards that enable applications to communicate with one another, providing seamless integration. Web services are likely to be the paradigm-busting instrument enabling enterprises to easily link ERP, legacy systems, and outsourced applications. These will influence dramatically the evolution of the next generations of applications and the roles and relationships among vendors and users.

> *The promise of Web services lies in its ability to resolve the differences among shared, networked applications. Applications from different vendors, of various vintages, written in different languages, running on disparate platforms, easily communicate and cooperate, resolving their differences to act in concert.*
>
> *Carl Jacobsen, June 2002*

Web services are significant in another way: they offer the prospect of making it far easier for staff within an organization to bypass knowledge silos and legacy IT systems that restrict access to internal information. One consequence is that people in the organization or in partner organizations can develop processes and systems, built on Web services, that help them to become aware of the needs and capabilities of their colleagues and to work as a community.

Next Generation ERP and CRM. In the future, ERP will cease being a software solution and will morph into a broad-gauged combination of product, services, and solutions. Rather than writing RFPs for large systems acquisitions, enterprises will be "sourcing blended business solutions" with solutions providers. Just as knowledge management has triggered broader consideration of knowledge ecology, "customer relationship management" has evolved from a standalone soft-

If you look today, very senior people are making decisions about technology, and they are viewing it as mission critical.

Carol Vallone

ware application to an integral part of the applications array enabling enterprises to sustain personalized interactions and relationships with a wide range of stakeholders. In the e-knowledge future, effective enterprises will develop *indispensable relationships* with their stakeholders.

Putting Knowledge Management into e-Learning. Awareness is growing of economic ways to augment today's limited kinds of information about data elements and learning objects. By adding semantic information, it becomes easier to share those assets and re-purpose them. The next big thing in learning management is the incorporation of content management tools and practices that make use of semantics. These will make it easier to infuse just-in-time knowledge into learning experiences.

Communities of Practice. Communities of practice will become an integral part of Knowledge Age enterprises. In learning enterprises, these communities will deal with learning and administrative services and will involve students, faculty, staff, alumni, suppliers, and other stakeholders. They will cut across organizational boundaries and connect to knowledge exchanges and marketplaces. Communities of practice will become much more intentional and part of active enterprise knowledge strategies.

Knowledge Resources Utility. Through the experience gateway, users will engage the enterprise's knowledge resources. These will include internal and external sources and resources, not just databases "owned" by the enterprise. Powerful search engines and intelligent agents will be available as part of the enterprise's solution to knowledge management. Knowledge resources will also include graphics, simulations, applications, community of practice "know-how," and a host of other knowledge resources. Knowledge management will be a key ingredient of both formal and informal enterprise learning experiences.

Users will have less reason to concern themselves with the location and original source of knowledge resources, which increasingly will function like a utility.

Network and Hardware Resources. Enterprises will deploy various levels of pervasive, ubiquitous computing environments in their own physical settings. But each enterprise's knowledge resources will be available anywhere, anytime, through wired and wireless interactivity. Pervasive technology environments will be advanced by next generation Internet and the rise of nomadic computing and interactivity.

Services: The Tie that Binds All Applications and Solutions. The e-enterprise infrastructure of the future will depend on a broad range of services, supporting the experience gateway, applications array and solutions, knowledge resources, and network and hardware resources. These services will be provided by enterprise staff and external sourcing relationships that include both expert consultation and technical support dealing with implementation, integration, co-sourcing and shared services.

Processes, Communities of Practice, Capacities, and Culture

In addition to enterprise infrastructures, applications, and solutions, the successful e-knowledge enterprise needs to reshape the social elements of its knowledge ecology.

- **Business processes** should be reinvented to produce e-knowledge-based relationships that will be demanded by customers, learners, and other stakeholders;
- **Communities of practice,** linked to business processes, need substantial development to serve as the creators and stewards of knowledge capital;
- **Individual and organizational capacities** perpetually grow to assimilate and share knowledge far more effectively and efficiently than today; and

- **Culture regarding knowledge** should be refashioned to reflect the emerging needs of customers, learners, suppliers, and other stakeholders.

These social elements of the knowledge ecology will receive greater attention in the future.

Knowledge is a social construct. For enterprises to change their knowledge ecology, they must understand the social dimension and make it simpler for people to use knowledge in their jobs. Knowledge resources and support must be fused with work in a manner that enhanced ease of use and ultimately achieves amenity. As part of this fusing, organizations should adopt best practice on minimizing the time and other resources needed by individuals to make what they know available to others. Surprisingly few knowledge-sharing programs recognize the importance of this. Yet by thoughtful process reinvention and innovation, taking greater account of the social elements of knowledge ecologies and the patterns of interactions that exist in those ecologies, the conscious effort needed to share knowledge can be reduced dramatically.

Knowledge-sharing programs often fail because they make it harder, not easier, for people to do their jobs.

Thomas H. Davenport and John Glaser

Tomorrow's Infrastructures: User-Centric, Flexible, and Cost Effective

Users

Members, Customers, Applicants, Suppliers, Managers, Students, Faculty, Friends and Family, Affiliated Organizations, Legislators and Policy Makers, Other Stakeholders

Experience Gateway

Interfaces through which users experience all of the organization's applications, services, interactivity, and knowledge. Web sites, portals, and specialized knowledge gateways will all provide these experiences. Portal-based interfaces provide personalized, secure, and customized experiences, accessible via multiple devices. Personalization capabilities also are available through individual or fused applications in the enterprise applications array.

The Enterprise Applications Array

Full range of enterprise applications, including a mixture of ERP and legacy systems (HR, finance, knowledge, and industry-specific applications.) Many will be external to the institution and linked through Web services. Users care about capabilities, not the means or provider.

Knowledge and Learning—Knowledge Asset Management, Digital Rights Management, Learning Management, Digital Rights Enforcement, Assessment
Industry-Specific—Course Management, Relationship Management, HR, Finance, Financial Aid, Procurement, Applications/Admissions, Fund Raising, Library Systems, Personal Portfolio, Supply Chain
Communities of Practice—Prospective Students, Working Groups, Learning Communities, Clubs, Alumni, Athletics, Associations, Intramural Sports
Shared Applications—Web services, Knowledge Management Utilities, Messaging, Search, E-mail, Calendaring

Knowledge Resources Utility

Internal and external knowledge repositories of all kinds, organizational databases, communities of practice, directory server, e-mail, calendar.

Network and Hardware Resources

Computing—Servers, Desktops, PCs, wireless devices of all kinds, embedded computing devices, the Grid, and technologies yet to be determined
Networking—LANs, wireless LANs, WANs, Routers, Hubs, Internet Access, Broadband Infrastructure

Closing the Gap Between Today and Tomorrow

Tomorrow's user-centric interoperable environments will place a premium on the ease and efficiency with which knowledge can be learned, shared, and flowed.

In a nutshell, our basic KM philosophy is Learn Once, Use Anywhere.

V.P. Kochikar

Enterprises have a long way to go in developing the knowledge ecology and supporting infrastructures necessary to succeed in the variety of likely e-knowledge futures. They have also learned a great deal about the limitations of the early generations of ERP, LMS, LCMS, portals, and community-building software. The list of "what has been missing" from enterprise ICT has included non-proprietary applications, interoperability, and transformative impacts on enterprise processes, dynamics, and culture. These elements are being included in the next generation of enterprise applications being developed by solution providers. Equally important, enterprise leaders are beginning to evaluate their investment in technology based on the potential to create genuine competitive advantage and open new relationships and markets.

In his book, *From Good to Great*, Jim Collins assesses why some enterprises persist over time and become true leaders in their industries. One of the central elements in the saga of great enterprises is their shrewd use of technology as an "accelerator" in the attainment of their mission.

"(These enterprises focus on) what they can be the best in the world at, a deep understanding of their economic engine and the core values they hold with deep passion. They then use technology to enhance these pre-existing variables, never as a replacement."

Jim Collins, 2001

And so it is with knowledge. Enterprises need to apply this same discipline to using investment in ICT to accelerate their attainment of their strategic goals for using e-knowledge to attain their mission, vision, and competitive position. The emergent concept of VOI can be a useful benchmark for the enterprise's strategic goals, which can be attained through use of ICT as an accelerator.

Enterprise Knowledge Ecology to Succeed in the e-Knowledge Future

	Today's Capabilities	Tomorrow's Vision and Requirements
Infrastructure, Applications and Solutions	Moving beyond first-generation proprietary enterprise applications (ERP, LMS, portal, community ware) in networked and early wireless environments.	Seamless, interoperable, and scalable enterprise application infrastructures and solutions accessible through mobile, ambient technology environments.
Processes	Business processes based on existing knowledge capabilities and relationships with members, learners, customers, staff, and other stakeholders. Superficial conversion to Web formats.	Business processes are transformed to the patterns and cadences of the Internet/Web. Provide essential products, services, knowledge, and experiences that are the basis for indispensable relationships with members, learners, customers, staff, and other stakeholders.
Communities of Practice	Developing communities of practice, supported by first generation interactivity and e-knowledge capabilities.	Communities of practice gain in capability, flexibility, and capacity to create and steward knowledge, seamlessly linked to business processes.
Knowledge Capabilities	Capacity for managing and sharing knowledge is underdeveloped in most enterprises for both individuals and organizations.	Competency and capacity development is a top enterprise priority. Major human resources challenges arise in creating enterprises that are e-knowledge savvy.
Enterprise Culture	Most enterprises are adapting their business practices to the Internet/Web, but have not transformed their knowledge cultures.	Tomorrow's successful e-knowledge enterprise will transform its knowledge culture to reflect the culture of the Internet. This requires changes from top to bottom, from grassroots to executive leadership.
Leadership	Knowledge is not treated explicitly as a strategic asset.	Knowledge is explicitly treated as a strategic asset through the enterprise's knowledge strategy and business plan.

Knowledge-based initiatives are often unfocused and not linked adequately to business outcomes. Leveraging knowledge assets effectively requires well focused initiatives clearly linked to business performance.

Marianne Broadbent

Value on Investment (VOI)—A New Benchmark

Gartner introduced the concept of *value on investment,* driven by its observation that in the Knowledge Economy, intangible assets such as knowledge, networks, collaborations, and communities of practice are the source of most new products, services, and experiences. Consequently, managing and leveraging these so-called intangible assets will become an imperative for all kinds of organizations. Business and governmental organizations have been early adopters of these concepts. Gartner (2001) predicts that "by 2005, 50% of Fortune 1000 companies will identify an owner for workplace initiatives, formally track and manage intangible assets, and measure investment vs. value creation on these initiatives (0.6 probability)." Other learning enterprises are likely to be following close behind.

The intangibles tracked by VOI are roughly the same elements that are needed to change enterprises' e-knowledge ecology. This suggests that most organizations can turn their existing processes for developing ICT infrastructure into a far more effective change agent by expanding the measurement standards from ROI to VOI. The following table compares the relationship between ROI and VOI concepts.

Return on Investment (ROI)	Value on Investment (VOI)
ROI is the measure of the value of "hard," tangible benefits from technology initiatives.	VOI is the measure of the total value of "soft" or "intangible" benefits derived from technology initiatives. ROI is part of VOI.
"Return" is generated by tangible, traditional outcomes such as conventional enhancement of productivity, cost reduction, enhanced revenues, and opening new markets. ROI focuses on traditional measures.	"Value" is generated through outcomes that enhance productivity, build collaboration, and enable innovation. Value-building initiatives change the organization's dynamics by: • supporting business process reinvention and innovation; • formalizing knowledge management; • enabling collaboration and increasing the capabilities to learn and develop communities; • increasing individual and organizational competencies; and • enabling new leadership capabilities Measurement of VOI typically uses non-traditional measures in combination with the traditional measures of ROI.
ROI is objective, based on concrete measures, although the assumptions driving ROI may be highly subjective and judgmental.	VOI is subjective and judgmental. It is also contextual, depending on the perspective and position of the evaluating party—president, provost, VP, CIO, manager, or steward of organizational processes.

Adapted from: Gartner, 2001.

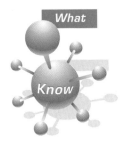

ROI is still an important component of VOI. In some tactical applications, ROI may be sufficient justification, by itself, to proceed with a technology investment. Consider the following examples from higher education settings:

- Rensellaer Polytechnic Institute's deployment of an e-procurement solution was justified on an ROI basis alone. It dramatically improved the productivity and efficiency of the purchasing process and increased the level of on-contract buying, providing a solid ROI.
- Many Web applications at the University of Delaware and other leading-edge institutions have reduced the cost and increased the convenience of administrative processing. These Web applications will soon be extended by the new generation of Web services. In their article, "Your Next IT Strategy," John Hagel III and John Seely Brown have cited corporate applications of Web services by the likes of General Motors, Merrill Lynch, and Dell that yield substantial ROI savings. Some of these examples include applications combining disparate databases and knowledge resources which dramatically reduced costs.
- ERP can be implemented to increase the efficiency of existing processes, using

workflow and productivity tools, better information flows, and improvement of individual performance. This can yield a reasonable ROI. But significant VOI will not be realized without an emphasis on achieving strategic direction, collaboration, and innovation.

So ROI is an important metric when ICT can be used to improve productivity and efficiency of existing academic and/or administrative processes. But VOI is necessary to assess the strategic potential of changing organizational dynamics and innovating better ways of doing things. VOI is a new benchmark for the strategic use of technology.

VOI is key to understanding the real strategic pay-offs from technology to enterprises over the next decade.

What are some examples of the value of intangible technology assets? And how will the new generation of enterprise applications solutions and systems facilitate the attainment of these values? Five elements contribute to the new value proposition for ICT infrastructure, solutions and applications:

- support process reinvention and innovation,
- formalize the management of knowledge and intellectual assets,
- enable collaboration and increase the capacity to learn and develop communities,
- increase individual and organizational competencies, and
- implement new leadership methods and capabilities.

Not coincidentally, these elements are also fundamental to preparing enterprises for success in the e-knowledge future. The following descriptions discuss these elements and provide examples of how enterprises are discovering these elements today.

Investment in technology must be part of an overall strategy to improve academic performance and achieve institutional goals.

Carol Twigg

Knowledge often walks out the door during downsizing.

Thomas Davenport and Laurence Prusak.

Support Process Reinvention and Innovation

Process reinvention and innovation are the most widely applied component of VOI. Enterprises have been using new enterprise application infrastructures and solutions to change what they are doing and how they are doing it. To achieve such reinvention, however, enterprises must get past memories of past experiences of business process reengineering.

Limitation of Business Process Reengineering. The knowledge management literature is awash with analyses of the failures of the round of business process reengineering (BPR) in the 1990s, which was supported by first-generation knowledge management tools and philosophies. Early BPR focused on productivity gain (efficiency), treated knowledge as a "thing," failed to recognize the richness of employees' tacit insight and underestimated the importance of the social elements of knowledge ecology. BPR failed to take a systemic perspective. The personnel reductions and reallocations of energies made by first-generation BPR helped enterprises trim costs, but many enterprise processes suffered.

Today's approach to process reinvention begins by taking a systemic perspective and understanding the importance of all elements of the knowledge ecology. Moreover, the focus is on not just enhancing productivity, but on changing the dynamics of enterprise processes through collaboration and innovation. Experience has shown that process reinvention can yield a wide range of advances, ranging from the incremental to the transformative.

Incremental Business Process Reinvention. The emergence of early examples of the next generation of enterprise application infrastructures and solutions provides many opportunities for process reinvention. Technology-driven process reinvention is enabling colleges and universities to refashion their processes, policies, organizational structures, and relationships with stakeholders of all kinds. For example, in the 1990s, the University of Delaware used technology-enabled process reinvention to create its ground-breaking "student one-stop shopping" facility and to reshape the dynamics of its relationship with students. This process of continuous reinvention has continued through today, using portal technology and Web services.

Even today, many enterprises have made process reinvention a fundamental element of their selection and implementation of ERP. They have discovered that process reinvention and measurement of the resulting changes in performance continue throughout the entire ERP project life cycle process. Some early successes in process reinvention are possible during the planning, acquisition and deployment phases. However, experience has shown that the full potential of incremental process reinvention will only be achieved after the enterprise has experienced the best practice processes embedded in mature ERP products. The full benefits of process reinvention will come through continuous improvement during the experience and improvement phases. Measurable improvements can be realized during the first two years of the process and can continue at significant levels for seven or eight years—or even more.

The University of Minnesota has used the development of its portal as a vehicle for reinventing its ERP-based processes. In the process, it has reshaped its relationships with students, faculty, and staff. Minnesota used portal-based e-business to simplify the ways in which users "experienced" the University's core processes and services. Focusing initially on essential core services (admissions, registration, communication, and the like) the University has progressively extended its reinvention to include other academic and administrative products, services, and functions. These innovations have changed the dynamics of how users engage university products, services, and knowledge, enabling individuals to "self-serve" more of their needs for knowledge and services.

e-Business is first and foremost about improving service to create enduring relationships with clients.

Robert Kvavik, 2001

Through this process, Minnesota also concluded that it could become its students' Internet Service provider (ISP) after graduation, extending the use of the experience gateway to which students had become accustomed during the period of their enrollment. This could lead to an enduring, daily relationship with alumnae. Other universities, like Virginia Tech and Weber State University, have articulated their aspirations to use portalized experiences to transform their lifelong relationships with alumni and their ongoing relationships with students, faculty, staff, donors, and other key stakeholders.

Progressing From Incremental to Transformative Process Reinvention. In the future, the enterprise's stakeholders will expect to experience a level of personalized convenience that Carl Berger of the University of Michigan calls WINWINI (What I Need, When I Need It). This is the next "killer app" in higher learning and is being evolved today through the experience gateway provided by the enterprise portal, shared tools, integrated applications, and process reinventions in learning enterprises across the globe.

The next killer app is a ubiquitous system for students, faculty, and support staff to carry out learning, instruction, and research.

Carl Berger, 2001

The continuing incremental development of these enterprise experience gateways will become truly transformative only when we change our perspectives on how stakeholders must access, assimilate, and share knowledge. Leaders at all enterprise levels, from CEO to grassroots, are beginning to articulate new visions of tomorrow's knowledge resource utilities and how they will be experienced by users of all kinds.

Over the next five years, enterprises will experience cascading cycles of reinvention in their best practices, business models, and strategies for e-learning and knowledge management.

Formalize the Management of Knowledge and Intellectual Assets

Of all the processes requiring reinvention, knowledge management may hold the greatest promise. For example, while colleges, universities, and training organizations are learning enterprises, they do not truly manage the knowledge and intellectual assets resident in individual faculty and researchers. Just like most courses or classes have been "cottage industries," created in the image of their faculty creator, knowledge resources have been treated like cottage industries as well. Publishers have organized and managed these resources, but not colleges and universities, acting on behalf of themselves, their faculty, and researchers. At least for now.

Knowledge asset management will be a central element of content and knowledge management systems, which will supersede today's generation of course/learning management systems. Knowledge and content management tools will be accessible through the enterprise's Web site, portals and within content management applications.

Example is not the main thing influencing others. It is the only thing.

Albert Schweitzer

Perhaps most importantly, institutions and their constituent groups would be empowered collectively as consumers in the digital content market.

Patrick McElroy

Knowledge management is becoming a key issue in enterprises that are successfully engaging in e-learning and in the archiving of research. Over the past few years, educational and training programs have made substantial progress in digitizing course materials for use in their learning management systems, aided by learning management system providers like WebCT and Click2learn. Successive advances in e-learning standards have been reflected in the interoperability framework for reusable content (SCORM) developed through the ADL Initiative and the ADL Co-Labs. These advances are making it possible to develop institutional data repositories that will enable the repurposing, combination, reuse, and exchange of data. These enterprise repositories will evolve from basic learning objects to include research, presentations, white papers, tradecraft, and other tacit knowledge. These repositories are part of the emergence of new, cross-cutting channels for sharing learning content that will be an important element in the reinvention of current models for publishing, textbooks, trade books, and other off-the-shelf content. These channels will enable the combination and repurposing of content held by different

enterprises, publishers, learning content management systems and digital content repositories in general.

Such initiatives are the precursors of *meta-marketplaces* that will span industries—education, publishing, learning management, associations, and professional societies—to create broad-based exchange of e-content and tacit knowledge through communities of practice. These meta-marketplaces will be driven by the aggregate power of consumers who will be empowered to support the business models and practices needed to serve their needs.

This is not just an issue for major research universities, R&D driven corporations, and research laboratories. Digital asset management and knowledge management will be important contributors to value for most enterprises as they develop their infrastructures. They will enable enterprises to personalize and enhance learning experiences, reduce the cost of digitized content, leverage e-knowledge resources, access previously unavailable sources of content and context, open new marketplaces for the enterprise's e-content, and establish their competitive position.

Enable Collaboration and Increase the Capacity to Develop Communities

The next generation of enterprise application infrastructures and solutions will enable new modes of collaboration at all levels:

- **Within enterprises.** In tomorrow's e-learning experiences, previously unattainable levels of collaboration will be achieved between and among learners, faculty and other support staff. These collaborations will change the dynamics of many existing processes.
- **Between enterprises and their suppliers, providers, and educational partners.** Tomorrow's enterprise application solutions will both require and support new levels of intimacy between enterprises and their suppliers and solution providers. In many cases, the staffs of these solution providers will function like extensions of enterprise staff, but with more structured performance agreements.
- **Between individuals in the enterprise and external peers.** Collaboration between individuals and peers outside the enterprise will be facilitated dramatically by enterprise application solutions, adding substantial value. Faculty and staff will be able to share insights more effectively with peers and colleagues.

The value of different kinds of collaboration will vary from process to process, setting to setting.

Collaboration will leverage technological and human networks to share tacit knowledge, develop insight, and make enterprise processes more responsive to client needs.

Communities of Practice. The ability to create communities of practice will be among the most important of the new competencies developed by faculty, staff, and other stakeholders. These communities will cross organization boundaries, fusing the power of professional societies and associations with the instrumental needs of individual organizations.

Consider just a few examples of the communities of practice enabled by the next generation of enterprise application solutions:

- **Applications implementation communities** are created by enterprises implementing ERP systems, LMS/ LCMS, or other major applications. They include online repositories of technical and process information, help desks, and communities of users, organized by functional or process subgroups. These communities are the foundation for participation in solution provider user groups.
- **Disciplinary communities of practice** would link learners in a discipline in ways that span and bridge experiences in individual courses. Such linkages could both complement course-based experiences and enable redesign of course experiences. These communities may not represent traditional disciplines at all, but emerging, hybridized disciplines or aggregations of integral, transpersonal knowledge that will constitute the curricula of the future.
- **Enrollment services communities of practice** linking an enterprise's cross-trained generalists in enrollment services (spanning admissions, recruitment, registration, advising, financial aid, and other support services) linked with professional societies and their bodies of knowledge and tradecraft. Similar communities could evolve for other academic and administrative support processes.
- **Adjunct faculty and consulting communities of practice** for consulting adjunct faculty, providing departmental management, support networks, and access to pedagogical resources and linkage to disciplinary learning resources.

The key to successful collaboration and knowledge transfer lies not in technology but in allowing people to build social networks connected by networks.

Martha Patillo-Siv

This community would link currently disjointed adjuncts into the mainstream of the learning community and change the dynamics of the adjunct faculty experience.

- **Purchasing/acquisition communities of practice** linking all those engaged in purchasing decisions, providing decision support and development, with linkages to cooperative buying and other resources not available at all enterprises.

However they accumulate knowledge, they become informally bound by the value they find in learning together. The value is not merely instrumental for their work. It also accrues in the personal satisfaction of knowing colleagues who understand each other's perspectives and of belonging to an interesting group of people. Over time, they develop a unique perspective on their topic as well as a body of knowledge, practices, and approaches. They also develop personal relationships and established ways of interacting. They may even develop a common sense of identity. They become a community of practice.

Etienne Wenger, 2002

The list of communities of practice could go on and on. These communities will multiply the impact of the social and technical networks that will be an essential element of the new enterprise application infrastructure. These communities of practice and collaborative interactions will be a key element of both process reinvention and changing the knowledge ecology of the institution to enable new levels of knowledge sharing.

Increase Individual and Organizational Competencies

Twenty-first century colleges and universities need to develop a wide range of new competencies, both as enterprises and for the individuals associated with them:

- **e-Learning.** Tomorrow's successful enterprise will need to be able blend physical and virtual learning resources and experiences, both on campus and to learners at a variety of settings, both physical and virtual. They will also need to fuse academic community and personal and administrative processes to support e-learners wherever they may be. The new generation of knowledge and content management applications will be essential to e-learning, enabling the introduction of just-in-time knowledge into learning.

e-Learning is the use of ICT to extend, enhance, and enrich every learning experience. Even the most traditional learning enterprise needs to develop the capabilities to support e-learning experiences.

- **Knowledge and content management.** Digitized content supporting e-learning will include not just virtual versions of the current generation of textbooks, course packs, and supporting expert resources. Topical content and context will need to be digitized, meta-tagged, and stored in institutional repositories for easy access, combination, and repurposing. Repositories of learning content such as MERLOT and those adopting the content interoperability framework developed by the ADL will be combining content from different sources. Over time, "marketplaces" will provide content from institutions, publishers, learning content companies, and professional societies and trade associations. Additionally, all of the instructor/mentor/navigator notes about how to manage and enhance learning experiences, syntheses of excellent questions and answers from past courses, assessment and evaluation, and other learning support materials will need to be made available to support e-learning.

- **Acquisition and e-procurement.** e-Procurement is about more than on-line purchasing. Supplier enablement and strategic purchasing will enable enterprises to reduce costs and enhance the quality of the purchasing experience. In the process they will yield a handsome ROI and VOI on their investment in e-procurement.

- **Other e-business applications.** e-Business is about using technology to transform how enterprises conduct their business. Tomorrow's e-learning experiences will need to be supported by transformed and fused versions of today's academic support and administrative processes.

- **Partnerships and relationships with suppliers/vendors/partners.** Tomorrow's relationships between colleges applications and universities and technology companies will be broader than today's. Leading-edge technology providers like SCT are evolving into solution providers specializing in "blended" enterprise application solutions that combine services and infrastructures, in-house and outsourced solutions, and legacy and new systems.

Iconographic enterprises and leading-edge technology-based solution providers are developing these new competencies today. The discovery of these new capabilities is both evolutionary and "expeditionary" as well. Even when guided by a well-conceived vision of the new competencies needed to succeed, leaders are discovering unexpected nuances and facets through a process of expeditionary inquiry. Enterprises will need to achieve a higher plane of individual and institutional capability in e-learning, knowledge management,

faculty and staff development, collaboration, and the use of communities of practice. These competencies will be essential to attaining the value on investment possible through changing the institutional dynamics of productivity, collaboration, and innovation. This will be a substantial challenge for the human resources development capabilities of colleges and universities, but necessary to their success.

Enterprises are developing their new enterprise application solutions as expeditions, discovering how to combine process and information integration, business process reinvention, and staff development as an ongoing process of continuous improvement and revelation. The new "killer apps" will emerge from this process of expeditionary discovery.

Implement New Leadership Methods and Capabilities

Developing the next generation of enterprise application infrastructures and solutions will require different kinds of leadership, from the CEO to vice presidents and the CIO to line managers and process owners. Consider the following examples:

- CEOs will coordinate the articulation of enterprise strategy that will deploy new enterprise applications, infrastructures and solutions to position their enterprises for competitive advantage and providing new experiences for stakeholders.
- Several strategies are needed:
  - Knowledge strategy articulates the centrality of knowledge to the enterprise's mission, vision and competitive position. It presents the enterprise's strategy for achieving knowledge-driven competitive advantage.

  - Knowledge management strategy details the enterprise's strategy for developing and using the infrastructure, processes and capacities necessary to maximize the stewardship and management of their knowledge assets.
- The fusion of academic and administrative applications will require broad collaboration on the development of most infrastructures and applications.
- CIOs and IT departments will experience especially dramatic changes. In the view of Hagel and Brown, IT departments will turn to outsourcing or co-sourcing relationships with external partners while leveraging distinctive internal capabilities. CIOs will need to substantially extend their skills as: 1) strategists and entrepreneurs, 2) knowledge brokers, 3) relationship managers, and 4) negotiators. Developing the enterprise application infrastructure will require new levels of partnership between the CIO and other campus executive officers.

In summary, VOI is a facile instrument for focusing an enterprise's ICT resources on strategic enterprise objectives, especially as they pertain to e-knowledge. VOI also focuses attention on the "social" elements of the enterprise's knowledge ecosystem.

In Japanese the "place" is "Ba" (shared space of interaction)—physical, intellectual, and emotional facets.

Processes, Communities of Practice, and Culture

Today's knowledge ecosystems are not bounded by organizational structures and enterprise borders. Portions of the enterprise knowledge ecosystem may be proprietary. But today's relationships and exchanges of knowledge are using new generations of communities of practice and emerging value webs that are unconfined, uncontrolled, and often uncontrollable.

The complexity of markets and learning systems in the knowledge economy has sparked a trend toward communities that are not confined to the boundary of a single organization. Rather, these communities help weave broader value webs created by relationships and exchanges both within and beyond the boundaries of the firm.

Etienne Wenger, et al., 2002

Taking a Systemic View of All Aspects of Knowledge Ecologies

Today's emerging practice of knowledge management takes a systemic view of knowledge ecologies. The next generation of knowledge infrastructures and tools will provide both the capacity and the stimulus to refashion all of the elements of the knowledge and hence social ecosystem.

Knowledge is not a 'thing' that can be 'managed' like physical assets, but a human and organizational capacity produced by collaborative relationships that can be nurtured and inspired.

George Por, 2001

It has become an article of faith among developers of organizational technology infrastructures that the ultimate value from technology investment lies in its capacity to enable/leverage the reinvention and innovation of business processes. But the term "process reinvention" does not do justice to the entire scope of innovation. In reality, the goal is reinvent the "conversational space" of the enterprise—the dynamics and relationships of the organization that are embedded in business processes, communities of practice, and other elements of the organizational system's social ecology.

Organizational Structures and Communities of Practice

Organizations function through intersecting patterns of relationships involving individuals and a differentiated set of organizational structures in which they participate. Most individuals participate in multiple structures and communities, both formally and informally—and many extend beyond the organizational workplace. These structures range from formal department, project teams, and operational teams to informal networks and communities of various kinds. In recent years, practitioners have come to recognize and articulate the importance of **communities of practice.**

The community of practice organizational structure exists to create, expand, and exchange knowledge and to develop individual capabilities. Individuals choose to belong through self-selection, based on expertise or passion for the topic. Communities of practice are bordered by "fuzzy" boundaries that extend beyond formal organizations and are held together by the passion and commitment of their participants. They evolve and last as long as there is relevance to the topic and value in learning together.

Communities of Practice and Other Organizational Structures

Organizational Structures	Purpose/Membership	Characteristics
Communities of Practice	Create, expand, and exchange knowledge and develop individual capabilities/Self-selection based on expertise or passion for a topic	Fuzzy boundaries Held together by passion, commitment and informal teaming through identification with community
Formal Departments	Deliver a product or service/Everyone who reports to group manager	Clear boundaries Held together by job requirements and common goals
Operational Teams	Take care of an ongoing operation or process/Membership assigned by management	Clear boundaries Held together by shared responsibility for the operation
Project Teams	Accomplish a specified task/People who have a direct role in accomplishing the task	Clear boundaries Held together by project goals and milestones
Communities of Interest	Be Informed/Whomever is interested	Fuzzy boundaries Held together by access to information and sense of like-mindedness
Informal Networks	Receive and pass on information, know who is who/Friends and business acquaintances	Undefined boundaries Held together by mutual need and relationships "Know-Who" is intellectual capital

Adapted from: Etienne Wenger, Richard McDermott, and William M. Snyder, Cultivating Communities of Practice, *2002.*

An Old Form, Elevated by Recent Forces. Communities of practice have existed for centuries. Commercial organizations, professional societies and trade associations, philanthropies, civic organizations, government agencies, non-profit organization, and other entities have displayed community of practice characteristics over centuries of development. But the strategic importance of communities of practice has been elevated in recent years by several interdependent forces:

1) The power of technology-supported interactivity to enable community participants to engage with one another and with knowledge resources anytime, anywhere, at greater speed, with greater ease, and in ways that change relationships;

2) The technology-supported capacity to assemble, synthesize, share, repurpose, and experience knowledge in new ways through communities of practice;

3) The capacity of communities of practice to deal with the fusion of "head, heart, and hand"—inquiry, interaction, and craft (Wenger, *et al*, 2002); and

4) The emerging understanding that communities of practice can lead to genuinely new patterns of organizing work and learning and new relationships, not just more efficient versions of the old.

Over the next five years, these forces will enable communities of practice to attain even higher planes of accomplishment and significance in meeting the needs of knowledge stewarding and sharing. The amenity experienced in tomorrow's communities of practice will make current practice seem primitive.

Domain, Community, and Practice. These three elements shape how a community of practice functions and how it links to the practice shared by members of the community. The body of knowledge developed by a community of practice and made available for sharing externally will become increasingly valuable.

Three Elements Shape a Community of Practice

Domain of Issues	Community	Practice
Creates common ground and a sense of common identity.	Creates the social fabric for learning.	A set of frameworks, ideas, tools, information styles, stories, and documents that community members share.
Legitimizes the community by affirming purpose and value.	Foster interactions and relationships built on mutual respect and trust.	The practice is the specific knowledge the community develops, shares, and maintains.
Inspires members to contribute, guides learning and gives meaning to their actions.	Encourages willingness to share ideas, expose one's ignorance, and listen.	When a community has been established for some time, it expects its members to have mastered the basic knowledge of the community.
Knowing the boundaries and leading edge of the domain defines what is worth sharing and to recognize the value in emerging, half-baked ideas.	Learning is a matter of belonging as well as intellectual activity involving the heart and the head	Body of shared knowledge and resources enables the community to proceed efficiently in dealing with its domain.

Adapted from: Wenger et al., Cultivating Communities of Practice, 2002.

Communities of practice are developing in virtually every organizational setting, often spanning traditional boundaries. Individuals typically participate in many communities of practice at once. For example, a mid-level employee of Sun Microsystems responsible for Java-based products might be an active participant in a variety of intersecting communities:

- an internal Sun community of practice dealing with Java standards and their relationships to international standards developments;
- communities of practice formed by IMS, IEEE, and other international bodies dealing with interoperability standards; and
- communities of practice formed by the Computer Society of the IEEE to build the body of knowledge on interoperability.

Leading-edge enterprises depend on all of these relationships with communities of practice, both internal and external.

Linking Communities of Practice and Processes. Successful Knowledge Age organizations manage to link communities of practice to business processes and project teams. Nonaka and Takeuchi refer to this linkage as "hypertext organization" because project teams "click on" the knowledge in the community of practice on an as-needed basis (1995). R. McDermott characterizes this relationship as a "double-knit" organization (1999), where persons interested in a particular domain participate both as creators/stewards of the domain's knowledge capital (community of practice) and as appliers and problem solvers using the knowledge capital (business process). In tomorrow's organizational

structure, as enterprises use their new generations of enterprise applications solutions to reinvent business processes and project team structures, the community of practice may be the most stable organization form in which individuals participate.

Wenger, McDermott and Snyder have generated the following graphic to capture the nature of the "double-knit" relationships between communities of practice and process teams.

Learning and Stewardship of Knowledge in the Double-Knit Structure. The double-knit structure is where directed/structured and autonomic learning meet the needs of the enterprise as was shown on page 57. Different variations on these themes exist in corporate, educational, governmental, and professional society settings.

Double-Knit Structures

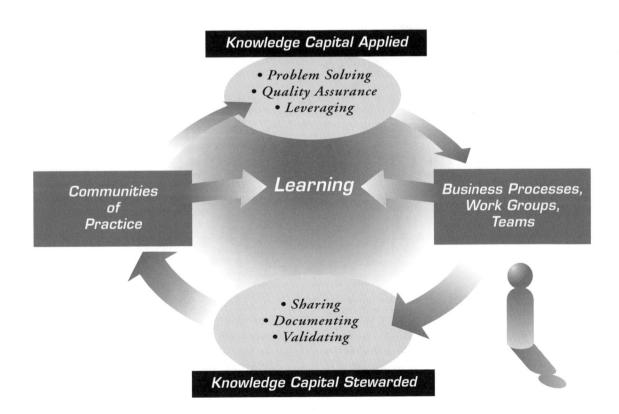

Adapted from: Wenger et al., Cultivating Communities of Practice, *2002.*

Consider the following example, illustrated in the graphic below: a distributed global university is rolling out a substantial revision of its successful learning programs in environmental sciences. This offering is a customizable series of learning experiences, which can result in for-credit or not-for-credit learning. The for-credit learning experiences can be part of a formal degree program, or they can be tailored to result in a series of special, customized certificates. The price of the learning experiences varies dramatically depending on the nature of the experience, the desired level of interactivity with faculty/ mentors/ and practitioners, and the type of certification required. This program can be offered in purely virtual or a blended learning mode.

The learning experiences are supported by two repositories of e-resources: 1) an extensive repository of learning objects, and 2) a knowledge management system. The learning object repository contains content and context created by instructional designers in collaboration with faculty, mentors, and practitioners. The knowledge management system contains a wealth of information on the tradecraft of learning this subject matter and its application in practical settings. A team of knowledge management specialists has created a system that links the klogs, notes, application reports, syntheses of past questions, and other resources from practitioners, faculty, and mentors.

The community of practice supporting this effort is a collection of faculty, mentors, and practitioners who have been contributing to the university's environmental sciences offering over the years. They have provided explicit content on the subject matter of environment science, which has been shaped by the supporting team of instructional development staff into learning objects. The upgraded offering is introducing a just-in-time knowledge component, provided through continuous editing of the contents of the knowledge management system and the existing learning objects, "push" technology updates to learners, and/or personal interactivity with practitioners to share emergent tacit knowledge.

Learning Meets Knowledge Management

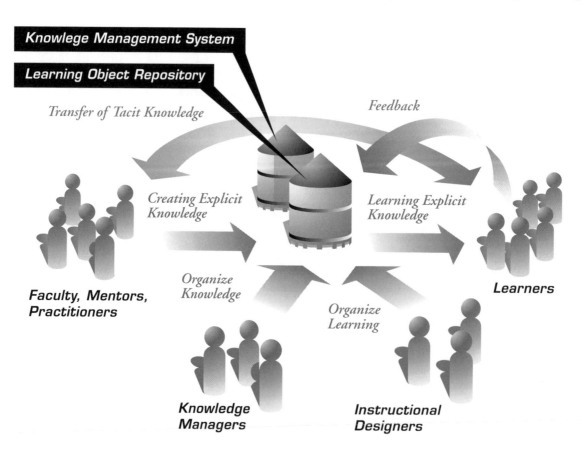

Adapted using Woelk/Agarwal techniques

Virtuous Circle

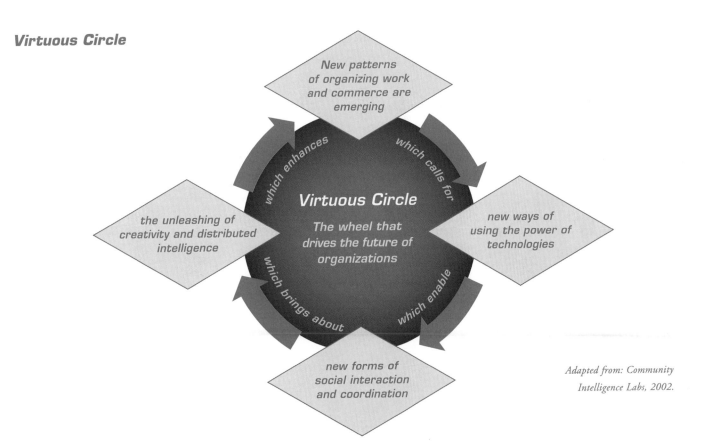

Adapted from: Community Intelligence Labs, 2002.

Learners participate in learning experiences in cohorts of 25, facilitated by a faculty or mentor, as appropriate. Most of their interactions are with the other learners, the repository of learning objects and the knowledge management system. To acquire new insight, they interact with their primary faculty/ mentor, other faculty/mentors who are available, and/or with artificial intelligence agents that synthesize responses based on past questions and answers on particular topics.

In upgrading the environmental sciences offering, the community of practice decided the extent of the upgrade, the changes in content and tradecraft to include, and the mechanisms for providing just-in-time knowledge. The knowledge management and instructional development staff provided insight on how to incorporate these materials into learning objects and the knowledge management system.

Unleashing Creativity and Creating New Patterns of Work and Learning

Communities of practice are deploying new technologies to enable new means of social interaction and coordination. Today, proof-of-concept versions of these new communities are being developed and refined. Over time, they will develop even greater amenity. These new communities combine powerful knowledge management tools with new interfaces and interactivity tools that make it easier to engage in a wide range of community activities. Examples such as Community Intelligence Labs (www.co-i-l.com) illustrate how they facilitate the community interaction process.

With time, the new forms of social interaction and coordination will unleash the creativity of the community members and the distributed intelligence that resides in communities of practice in tactic, explicit, and evolving forms. In turn, this will enhance the new patterns of work and learning that will be emerging from advances in knowledge sharing. This circular process is self-reinforcing; new forms of social interaction, creativity, and patterns of work and learning accelerate the development and application of new technologies, which restart the cycle all over again.

Evolving a Distinctive Knowledge Culture

While all enterprises have a distinctive knowledge ecology, they also are part of a greater knowledge ecology that extends beyond their boundaries. This knowledge ecology influences the enterprise knowledge culture, since successful enterprises must participate in knowledge sharing and exchange that transcends the boundaries of the enterprise. However, every

People-first organizations, not task-first ones, spawn hot groups that focus tirelessly on tasks.

Harold J. Leavitt and Jean Lipman-Blumen

enterprise knowledge culture has distinctive elements. For example, Richard Hames believes that enterprises are characterized by a distinctive blending of competing knowledge metaphors, mixing elements of "the cathedral" and "the café." To some extend, this blending is a sort of "brand" portraying the role and flow of knowledge in the enterprise and beyond. Over the next decade, successful enterprises will change the dynamics of their knowledge ecosystems. To do so will require new levels of individual and organizational competencies and changes in leadership, processes, infrastructures, and cultures as summarized below.

The Cathedral	The Café
Ordained leaders	Leaders at all levels
Sacred dogma	Heretical ideas and passion
Code and protocols	Open source activity
Prescribed culture	Networked community
The "official story"	Emergent stories

Adapted from: Richard Hames, 2002.

Enterprise Knowledge Ecology to Succeed in the Knowledge Age

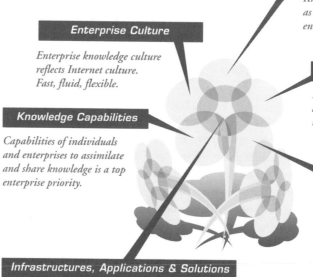

Leadership
Knowledge is explicitly treated as a strategic asset through the enterprise's knowledge strategy.

Enterprise Culture
Enterprise knowledge culture reflects Internet culture. Fast, fluid, flexible.

Processes
Processes reinvented to fit patterns and cadences of the Web and forge indispensable relationships.

Knowledge Capabilities
Capabilities of individuals and enterprises to assimilate and share knowledge is a top enterprise priority.

Communities of Practice
Gain in capability, flexibility and capacity to create and steward knowledge.

Infrastructures, Applications & Solutions
Seamless, interoperable and scalable solutions accessible through mobile, ambient environments.

Building Individual and Organizational Capabilities

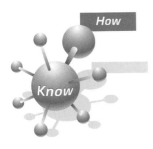

Becoming successful Knowledge Age enterprises is a substantial developmental challenge. It will require a commitment to individual and organizational learning far beyond today's norms. And it will require a commitment to understanding, building, and measuring new capabilities —the capacity of individuals and organizations to develop, acquire, share, and deploy just-in-time knowledge to drive decision making, strategy setting, product and service development and enhancement, and customer satisfaction.

Education in the twenty-first century will be about . . . who can DO what . . . not who KNOWS what.

Roger Shank, 2002

Making Capability Development an Organizational Priority

This challenge is greatest for enterprises that have not taken an enterprise-wide approach to the development of personal and organizational competencies. The systems, processes and procedures necessary to support competency development are the heart of an enterprise approach to strategic learning.

Firms that understand how to translate the power of communities into successful knowledge organizations will be the architects of tomorrow—not only because they will be more successful in the marketplace, but also because they will serve as a learning laboratory for exploring how to design the world as a learning system.

Etienne Wenger, Richard McDermott, and William M. Snyder, 2002

The more original a discovery, the more obvious it seems afterwards.

Arthur Koestler

Focusing on key business processes that are closely linked to strategic imperatives may offer better returns —at least at the outset —than attempted all-encompassing, enterprise-wide initiatives.

Deloitte Consulting

Balancing Organizational & Individual Perspectives on Knowledge

Organizational	Individual
Flexible delivery	Flexible access
Brand X-Portal	My-Portal
Corporate/enterprise knowledge	Individual learning and expertise
Systems perspective	Functional perspective
Defined palette of offerings	Open palette of choice
Data-centric service models Knowledge management: streamlining workflow and management of knowledge capital	Needs-based service models Learning management: easy integration of disparate information and communications sources/services

Specs matter . . . you indirectly commit to specs when you go online.

Tim Berners-Lee

Developing enterprise and individual capabilities are different issues. They have different orientations and mechanisms.

The dramatic enhancement of individual and organizational capabilities to acquire and share knowledge is the major human resources challenge—and opportunity—of the twenty-first century. The challenge can be met in small stages, each of which is easily possible today. As an example, one of the barriers to sharing knowledge is the present requirement that someone should add metadata to each "knowledge object" before it is placed in a database. This is rightly perceived as a chore, yet much of the effort is unnecessary.

Simple solutions abound. As an illustration, we know of one computer network administrator who added some software to the print server that handled all requests for printed documents. The software kept copies of each document on the network. The identity of the originator of the print request was known from their login details, therefore it did not need to be re-keyed (enter data only once, then re-use it). If the document was not on the list of previously printed documents, the software automatically created metadata for the document, by analyzing its content for key words and phrases. The originator of the print request received an automatic email telling them where they could find the copy of their printed document, if they wanted to reprint it, and also what metadata had been added to it. This provided each person with a personal database of their own documents plus annotations. They could also choose whether to add the document to the department's knowledge base, comprising documents explicitly made available for sharing.

Cascading cycles of development of such practices, along with powerful content recognition and patterning software to support them, will soon facilitate e-knowledge processes.

Knowledge sharing is becoming the central driver of the twenty-first century economy. Among the many companies which now recognize their stock of human capital as the major asset to business success; access to knowledge and just-in-time learning are more important than ever before . . . those countries, sectors, and organizations that can adapt will be the winners of the 21st century.

Steve Denning, Michel Pommer, Lesley Schneier, 2002

In conclusion, enterprises of all kinds must change their knowledge ecologies if e-knowledge is to be transformed. Enterprise strategies should include a knowledge strategy that identifies the salience of e-knowledge to strategic relationships and how the enterprise plans to use e-knowledge to establish competitive advantage. Enterprise initiatives dealing with every aspect of knowledge ecology—infrastructures, processes, capabilities, and culture—must be shaped in the image of the enterprise's knowledge strategy. All enterprises are affected—corporations, colleges and universities, trade associations and professional societies, government agencies, and other non-profits.

CHAPTER 6

Best Practices, Business Models, and Strategies

- Best Practices in Changing Times
- Time Frames for e-Knowledge
- Experiencing Continuous Reinvention

The next several years will witness dramatic advances in Web technologies, standards, e-knowledge marketplaces, enterprise infrastructures, processes, as well as individual and organizational capabilities to handle e-knowledge.

As a result enterprises will experience cascading cycles of reinvention in their best practices for e-learning and knowledge management. e-Learning and knowledge management will be pervasive, integrated into enterprise activities, and for all practical purposes, fused. These cycles of reinvention are starting today in leading-edge enterprises. They will accelerate and continue for decades. Many of the new practices will come from new competitors and from outside North America.

New business models and strategies will emerge that capitalize on the changing value nets for knowledge. The new business models will reduce the unit cost of content and knowledge and create new combinations of knowledge, experience, and performance that can command market premiums from users. As revenue streams are readjusted, enterprises will need to aggressively open new marketplaces for their knowledge. Communities of practice will become the dominant organizational form for creating and stewarding knowledge, spawning new mechanisms for creating insights and synthesis.

In the process of these cycles of reinvention, enterprises will reinvent their knowledge ecosystems— infrastructures, processes, competencies, and cultures.

Vision is the art of seeing things invisible.

Jonathan Swift

Terms & Concepts

Cascading Cycles of Reinvention: The dual forces of new Web technologies and e-knowledge standards and seamless, portalized enterprise applications infrastructures will accelerate the reinvention of processes and practices for e-knowledge. Iterative cycles of reinvention will cascade for decades.

Best Practices: What does best practice mean during a period of reinvention and transformative change? It means existing conceptions of "best practice" will be challenged by new alternatives. Given the wide range of global knowledge environments, best practice will likely take radically different forms around the globe.

Business Models: The business models for e-knowledge are the combination of services, experiences and prices offered to acquire e-knowledge. These are likely to change significantly. Already, the unit cost of e-content is being driven downward. Low-cost e-learning practices are being developed in Asia, and those practices will likely be adapted to application in developed markets in North America and Europe.

Strategies: Enterprises will need to develop enterprise-wide strategies for knowledge and for their various activities supported by e-knowledge. Enterprise strategies for e-learning, for opening new secondary marketplaces for e-knowledge, and for using knowledge as an instrument of competitive advantage will become important.

Knowledge Management Strategy: Enterprises develop strategies for developing the infrastructure, processes, and capacities necessary to maximize the stewardship of their knowledge assets.

Knowledge Strategy: Articulates the centrality of knowledge to the enterprise's mission, vision, and competitive position. It presents the enterprise's strategy for deploying its knowledge to establish competitive advantage.

Automatic Tagging and Automatic Sequencing: Use of automated tools to assess content/context and automatically determine tags for reusable learning objects.

Portfolio of Initiatives: Every enterprise has a portfolio of initiatives, with various levels of risk and transformation potential ranging from improvement to incremental reinvention to radical transformation.

Enterprise Plans and Initiatives: The organization's regular business plan and initiatives which must explicitly reflect the enterprise knowledge strategy.

Best Practices in Changing Times

During changing times, we experience the past, present, and future, all at the same time. How can we engage the different visions, sights, and sounds? And how can we each understand, in terms meaningful to our individual frames of reference and experience, what the future for e-knowledge may hold? The future is not a message to be conveyed from the prescient to everyone else; it is visions and experiences to be engaged in an evocative manner by everybody.

In this new world, the search for simplicity is tantamount to coming to the core understanding of how something is. I find the old cliché, 'You don't really understand something until you can say it in a simple way,' to be incredibly true and unbelievably useful. And I think today, in the era where the economy of attention reigns supreme, the ability to get to the very essence of what's going on very rapidly also provides tremendous leverage.
The power of saying simply makes all the difference in the world. The key to me is learning how to craft evocative objects: they could be metaphors, sayings, or experiences which rapidly help the other person rapidly construct their own understanding. Again, not provocative as much as evocative, so that it evokes the right kind of ideas in the listener. Great learners are, of course, great listeners, and if you learn how to listen to and through an evocative object, you learn how to leverage your emotional side as well as your cognitive side.

John Seely Brown

The future is conditional, not deterministic. It depends on what we do, as well as major trends, external forces, and developments. We have the power to derail the future as well as enable it. Over the next several years, advances in the tradecraft of e-knowledge will enable significant reinvention in e-learning and knowledge management, but only among those enterprises and practitioners who have the means, the vision, and the will to make it so.

The only way to predict the future is to have power to shape the future.

Eric Hoffer

Over the next few years, we will witness the existence of past, present, and future versions of "best practices," all existing concurrently in different settings and often in the same setting. Most enterprises will hedge their bets as they migrate their initiatives toward the e-knowledge paradigm without fully abandoning the existing paradigm. Under such conditions, the term "best practice" becomes especially problematic.

The future is called 'perhaps,' which is the only possible thing to call the future. And the important thing is not to allow that to scare you.

Tennessee Williams

The simple fact is that even highly innovative enterprises maintain a portfolio of initiatives ranging from "improvement" to "incremental innovation" to "radical innovation." Under such conditions, their notion of "best practice" is highly situational. Our challenge is to identify the emerging best practices, business models, and strategies that are likely to emerge as the e-knowledge paradigm matures and tradecraft develops.

Out of intense complexities intense simplicities emerge.

Winston Churchill

Time Frames for e-Knowledge

Predicting the future is uncertain. Predicting a calendar for transformation is uncertainty squared. *Transforming e-Knowledge* aims to mobilize the energies of policy makers and practitioners to accelerate and facilitate the development of e-knowledge, not create a precise road map to the future. Nevertheless, it is useful to paint in broad strokes the time frames during which enterprises could expect to capitalize on the forces described in this book. Rather than providing precise milestones, this description is meant to stimulate the realization that most of the technologies needed are available today and can be substantially deployed by 2010.

> *Perhaps the most plausible prediction is that any prediction about serious matters is likely to be off the mark, except by accident.*
>
> *Noam Chomsky*

The overall time frames have been drawn from a set of resources describing the evolution of ambient intelligence environments, learning and knowledge standards, knowledge exchanges and marketplaces, enterprise applications infrastructures, advances in communities of practice, intelligent agents and search engines, and related developments. Between today and the year 2010, all of the primary elements enabling the full emergence of e-knowledge have the capacity to develop and be put in place.

> *The future is like heaven. Everyone exalts it, but nobody wants to go there now.*
>
> *James Baldwin*

This is not speculation in the style of Jules Verne or Arthur C. Clarke, reaching far beyond the capabilities of current technologies and into the long-term future.

The technologies, standards, infrastructures, and e-knowledge marketplaces needed to make e-knowledge a reality are either possible today or will be within a few years. What is missing? The vision, perspectives, policies, procedures, routines, partnerships, cost structures, capabilities, experience, strategies, and will that is necessary to make e-knowledge happen. Our belief is that the greatest challenges to the development of e-knowledge will emerge within the human and relationship dimension. The table on the facing page summarizes the time frames for the arrival of technology, standards, and e-knowledge marketplaces necessary to transform e-knowledge.

Technology, Standards and e-Knowledge Marketplaces

Most of the technologies and standards needed to support e-knowledge sharing exist in proof-of-concept form. Over time, they will spread among enterprises and spawn the development of exchanges and marketplaces that should progressively achieve economic viability by 2009.

e-Knowledge Standards. Learning object standards are in place today (metadata and modular content). A broader suite of knowledge interoperability standards will come into use, on a *de facto* or *de jure* basis, during 2003–2004.

Proof-of-Concept Repositories. MERLOT, SCORM-compliant repositories, scholarly e-prints, and a host of enterprise and cross-enterprise repositories exist today. Typically, these pioneering efforts are still expensive and have not automated and made routine the tagging process sufficiently to bring costs into an acceptable range.

Proof-of-Concept of Automatic Tagging and Enterprise Reusability. In some settings, enterprises have achieved reusability of learning objects and content in different contexts. For example, Knowledge Media, Inc. and Autonomy have deployed auto indexing and auto tagging, auto sequencing of reusable knowledge objects using Bayesian algorithms/Shannon's theorem for conceptual search, and indexing methodologies. They have also deployed auto-indexing of multimedia using voice recognition utilities and subsequent indexing. Proof-of-concept exists today.

Proof-of-Concept Enterprise Accounting and Costing of e-Knowledge. As they develop experience in e-knowledge, leading-edge enterprises are adapting their cost accounting systems and procedures to cost-out e-knowledge practices and products. Over the next two years (2003–2004), new model practices will emerge.

Model Protocols for Enterprise Knowledge Asset Management. Current, first-generation approaches to knowledge asset management are too costly to be attractive for the full range of enterprise knowledge assets. This includes the cost of policy and protocol development and the cost of tagging, content management, and support. In response, enterprises have digitized their most strategic and/or often used resources. Over the next several years (2003–2004), exemplary policies, protocols and automated tagging, and similar means will be used to develop models that can be adapted by a wide range of enterprises. Associations like NACUBO, EDUCAUSE, NACUA, ASTD, ARL, and others are likely to play a major role in the development and promulgation of models and the reduction of costs.

Time Frames for e-Knowledge: Technology, Standards, and e-Knowledge Marketplaces

Technology, Standards and e-Knowledge Marketplaces	Description	Projected Time Frames
Knowledge interoperability standards	Knowledge interoperability standards in place, de facto or de jure	2002–2004
Proof-of-concept repositories	MERLOT, ADL co-labs, SPARC e-prints	2002
Proof-of-concept of automatic tagging and reusability	Current examples—KMI/Autonomy applications	2002
Proof-of-concept of enterprise accounting and costing of e-knowledge	Leading-edge enterprises develop accounting systems and procedures to cost out e-knowledge practices and products	2003–2004
Model protocols for enterprise knowledge asset management and external sharing	Enterprises develop model protocols	2003–2004
Digitizing of current knowledge resources in vertical channels	Enterprises (publishers, associations, corporations, colleges, and universities) digitize their existing knowledge resources in vertical channels	1997–2007
Emergence of horizontal e-knowledge marketplaces	Horizontal marketplaces emerge to link the content in vertical repositories	2002–2005
	Horizontal marketplaces achieve economic viability and substantial market penetration	2005–2009

In all affairs, love, religion, politics or business, it's a healthy idea, now and then to hang a question mark on things you have long taken for granted.

Bertrand Russell

Digitizing of Current Knowledge in Vertical Channels. Since the late 1990s, textbook and trade book publishers, university presses, association presses, and other enterprises have been digitizing their existing knowledge resources. They have used these digital assets to extend and complement their print offerings and to anticipate fully virtual products. The repurposing of existing content in e-learning formats has been given a major stimulus by new defense contracts through the U.S. Defense Department's ADL initiative. The size of this opportunity is US $48 million today and is expected to grow to over $300 million by 2003. The Association of American Publishers has sponsored a workshop in conjunction with the Learning Objects Network (LON) to explore how to leverage these opportunities. Over the next decade, repurposing content for e-learning through vertical publisher channels will be a major market opportunity.

Someday, objects will have wide-ranging and deep conversations with other objects, and their silent form of commerce will be the rule.

Glover T. Ferguson

Emergence of Horizontal Marketplaces. The multi-enterprise repositories described in Chapter 4—ARL's Scholar's Portal, MERLOT, RDN, SMETE, SMC, and commercial entities like Learning Content eXchange, XanEdu, and LON—are harbingers of non-profit and for-profit marketplaces that will emerge to slice across current vertical channels. Between 2002 and 2005, we expect a number of these marketplaces to evolve from existing ventures or enter the marketplace afresh. If properly constituted and funded, these marketplaces could achieve economic viability by 2005–2006 (also with the right business model). They could achieve widespread market penetration by 2008–2009.

Infrastructures, Processes, Capabilities and Cultures

Most of the technologies necessary to support enterprise application infrastructures and solutions, and e-knowledge ecologies are available in current or emerging generations of products, services, and solutions. What remains to happen is widespread deployment and enterprise adaptation. The table on the following page summarizes the timeframes for developing enterprise infrastructures and knowledge ecologies necessary to support e-knowledge.

Portalized Experience Layer Develops. Most enterprises have deployed portal and intranet capabilities and are refining them as platforms for interacting with their stakeholders. Early, proprietary portal products will have been replaced by interoperable, low-cost portal solutions by 2003–2004. This expeditionary process will then continue. By 2004–2005, the evolution of portals should have proceeded to the point where proof-of-concept is achieved of the "killer app:" the experience gateway through which stakeholders will experience the products, services, and knowledge the enterprise has to offer.

Fusion of Mission Critical Applications. Most industries have demonstrated the "fusion" of mission critical applications though the enterprise portal/intranet. For example, in higher education, the full integration of learning management, content management, and ERP, through the enterprise portal, has been achieved through SCT's Banner product in conjunction with WebCT and CampusPipeline. In the association industry, associations such as the American Health Information Management Association (AHIMA) have fused their "body of knowledge," e-learning, and communities of practice into a singular experience available to members and other stakeholders through the enterprise portal. Government and corporate demonstrations of this proof-of-concept are too numerous to recount.

Web Services Development. Over the next three to five years, Web services will be one of the hottest areas of applications development. By 2006–2007, Web services will likely have enabled the seamless integration of "best-of-breed" applications, plus the reclamation of many "legacy" systems that can be made much "smarter" through Web services applications.

Time Frames for e-Knowledge: Infrastructures and Knowledge Ecology

Infrastructures and Knowledge Ecosystems	Description	Projected Time Frames
Portalized experience gateway develops	Widespread, expeditionary development of portal capabilities	2002 onward
	Proprietary portals replaced by open, interoperable platforms	2003–2004 and onwards
	Proof-of-concept of highly personalized WINWINI experiences	2004–2005
Fusion of mission critical applications through portal	Most industries have demonstrated this capability	2002
Progressive Web services development	Web services making major headway in corporate settings today; major development in all sectors in next three to five years	2003–2007
Enterprise applications infrastructures and solutions	EAIS will create powerful enterprise infrastructures and solutions of all kinds	2003–2007
Development of community of practice infrastructures and experiences	Communities of practice become recognized as the dominant structure for knowledge creation and sharing	2003–2008
Mobile work and learning pilots	Many enterprises have launched mobile pilots. Over the next two years, leading enterprises will develop work and learning pilots to explore the impact of wireless technology	2003–2004
Enterprise-based development of pervasive technology, ambient intelligence	Pilots will lead to more ambitious ambient intelligence applications	2004–2008
Full ambient intelligence environments as described in ISTAG Report	Five ISTAG elements come together sufficiently to support ambient intelligence: 1) very unobtrusive hardware, 2) seamless mobile/fixed Web-based communications infrastructure, 3) dynamic and massively distributed device networks, 4) natural feeling human interfaces, and 5) dependability and security	2009–2010

There is nothing worse than the sharp image of a fuzzy concept.

Ansel Adams

Enterprise Applications Infrastructures and Solutions. The interoperable enterprise applications and solutions array of the future is possible with the capabilities present in the latest releases of today's generation of technology products. What is lacking is enterprise capability to deploy these new solutions, guided by VOI and strategic intent. Over the next five years (2003–2007), enterprises will develop the solutions, capabilities, and relationships necessary to achieve this goal.

Development of Community of Practice Model. Communities of practice are the dominant organizational models for knowledge creation and sharing. The level of awareness of community of practice principles varies from industry to industry, but between 2003–2008, this concept will prosper in all settings.

Mobile Work and Learning Pilots. Today, leading-edge enterprises are developing wireless environments and launching pilot programs to facilitate mobile work and learning activities. Over the next two years (2003–2004), most enterprises will use such pilots to develop mobile and even ambient environments.

Enterprise-based Development of Ambient Intelligence Environments. The mobile work and learning pilots will lead to more ambitious infrastructure and application development in 2004–2008.

Full Ambient Intelligence Environments as Described in ISTAG Report. By 2009–2010, the fully functional ambient environment could be put in place, as described by the European IST Advisory Group in its scenario report (supported by inputs from 35 European experts). Five ISTAG elements come together sufficiently to support ambient intelligence: 1) very unobtrusive hardware, 2) seamless mobile/fixed Web-based communications infrastructure, 3) dynamic and massively distributed device networks, 4) natural feeling human interfaces, and 5) dependability and security.

Reinvention of Best Practices, Business Models and Strategies

Even today, some leading-edge enterprises are engaged in the first waves of reinvention enabled by knowledge interoperability standards and infrastructure development. By all reasonable accounts, we can expect a significant acceleration in the reinvention of best practices for learning and knowledge management after 2005–2006. In addition, reinvention in business models will be driven by the emergence of new best practices, probably after 2002–2007. Finally, enterprise strategies for knowledge are beginning to be reinvented now and will have substantially developed by 2007–2008. These processes of reinvention will be continuous and ongoing.

Put simply, the prevailing judgment of practitioners and technologists is that by 2010, it is feasible that all of the pieces will be in place to support ambient environments and the new ways of experiencing knowledge presented in Chapter 1. There remains the prevailing question: to what extent will enterprises reinvent their knowledge ecologies, business practices, business model, and strategies to take advantage of their e-knowledge opportunities?

Resources on Timeframes for Reinvention

K. Ducatel, M. Bogdanowicz, F. Scapolo, J.Leijten, and J-C. Burgelman. 2001. *Scenarios for Ambient Intelligence in 2010.* IST Advisory Group, European Commission Community Research, February.

John Hagel and John Seely Brown. 2001. Your Next IT Strategy. *Harvard Business Review.*

Taylor, James C. 2001. *Fifth Generation Distance Education.* Australian Department of Education, Training and Youth Affairs, Higher Education Division, Higher Education Series, Report No. 40, June.

Hunter, Richard. 2002. *A World Without Secrets.* New York: John Wiley & Sons.

Experiencing Continuous Reinvention

The following discussion explores the continuous stream of reinvention for best practices, business models, and strategies that will occur between now and 2010 and beyond. It provides greater detail on the nature of the reinventions and how practitioners will experience such changes.

Reinventing Best Practices

What will it be like for an e-knowledge practitioner to experience the past, present, and future all at once? To witness cascading cycles of best practices in e-learning and knowledge management? To hear of interesting new practices and approaches from institutions and enterprises half way around the globe? And to try to make sense of the many choices and options in attempting to reinvent and innovate one's own e-knowledge initiatives?

How do companies spot and manage promising opportunities? They do it as surfers ride waves or scientists conduct research. They observe selected environments systematically and scan ripples of opportunity on multiple horizons. They learn to recognize patterns of impending change, anomalies, or promising interactions, then monitor, reinforce, and exploit them.

James Brian Quinn, 2002

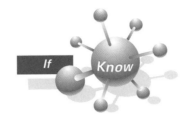

Making Innovation Easier—Yesterday, Today and Tomorrow. Even today, mass systems for education and training offer little more by way of personalization than did Henry Ford's pioneering system for mass production of vehicles: "You can have any color you like as long as it's black." Ford's system, remarkable for its day, had its R&D equivalent in Thomas Edison's laboratories at Menlo Park. Edison is famously credited with the insight that invention was 99% perspiration and 1% inspiration. He needed thousands of experiments before he was able to devise a long-lasting electric light. His studies of other inventors convinced him that sudden flashes of inspiration—'Eureka' moments—were the exception. Most of the time, small steps were all that was needed to make valuable advances. He isolated the processes that were common to the mass of inventive steps, and established the world's first production line for inventions and innovations.

What was admirable about that approach was the way in which people who would not have considered themselves to be creative were enabled to be creative and to come up with ideas for products that changed their society. Today, comparable vistas are emerging. The difference between now and Edison's time is that today "we have the technology," such as computer-supported ways to develop personalized knowledge bases specific to our needs, which can be combined with databases of processes that are proven to be helpful. As an early illustration, consider the success of NASA. They were an early

user of a system for managing invention and innovation, developed in the former Soviet Union under its Russian acronym TRIZ. The inventor of TRIZ looked for patterns in many thousands of patents, and determined the physical effects that were the basis for each invention. From this, he was able to come up with generalized processes that anyone could use to create new inventions.

In the West, the system is now available commercially under such names as the Invention Machine. It provides a decision-support system that incorporates links to relevant databases, covering such areas as constraints (e.g., physical and chemical properties of materials) and possibilities (e.g., known physical effects and phenomena). We see it as a precursor of the kinds of tools that will become widely available in the knowledge economy for managing knowledge of all kinds and seeing patterns that can be put to use in new contexts.

The key to success is to bake specialized knowledge into the jobs of highly skilled workers—to make knowledge so readily accessible that it can't be avoided."

Thomas H. Davenport and John Glaser, July 2002

Such tools will need to be embedded into people's knowledge space in a highly amenable manner.

Emergent Best Practices. Two benchmarks guide our vision of emerging best practices for e-knowledge: 1) current e-knowledge practices that are gestating in different settings across the globe, and 2) the impact of impending changes in standards, technologies, marketplaces, infrastructures, and knowledge ecologies. The leading edges of many of these best practices are evident today.

Generalizations are generally wrong.

Butler Lampson

Reinvention of Best Practices

- ***New e-knowledge forms and capabilities achieve wide acceptance.***
  - Digitized *context* joins content as key element in the value web of modular content
  - New generations of learning objects are managed within knowledge ecologies where 'know-what' and 'know-how' come into closer alignment
  - Content embedded in experiences and performances commands a value premium
  - Just-in-time and just-in-case knowledge management systems (ability to reflect new knowledge in learning experiences) are used to create new and re-purpose existing learning objects
  - Ability to track the knowledge to which people have been exposed and to which they have demonstrated competencies enables continuous recertification
  - Tradecraft-rich approach to learning objects is valued by most enterprises

- ***Knowledge repositories, services, and marketplaces are established as foundations for e-knowledge.***
  - Change the dynamics and power relationships of publishing
  - Open secondary markets for e-knowledge from particular providers
  - Empower non-traditional providers and supply aggregators

- ***Communities of practice become the epicenters of knowledge stewardship and autonomic learning.***
  - Achieve amenity in the experience of facilitating knowledge sharing among peers
  - Also provide regular syntheses of new knowledge to outside consumers

- ***Impacts of new infrastructures and environments reshape knowledge ecologies.***
  - New knowledge ecologies reshape relationships with learners, customers, members, and other stakeholders
  - Ambient intelligence environments provide new opportunities for individual and community-based knowledge sharing experiences
  - Relationships are the foundation for learning experiences and the fulcrum for leveraging them.

New e-knowledge forms and capabilities achieve wide acceptance. "Context" joins content as an important enabler of learning objects, generated through a value web of interconnecting knowledge sources. "Know-what" and "know-how" come into closer alignment as drivers of value from knowledge. The experiences and/or performances in which content/context are embedded are recognized as a source of premium value. Just-in-time and just-in-case knowledge management systems provide the capacity to continuously reflect emergent knowledge in existing and new learning objects. Pervasive, easy-to-use content management capabilities will enable enterprises and communities to track the knowledge which people have experienced and to create continuous re-certification capabilities. Most enterprises and individuals beyond basic educational levels will place a premium value on tradecraft-rich learning objects and experiences.

Any technology gradually creates a totally new human environment.

Marshall McLuhan, 1967

e-Knowledge repositories, marketplaces, and exchanges become the foundation for e-knowledge. The sharing and exchange of e-knowledge becomes an essential element of the e-Knowledge Industry. Horizontal marketplaces change the dynamics of publishing and learning support, increasing customer satisfaction and driving down both the cost and price of content. These marketplaces open secondary markets for enterprise knowledge, which creates a significant revenue stream for associations, universities, many enterprises, and individual faculty, researchers, and practitioners. These marketplaces also empower providers and demand aggregators who leverage their established relationships with learners in various settings.

Communities of practice become the epicenters of knowledge stewardship and autonomic learning. Communities of practice achieve amenity in facilitating knowledge sharing among peers. They also provide syntheses of insights to outsiders. Communities of practice become the epicenters of autonomic learning; directed/structured learning uses cohort-based models, drawing its learners from the community of practice and/or working groups.

Impacts of new infrastructures and knowledge environments reshape knowledge ecologies. Cycles of process reinvention create new knowledge ecologies that reshape the relationships between enterprises and their members, learners, staff, customers, and other stakeholders. These relationships are the basis for creating and sharing knowledge. They are also the foundation and fulcrum for leveraging learning relationships. Ambient knowledge environments provide new opportunities for knowledge sharing—involving individuals, teams, and communities.

Reinventing Business Models

The principles and practices of e-knowledge enable individuals and enterprises to "unbundle" their learning and knowledge sharing experiences. This is one of the greatest powers of e-knowledge. It appeals to the aspirations and motivations of individuals and most enterprises and enables dramatic changes in business models involving knowledge and learning.

The future of intellectual property industries lies in selling performances and relationships, not digital objects. Attempts to sell digital objects at increasingly higher prices can only succeed when the seller has a de facto monopoly. . . . Revenues for manufacturers and distributors of digital objects will drop steeply in the next 10 years in the World Without Secrets. It's a good time for those players to think about how they are going to make a transition to a new business. They might start by thinking about what makes a company exceptional, or not, beginning with its relationships.

Richard Hunter

A good business model begins with an insight into human motivations.

Joan Magretta, 2002

As for the future, your task is not to foresee, but to enable it.

Martin Gilbert

Unbundling Resources and Experiences for Learning and Knowledge Sharing.

The act of unbundling resources and experiences enables individuals to shape the nature and source of content, context, and associated tradecraft and the experience in which it is embedded. Unbundling, choice, and personalization are quintessential principles of the e-knowledge culture and the Internet culture on which it is based.

Universities are locked into supply-side thinking; they are out of step with the network economy. Changes in academic culture and university programs will be driven by the demand side (students, alums, employers, marketplace realities), not from institutional supply-siders (professor, administrators). The supply-side model sustains the 'control culture' of academe when the network economy has embraced a 'service and value culture.' The goal should be providing increased value to students and alums, not control.

Martin Irvine, 2001

Changes in Interactivity.

e-Knowledge enables reinvention in the patterns and cadences in the interactivity between learners, faculty, mentors, expert practitioners, and supporting staff in instructional development and knowledge management. For example:

- e-knowledge resources enable faculty to refashion their role toward knowledge navigator and judgment builder and away from human knowledge repository;
- e-knowledge encourages the development of resources by teams of faculty, instructional development staff and knowledge management experts;
- cohort-based learning using e-knowledge resources encourages greater dialogue among and between learners, changing the extent and nature of faculty or mentor involvement;

Reinvention of Business Models

- *e-Knowledge enables unbundling of knowledge, learning resources, and experiences.*

- *e-Knowledge enables changes in interactivity. It enables reinvention in the patterns and cadences in the interactivity between learners, faculty, mentors, expert practitioners, and supporting staff in instructional development and knowledge management.*

- *e-Knowledge drives changes in the economics of knowledge sharing and learning.*
  - **Sources, types, and combinations** of digital knowledge assets will increase exponentially, enabling greater choice and personalization;
  - **Unit costs** of producing digital assets will decline as enterprises refine routines, policies, protocols, use of auto-tagging tools and agents, and explore alternate sources of e-knowledge;
  - **Price** of individual units of digital knowledge will decline dramatically in the face of competition (including excellent sources of free e-knowledge), diminishing costs of production;
  - **Premium prices** will be accepted by individuals for particular combinations of content, context, and tradecraft embedded in performances and experiences;
  - **New markets for an individual's or enterprise's** e-knowledge will be opened by e-knowledge marketplaces;
  - **Creation and use of knowledge** will be combined in many settings (e.g. communities of practices) resulting in a sort of barter and free access for insiders; and
  - **New patterns of interactivity** will enable dramatic reductions in the cost and price of cohort-based learning experiences.

- *e-Knowledge enables disruptive offerings from new competitors. Lower-cost learning practices are developed in emerging markets in Asia and in Central and South America. Lower-cost models are selectively applied in markets in North America and Europe, further driving down prices for content and learning.*

- *Relationships with learners, customers, members, and other stakeholders can be leveraged to create new, personalized combinations of products, services, and experiences.*

- e-knowledge and ambient interactivity will enable the participation of expert practitioners in tradecraft-rich learning; and
- autonomic learning within communities of practice will create perpetual, sustainable patterns of interactivity around knowledge sharing and learning.

These changes in interactivity will expand the range of choices available to learners and knowledge seekers. Premium, high-cost options will be available, as they always have been. But lower-cost, rein-vented options will prove more attractive to many individuals and enterprises.

Changes in the Economics of Knowledge Sharing and Learning.

e-Knowledge will change the economics of knowledge sharing and learning in several ways:

- **sources, types, and combinations** of digital knowledge assets will increase exponentially, enabling greater choice and personalization;
- **unit costs** of producing individual units of digital assets will decline as

enterprises refine routines, policies, protocols, use of auto-tagging tools and agents, and explore alternate sources of e-knowledge;

- **price** of individual units of digital knowledge will decline dramatically in the face of competition (including excellent sources of free e-knowledge), diminishing costs of production;
- **premium prices** will be accepted by individuals for particular combinations of content, context, and tradecraft embedded in performances and experiences;
- **new markets for an individual's or enterprise's** e-knowledge will be opened by e-knowledge marketplaces;
- **creation and use of knowledge** will be combined in many settings (e.g. communities of practice) resulting in a sort of barter and free access for insiders; and
- **new patterns of interactivity** will enable dramatic reductions in the cost and price of cohort-based learning experiences.

One cannot precisely predict with elegant precision the combination and range of choices that will constitute the e-knowledge and e-learning marketplace of the future. One thing is clear: e-knowledge will enable a new range of choices that will put the learner and knowledge seeker in the driver's seat.

What are the top three success stories you have come across of e-learning in action? 1) Jones International University, which is the first fully accredited entirely online university in the USA and possibly the world; 2) Duke University Fuqua School of Management for running the most expensive online MBA program with a tuition fee of US $85,000—proving that people will pay for quality online education; and 3) MasterTutor.com, a little known but genuine effort which has a few thousand middle-class Indian students paying a few thousand rupees as fees per course.

Madan Pant,
Interviewed by Madanmohan Rao.

Disruptive Reinvention from New Competitors and Innovators. For some time, traditional learning models have been challenged by open universities, many of which enroll hundreds of thousands of physical and virtual learners. Today, lower-cost, cohort-based learning practices are being developed in emerging markets in Asia and in Central and South America by MasterTutor.com, NTT, NextEd, ITESM, Unisys, and others. These models are driving down the cost and price of e-learning and knowledge sharing. They will be refined in these settings and progressively applied to markets in developed nations. The processes, routines, and tradecraft used by these pioneering providers will be utilized by other providers.

When a new model changes the economics of an industry and is difficult to replicate, it can by itself create a strong competitive advantage.

Joan Magretta, 2002

Leveraging Relationships. The most successful business models in the e-Knowledge Economies will be based on leveraging and extending existing relationships. Whether it involves creating or

He who wishes to teach us a truth should not tell it to us, but simply suggest it with a brief gesture, a gesture which starts an ideal trajectory in the air along which we glide until we find ourselves at the feet of the new truth.

Jose Ortega y Gasset

sharing knowledge or learning, relationships with learners, members, customers, staff, suppliers, and other stakeholders are at the center of the picture.

What does this suggest for future prospects of knowledge and learning enterprises? The future belongs to knowledge and learning enterprises whose relationship is grounded on highly motivated stakeholders who are co-creators of the learning/knowledge sharing processes. Consider these examples:

- The American Health Information Management Association (AHIMA) has defined the "body of knowledge" for HIM professionals, which is accessible from the AHIMA portal. Learning and knowledge seeking/creating experiences are also available through the portal. The association has reinvented its governance structure along a community of practice model, creating self-defining, emergent communities.
- Claus Unger of Fern Universitaet in Germany (an open university) has described the "learning spaces" his institution hopes to create. Students could use them repeatedly throughout their careers, pursuing different paths, pursuing learning at different depths, making use of sharable materials from across the Web that would be reconfigured in real time for different purposes.

The future epicenter of e-knowledge sharing/e-learning appears to be: proprietary learning and knowledge providers, associations and professional societies, corporations with strong enterprise learning and communities of practice, open universities focusing on lifelong learning relationships, and traditional universities using relationships through alumni, extension and continuous learning channels.

To paraphrase, the epicenter of knowledge may be with the individual but the epicenter of leverage is with the organization.

Rudy Ruggles and Dan Holthouse

Reinventing Strategies

To assure success in the e-knowledge future, enterprises must redirect their strategies—not just for knowledge, but for all business processes, products, services, and experiences that depend on knowledge. Some of that redirection can start immediately, while other refinements must await new technologies, standards, marketplaces, changes in infrastructures, and reinventions of best practices and business models. The point is that the emergence of e-knowledge should affect every aspect of enterprise strategy and business planning.

Take Immediate Actions to Improve Your Readiness for e-Knowledge. In Chapter 7, we recommend 10 actions that your enterprise can undertake immediately to enhance its readiness for e-knowledge.

Craft an Enterprise Knowledge Strategy. Reinvention of enterprise strategy can start immediately through the crafting of an explicit knowledge strategy. At its first level, this strategy identifies the centrality of knowledge to the enterprise's mission, vision, and competitive position. At present time, enterprises bury their knowledge strategy implicitly within strategic and business plans. The enterprise must explicitly state its knowledge strategies and link those strategies explicitly to unit business plans. Chapter 7 illustrates how to create a knowledge strategy that drives enterprise initiatives.

Success in global markets depends on communities sharing knowledge across the globe. . . . Knowledge-driven markets make it imperative to develop a "knowledge strategy" along with a business strategy. Yet many organizations have no explicit, consolidated knowledge strategy. Rather, it exists implicitly at best, dispersed in strategic plans, human resource reports, or system-improvement proposals. A knowledge strategy details in operational terms how to develop and apply the capabilities required to execute the business strategy. Therefore, a knowledge strategy eventually depends on communities of practice."

Wenger et al, 2002

Take Advantage of Changes in the Mobility of Networked Knowledge. The pervasive spread of networks through enterprises has changed the mobility and distribution of knowledge. Mohanabir Sawnhey and Deval Parikh (2001) point out that back-office knowledge is often embedded in the network's shared infrastructure, while the front-office knowledge resides at the network's periphery, where the users are. Significant units of formerly disconnected or isolated knowledge become available to users wherever they are needed. These developments enable enterprises to consider a combination of four strategies for profiting from knowledge mobility:

- *arbitrage*—moving knowledge to locations where maintenance costs are lower;
- *aggregation*—combining formerly isolated knowledge into a pool of shared knowledge;

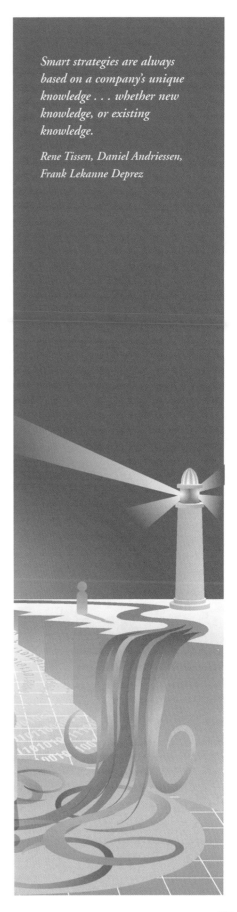

Smart strategies are always based on a company's unique knowledge . . . whether new knowledge, or existing knowledge.

Rene Tissen, Daniel Andriessen, Frank Lekanne Deprez

Reinvention of Strategies

- **Take immediate action to improve your enterprise's readiness for e-knowledge** (See Chapter 7 for 10 immediate actions).

- **Develop an explicit enterprise knowledge strategy.** Develop an explicit enterprise knowledge management strategy to tie knowledge asset management and reinventing knowledge ecology to business plans. (See Chapter 7 for examples)

- **Develop strategies to take advantage of changes in the mobility of networked knowledge:**
  - *arbitrage*—moving knowledge to locations where maintenance costs are lower;
  - *aggregation*—combining formerly isolated knowledge into a pool of shared knowledge;
  - *rewiring*—connecting islands of intelligence by creating an information backbone; and
  - *reassembly*—organizing pieces of knowledge from diverse sources into coherent, customized packages for customers.

- **Prepare to use expeditionary strategies to take advantage of opportunities.**

- **Develop a strategy portfolio dealing with productivity improvement, incremental innovation and radical innovation (transformation)** (See Chapter 7 for portfolio strategy methodology).

- **Enterprises leverage their relationships with learners, members, customers, and other stakeholders to provide new, personalized versions products, services, and experiences.**

If your knowledge category has substantial competition, a "less is more" strategy works best.

Thomas H. Davenport and John C. Beck.

• *rewiring*—connecting islands of intelligence by creating an information backbone; and

• *reassembly*—organizing pieces of knowledge from diverse sources into coherent, customized packages for customers.

Enterprises can fashion strategies for taking advantage of these opportunities to advance the enterprise mission through networked e-knowledge.

It may now make more sense to talk about a company's distributed capabilities' instead of 'core capabilities'.

Mohanabir Sawnhey and Deval Parikh

Prepare to Use Expeditionary Strategies to Take Advantage of New Opportunities. Corporations, associations, government agencies, and even universities have discovered the wisdom of taking an "expeditionary" approach to developing strategies, products, services, and experiences for today's market. They realize that during

periods of technology disruption, "killer apps" are discovered not through flashes of revelation, but through expeditionary initiatives that use product platforms as continuously adapting probes into the future. The killer apps for e-knowledge will emerge over time, not in a flash of dot.com brilliance.

In the words of James Brian Quinn, companies spot promising opportunities like surfers ride waves or scientists conduct research: by systematically observing environments, scanning ripples of opportunity on multiple horizons, and learning to recognize patterns of impending change, anomalies, or promising interactions that can be monitored, reinforced, and exploited. Enterprises need flexible knowledge platforms and the entrepreneurial skill to seize opportunity waves. This requires the systematic dissemination and trading of knowledge, even proprietary knowledge if necessary, to enable larger innovations that will leverage their own innovation's value by an order of magnitude (Quinn, 2002).

Dialectic of Enterprise Knowledge Initiatives

Stability	**Dynamism**
Operate in current environment	*Vision future environment*
Aggressively serve customers, learners, members, and stakeholders under current value propositions	*Rethink value propositions for customers, learners, members, and other stakeholders*
Make current processes more efficient—enhance productivity and optimize workflow	*Reinvent current processes using collaboration and innovation to change enterprise dynamics— rethink everything*
Structured/directed learning	*Autonomic learning*

Reinvention of Best Practices, Business Models and Strategies

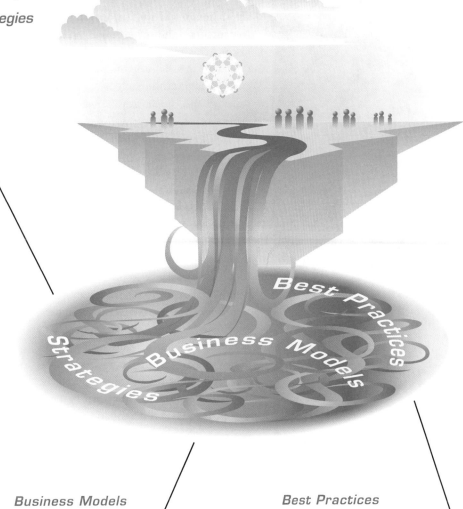

Strategies

- *Take immediate action to improve enterprise readiness for e-knowledge.*
- *Develop an explicit enterprise knowledge strategy.*
- *Develop strategies to take advantage of changes in the mobility of knowledge.*
- *Develop a strategy portfolio dealing with productivity improvement, incremental innovation, and radical innovation.*
- *Enterprises leverage relationships to provide indispensable products, services, experiences, and knowledge.*

Business Models

- *e-Knowledge enables unbundling of knowledge, learning, resources and experiences.*
- *e-Knowledge enables changes in interactivity between faculty, mentors, learners, and practitioners.*
- *e-Knowledge drives changes in economics of knowledge sharing and learning.*
- *e-Knowledge enables disruptive offerings from new competitors.*
- *Relationships with learners, customers, members, and other stakeholders can be leveraged.*

Best Practices

- *New e-knowledge forms and capabilities achieve wide acceptance.*
- *Knowledge repositories, services and marketplaces are established.*
- *Communities of practice become the epicenters of knowledge stewardship and autonomic learning.*
- *Impacts of new infrastructures and environments reshape knowledge ecologies.*

Someday, in the distant future, our grandchildren's grandchildren will develop a new equivalent of our classrooms. They will spend many hours in front of boxes with fires glowing within. May they have the wisdom to know the difference between light and knowledge.

Plato

Develop a Strategic Portfolio of e-Knowledge Initiatives. At any point in time, an enterprise will need to manage a portfolio of initiatives having varying objectives, ranging from improvement to incremental innovation to radical innovation. This will enable your enterprise to deal with the dialectic of enterprise initiatives, maintaining a balance between stability and dynamism, between operating in today's environment and making a jump shift in vision to the e-knowledge future.

Leverage Relationships to Create New Products, Services, Knowledge Resources and Experiences. Like best practices and business models, enterprise strategies should begin and end with relationships. Mobile, networked e-knowledge provides a powerful instrument for establishing ***indispensable relationships*** with members, customers, learners, staff, suppliers, and other stakeholders who not only want it, they want to participate in its creation. So what is it about the relationship and the associated experiences that can be both indispensable and differentiating?

> *Relationship is the only thing strong enough to resist the siren call of ten million other sites that are just a click away . . . In the digital world, the one with the best conversation usually wins. And I assure you that there are many dialogues out there still in search of a village square.*
>
> *Mikela Tarlow, 2002*

There are as many answers to this question as there are individuals seeking knowledge or engaging in learning. It seems clear, however, that in the information surfeit of the attention economy, most individuals will forge indispensable relationships with a relatively small number of trusted organizations, associations, institutions, and enterprises whose brand has been affirmed as meaning "giving me the knowledge

I want, when I need it, efficiently, and as part of an engaging experience." Sounds like a strategy for success.

In Chapter 4, we introduced a quote by H.G. Wells expressing the potential for marshalling the fragmented knowledge resources around the world to address the difficulties of the age. This grand idea could not be implemented 60 years ago because we lacked the technology and the capacity, let alone the will. In the near future, we shall possess the technologies and tradecraft to attempt Wells' vision. We have come to comprehend the complexity of knowledge and the importance of culture and knowledge ecology in establishing meaning. What will the future of e-knowledge hold for the receiving, sorting, summarizing, digesting, clarifying, and comparing of the knowledge and ideas of our time? We shall all participate in crafting the answer.

> *An immense and ever-increasing wealth of knowledge is scattered about the world today; knowledge that would probably suffice to solve all the mighty difficulties of our age, but it is dispersed and unorganized. We need a sort of mental clearing house: a depot where knowledge and ideas are received, sorted, summarized, digested, clarified, and compared.*
>
> *H.G. Wells, 1940*

CHAPTER 7

Achieving Success in the Emerging e-Knowledge Industry

- *10 Ways to Accelerate Your Readiness for e-Knowledge*
- *Mobilizing Leaders, Policy Makers, and Practitioners*
- *Developing a Knowledge Strategy that Drives Enterprise Initiatives*

This book concludes as it began, with a simple vision:
In the Knowledge Economy, individuals and enterprises that share and process their knowledge most effectively have a great advantage. To keep up, most of us will need an order-of-magnitude leap in our ability to handle knowledge. This won't happen without a genuine transformation in the ways in which knowledge is created, managed, repurposed, combined, exchanged and experienced. This transformation is underway. Participation is mandatory for all hoping to achieve success in the Knowledge Economy. We offer three instruments to help in preparing you and your enterprise for success in the Knowledge Economy.

10 Ways to Accelerate Your Readiness for e-Knowledge. Individuals and organizations need practical, yet visionary actions that they can take to accelerate their capacity to develop infrastructures and capabilities and participate in the cascading cycles of reinvention.

Mobilizing Leaders, Policy Makers, and Practitioners. The time is ripe to mobilize leaders, policy makers, and practitioners to shape the e-knowledge revolution.

Developing a Knowledge Strategy that Drives Enterprise Initiatives. A concise knowledge strategy states how knowledge is essential to competitive advantage. It shapes the enterprise knowledge management strategy and initiatives that build competitive advantage.

The three [knowledge-sharing] myths are (1) build it and they will come, (2) technology can replace face-to-face, and (3) first you have to create a learning culture.

Nancy M. Dixon

Terms & Concepts

Accelerating Readiness for e-Knowledge: Enterprises can gain a competitive advantage by accelerating their development of the perspectives, visions, infrastructures, processes, and capabilities needed for e-knowledge.

Digital Rights Management (DRM)/Digital Asset Management: Enterprises develop the policies, protocols, and infrastructures needed to manage, meter and exchange their knowledge.

e-Business: e-Business is more than e-commerce. It is the use of ICT to transform the way organizations conduct their business. e-Business enables enterprises to fundamentally change their relationships with customers, members, learners, suppliers/partners, and/or other stakeholders.

Organizational Storytelling: The essential tool of leadership wishing to engage their enterprise in understanding the future, disruptive technologies, and how they feel about change.

Activity Based Costing (ABC): Accounting practices that enable measurement of the cost of enterprise activities.

Non-Governmental Organizations (NGOs): Nonprofit organizations that are not governmental entities.

Co-Creation: When customers, members, or learners not only **consume** products, services, experiences, and knowledge, but **participate** in their creation, that is called co-creation. By definition, co-created knowledge is personalized to the needs of the co-creators.

Operational Excellence: Providing world-class efficiencies, timeliness, and cost/price.

Great Products: Providing excellence and leadership in product quality and innovation.

Customer Intimacy: Developing intimate indispensable relationships with customers, members, learners, and other stakeholders.

10 Ways to Accelerate Your Readiness for e-Knowledge

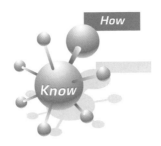

Discovery and discernment are the cornerstone skills of the New Economy.

Van B. Weigel

There is no cookbook for preparing your organization for e-knowledge transformation. No formulaic process or canned consulting methodology will guarantee success. Building the perspectives, visions, infrastructures, processes, and capabilities needed to transform current practices to embrace e-knowledge is an expeditionary venture requiring years to accomplish. And the jump shifts required may necessitate discontinuities in current practice.

A number of actions at key pressure points can make a dramatic difference, starting immediately. Some can enable your enterprise to engage its leadership, staff, faculty, learners, members, and other stakeholders in formative conversations that will elevate their e-knowledge perspectives and build capabilities. Others will develop plans, pilot projects, and new infrastructures and capabilities. Some will collect and reflect on best practices and competitive intelligence. The sum total of such actions can accelerate your organization's readiness for e-knowledge. They can also stimulate the expected cycles of reinvention in e-knowledge strategies, business models and best practices.

These initiatives should not be treated as independent, one-time, or even sequential activities. Rather, they should be integrated into organizational processes for planning, development, management, and operation. Moreover, they should be used as the instrument for reinventing those processes to reflect the strategic importance of e-knowledge. To succeed in the Knowledge Economy, your organization must harness and transform the capacity of individuals and the organization as a whole to acquire, manage, and share knowledge. Such expeditions require changes in your enterprise's knowledge ecology.

These initiatives are organized using the structure of the three-part model of the indicators of the e-Knowledge Economy. We have purposefully reversed the order, beginning with best practices, business models, and strategies. This formulation is a superior instrument for capturing the attention and evoking understanding from everyone in the enterprise from grassroots to top leadership.

Tracking the Indicators of the e-Knowledge Economy

Technologies, Standards and Marketplaces for e-Knowledge

Best Practices, Business Models and Strategies

Infrastructures, Processes, Capabilities and Cultures

*Envisioning the end is enough
to put the means in motion.*

Dorothea Brande

Best Practices Business Models and Strategies

The next few years will witness dramatic changes in best practices, business models, and strategies for e-knowledge. While these cycles of reinvention will continue for years, enterprises should move out immediately on five actions to enhance their readiness for e-knowledge.

1.

Storytelling

Engage everyone in the enterprise on the subject of e-knowledge. Use storytelling to explore how individuals will experience knowledge. Mobilize energies from grassroots to the CEO and Board.

e-Knowledge is not the subject of a momentary conversation, a fad, the business school topic *du jour*. Your enterprise's response to this topic may define your enterprise's success in the next five years. The challenge for leadership is how to make e-knowledge a central topic in engaging conversations that mobilize energies and release creativity.

Talk the talk. The strategic conversations about knowledge can focus on a variety of themes:

- Using storytelling to engage broad cross-sections of your enterprise in addressing the e-knowledge future and sharing real-life success stories;
- Developing a range of future scenarios about the use of knowledge and the changing roles of organizations and individuals;
- Using these stories and scenarios to explore the possibilities of truly transformational, and likely disruptive, changes in the existing knowledge value chain and power relationships; and

- Exploring the ecology, roles, and interactions of different knowledge entities—individuals, teams and work groups, communities of practice, and knowledge networks of various kinds.

Strategic, enterprise-wide conversations about knowledge should balance visioning with stories of successful transformation already achieved.

Walk the talk. It's not just about storytelling. Enterprises should begin to utilize technology-supported tools for sharing knowledge, such as those using the Semantic Web and intelligent agent capabilities.

**Exemplary Resources:
Engage the Enterprise**

- *The Squirrel: The Seven Highest Value Forms of Organizational Storytelling,* Stephen Denning. www.stevedenning.com/squirrel.htm
- Eastern Michigan University storytelling about technology-driven change. www.transformingeknowledge.info
- Collaborative Decisionmaking and Personal Knowledge Management with R-Objects Pepper . www.r-objects.com/papers/www2002 /jernst-www2002.pdf

2.

Knowledge Strategy

*Develop a knowledge strategy for the enterprise that brings into alignment:
1) management of the enterprise's knowledge assets, and
2) the enterprise's business plans to achieve its mission and goals.*

Develop a contemporary perspective on the strategic importance of knowledge, complementing the VOI perspective on the strategic importance of technology. In the past, a laissez-faire approach to knowledge was sufficient, but no longer.

It is not communities of practice themselves that are new but the need for organizations to become more intentional and systematic about 'managing' knowledge . . .

Etienne Wenger, Richard McDermott and William M. Snyder, 2002

A knowledge strategy is a concise, clear articulation of the role of knowledge in the enterprise's mission and goals and in achieving competitive advantage. It drives a strategy for knowledge management that is aligned with the enterprise's business initiatives. Every enterprise should have such strategies.

a. Develop a knowledge strategy—a clear concise articulation of the role of knowledge in achieving the enterprise's mission, goals, and competitive advantage. Every enterprise should use such a strategy to align knowledge management strategy and the enterprise's business initiatives.

b. Develop a knowledge management strategy that balances the dialectic of stability and change. The knowledge management strategy will identify e-knowledge capabilities that must be achieved to deliver on the enterprise's knowledge strategy. These 10 action items are all part of a knowledge management strategy. This strategy must simultaneously operate in the current value proposition and prepare for dramatically different value propositions in the future.

c. Integrate knowledge-based initiatives into enterprise business plans; plan for impending reinvention of best practices. To succeed, knowledge initiatives must be an explicit part of the enterprise's business plans, not stand-alone initiatives. Current approaches in e-learning and knowledge management should be scrutinized and compared to emerging best practices in other settings.

Exemplary Resources: Knowledge Strategy

- AHIMA Case Study. www.transformingeknowledge.info

3.
Pilot Projects

Support a wide variety of knowledge management and community of practice pilots throughout the enterprise. Support different expeditions and multiple trajectories in parallel to determine what works.

Each enterprise should establish a single, integrated, applications infrastructure for sharing knowledge and this should be an enterprise priority. However, there are many different approaches to creating and sharing knowledge. An assortment of distinctive communities of practice and communities of inquiry can yield valuable insights.

An enterprise must understand its knowledge ecology and reflect on what makes communities of practice effective under different circumstances. Storytelling can be used in dissecting and understanding the dynamics of knowledge and communities of practice.

Exemplary Resources: Support a Variety of Knowledge Management and Community of Practice Pilots

- UNESCO Education For All— Grassroots Stories. www.unesco.org/ education/efa/know_sharing/grass-roots_stories/

4.
Environmental Scan

Scan the environment for examples of changing best practices, business models, and strategies regarding e-knowledge; collect competitive intelligence on market leaders and innovators from outside the industry. Benchmark e-knowledge practices.

Organizations need to become active and reflective environmental scanners regarding e-knowledge. This should include identifying and evaluating changes in best practice, business models, and strategies for e-knowledge. For most industries, these efforts should take a global perspective in understanding potential challenges from unfamiliar innovators. Standard practice of benchmarking performance against familiar market leaders will prove inadequate during periods of disruptive change when the rules are being rewritten by new competitors as described in Chapter 6.

How can an organization know it is succeeding in raising its knowledge sharing capacity and competencies, and gaining ground against competitors? One of the best instruments is to use the enterprise knowledge strategy to focus on how knowledge contributes to competitive advantage, creating indispensable relationships and/or experiences. Benchmark your enterprise's ability to create indispensable relationship and experiences for members, learners, customers, suppliers, and/or other stakeholders.

Exemplary Resources: Environmental Scanning for Best Practices, Business Models, and Strategies

- UNESCO Education For All—Grassroots Stories. www.unesco.org/education/ efa/know_sharing/grassroots_stories/
- American Productivity and Quality Center. www.apqc.org

The necessary knowledge is that of what to observe.

Edgar Allen Poe,
The Murders in the Rue Morgue.

5.
Cost of Knowledge

Establish reducing the cost of knowledge sharing as an important enterprise goal. Put the infrastructures, policies, processes, and mechanisms in place to achieve that goal.

e-Knowledge has the potential to significantly reduce the unit cost of knowledge and to create new, knowledge-rich learning experiences. Moreover, linking perpetual learning and performance support to enterprise processes can dramatically reduce the cost of activities associated with those processes. Government agencies and corporations have been leading the way in applying activity-based-costing to learning, knowledge management, and performance support. However, this issue will be so important in the Knowledge Economy that no enterprise can pass on becoming reflective practitioners of knowledge costing.

The integration of enterprise processes, knowledge management, and cost accounting is a very new practice. Consequently, even those enterprises attempting this integration are using a patchwork of systems that do one or the other well, with significant gaps. Some companies, like KMI, are providing first-generation products that enable enterprises to align their processes and activities, then associating processes with knowledge. This leads to activity-based costing (ABC) that can be used to create metrics for process cost effectiveness.

Many colleges and universities have not considered the issue of the cost of knowledge, interactivity, certification, and the other elements that are bundled together in courses and degrees. However, most for-profit learning enterprises, the open universities, and corporate learning and performance support practices have been dealing with such cost issues for years. To jump-start their knowledge on these prac-

tices, most colleges and universities, associations, and other NGOs should learn from more advanced practitioners.

Exemplary Resources: Reducing the Cost of Knowledge Sharing

- Army Corps of Engineers CRMS project. www.usace.army.mil/
- Course on economic analysis issues. www.knowledge-media.com/saba/menu/menu.cfm?curr_id=25&student_id=25

Organizational Infrastructures, Processes, Capabilities and Cultures.

Changing enterprise infrastructures and knowledge ecologies will be a strategic priority over the next decade, as reflected in the following three actions.

6.
Value on Investment

Take a "value on investment" (VOI) perspective to planning for your organization's ICT infrastructure and knowledge ecology. Develop visions, plans, and strategies for your Enterprise Applications Infrastructure and Solutions (EAIS), shaped by VOI and guided by perspectives on potential e-knowledge jump shifts.

VOI forces organizations to focus on both the tangible and intangible results of technology investment, including the following five actions that are critical to sustaining e-knowledge development:

- support process reinvention and innovation,
- formalize the management of knowledge assets and intellectual capital,
- enable collaboration that increases the capacity to learn through sharing knowledge and expertise,

- increase individual and organizational capabilities, and
- implement new leadership methods and capabilities.

There are many strategic reasons for deploying ICT infrastructures, and VOI gives voice to all of them. However, it is especially germane to e-knowledge. VOI can be used to raise consciousness throughout the organization. The VOI perspective should be deployed by the CIO and the enterprise's technology planning process/organization. However, the VOI perspective should pervade the entire enterprise, not just the information technology division.

Develop visions, plans, and strategies for your organization's evolving Enterprise Application Infrastructure and Solutions (EAIS). Tomorrow's enterprise infrastructures and solutions will be easily integrated and will fuse administrative and academic applications. Organizational visions, plans, and strategies should use the EAIS model to shape the development of all of its components:

- experience gateway,
- enterprise applications and solutions array,
- knowledge resource utility,
- network and hardware infrastructures supporting pervasive knowledge environments, and
- new kinds of services, solutions, and relationships with technology partners.

Leading-edge academic organizations have articulated a vision for such an infrastructure architecture, which is driving their efforts to transform learning and knowledge management. Most enterprises need to elevate their thinking on this score.

Exemplary Resources: VOI-Based Strategies and ICT Plans

- Donald M. Norris. 2002. *Assuring Value from Your ICT Investment.* White Paper. www.transformingeknowledge.info

7.
Infrastructure

Focus on key elements of EAIS:
a) Web site and portal capabilities to create the "experience gateway", enabling progressive discovery of WINWINI;
b) fusion of mission critical applications;
c) progressive implementation of Web services; and d) wireless initiatives and mobile work/learning pilots.

a. Portalizing User Experiences. The next killer app in knowledge-centric organizations will be discovered through the experience gateway through which organizations will reinvent their relationships with customers, employees, members, suppliers, and other stakeholders. Most organizations are undertaking versions of this approach. This initiative is obvious to everyone in the enterprise using the Web site and portal capabilities.

However, the efforts of most organizations to develop personalized customization of an experience gateway need enhancement and acceleration.

- First, the strategic importance of this initiative and its impact on the enterprise must be understood and reflected on at all levels. For most organizations, it may be the most important single expedition in their development of e-knowledge capabilities.
- Second, continuous improvement and assessment of user satisfaction need to be integral elements of this expedition, and the pace of adaptation needs to be accelerated.
- Third, the experience gateway needs to be a central part of planning for programs, products, services, and experiences.

b. Begin to fuse key knowledge functions/ processes/technologies, building toward EAIS. This evolutionary process is at work today. Colleges and universities are fusing portal, ERP, and learning manage-

Take nothing on its looks. Take everything on evidence.

Charles Dickens

ment systems to create robust, integrated e-learning platforms and experiences. They are beginning to incorporate greater content management solutions into the early-generation course management systems to enhance knowledge management capabilities. This is creating a core of integrated academic and support services that provides a glimmer of the future EAIS that will fuse all academic and administrative systems and services. Solutions providers serving corporations, government agencies, and associations are fusing e-learning, learning management, knowledge management, and performance support to evolve the leading edge of enterprise application solutions. These efforts need support and acceleration. In particular, the strategic importance of knowledge and content management needs to be elevated to enterprise-level planning activities and become a topic of interest for organizational leaders.

c. Develop Web services capabilities and reshape the EAIS vision to incorporate Web services. Enterprises typically develop Web applications as an adjunct to their current systems. Through the process of node enablement, Web/application servers are used to connect traditional applications, one at a time, to the outside service grid, turning them into nodes on the Internet. Enterprises should re-evaluate their service models and begin to incorporate the Web services vision into their plans for the EAIS of the future.

A working group in the IT division should be formed to focus on the issue of Web services and identify the first pilots, working with functional managers. The pilot projects should be discussed broadly.

d. Launch mobile work and learning pilots and pervasive knowledge environments. Every enterprise needs active pilot projects in wireless computing and pervasive technology/knowledge environments. These pilots need to focus on both the technical issues of providing robust,

secure service and the more complex issue of how these capabilities change the work and learning experience.

A variety of Web sites and nascent communities of practice on mobile learning, some supported by corporate sponsors, are developing. The results of mobile work and learning pilots need to be assembled, assessed, synthesized, and made available to shape the evolution of these developments.

Exemplary Resources: Portalization, Web Services, and Mobile Work and Learning

Portalization
- Uportal. http://mis105.mis.udel.edu/jasig/uportal/

Mobile Computing Pilots, Mobile Work and Learning Pilots, and Related Resources
- Mobile Computing for Teaching and Learning at Wake Forest. www.cren.net/know/techtalk/events/mobile2.html
- Mobilearn Project. www.mobilearn.org

8.

Knowledge Ecology

Initiate change in the enterprise knowledge ecology: a) process reinvention and innovation; b) change the knowledge culture; c) elevate the understanding of knowledge flows, communities of practice, and knowledge as social interaction; and d) make the enhancement of individual and enterprise e-knowledge capabilities an organizational priority for human resources development.

Getting your enterprise to understand the "social side of knowledge" is an essential developmental step in becoming reflective about your knowledge ecology.

a. Practice process reinvention and innovation. Unlike 1990s reengineering, today's process reinvention takes a more sophisticated view of knowledge management, recognizing and incorporating the importance of organizational culture, embedded knowledge, and knowledge flows, in addition to organizational processes. The VOI from technology investments are unleashed by changing the dynamics of how enterprises interact with and serve customers, learners, members, staff, suppliers, and other stakeholders. Some of these changes are achieved through incremental improvement and others through adapting the best practice processes embedded in ERP and other application solutions. These perspectives need to be established in the programmatic planning efforts at all levels in the organization.

b. Change the knowledge culture. This is not an abstract exercise. Enterprises change their culture by creating solutions to problems, then showing those solutions to people in highly concrete ways. People change the way they feel about the change, then their behavior, and eventually their underlying values concerning knowledge (Kotter, 2002). The goal is to create a knowledge culture that values e-knowledge as a key to competitive advantage, and understands how enterprises must function like knowledge utilities, able both to share knowledge internally and externally, and to mobilize the special kinds of internal knowledge that make them distinctive in the marketplace.

So changing the knowledge culture requires a blend of storytelling, pilot projects that use e-knowledge to establish competitive advantage, environmental scanning that identifies other enterprises that are using e-knowledge strategically, gleaning of insights from the enterprise knowledge strategy, and other practical manifestations of how e-knowledge matters. These conversations and actions need to occur at all levels in the enterprise.

c. Elevate the understanding of knowledge flows, communities of practice, and knowledge as social interactions. The evolving Knowledge Age enterprise depends on a variety of formal and informal structures, knowledge flows, and communities to create organizational intelligence. Over time, the increasing capacity of the enterprise and individuals to acquire and share knowledge will encourage even greater development of communities of practice for learners, staff supporting particular processes, alumni, and other stakeholders.

Individuals and enterprises need to become more sophisticated in the understanding of the importance and interdependence of these structures, knowledge flows, and communities. This is best achieved in practical ways through the support, evaluation, and discussion of actual communities of practice such as those discussed in Chapter 5.

d. Make the enhancement of individual and enterprise e-knowledge capabilities an organizational priority for human resources development. Organizational readiness must be achieved in concert with individual capacity. Individuals will need to acquire new skills so they can discern, decide, and act in an e-knowledge rich environment. As a such, enterprises will need to provide more effective learning opportunities for employees and other stakeholders. This will require formal training and learning that is fused with work and depends on communities of practice for support and insights in the development of knowledge competencies. Enterprise learning will need to balance organizational and individual perspectives on knowledge.

Exemplary Resources:
Changing Enterprise Ecology

- American Productivity and Quality Center. www.apqc.org
- Community Intelligence Labs. www.co-i-l.com

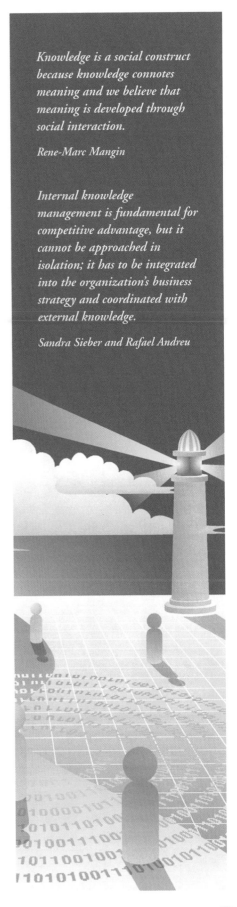

Knowledge is a social construct because knowledge connotes meaning and we believe that meaning is developed through social interaction.

Rene-Marc Mangin

Internal knowledge management is fundamental for competitive advantage, but it cannot be approached in isolation; it has to be integrated into the organization's business strategy and coordinated with external knowledge.

Sandra Sieber and Rafael Andreu

The micro-modular-based model is a revolution coming in the world of content that promises to be as radical and as profound as any that have preceded, including the printed word, the Gutenberg press, and HTML on the Web.

Wayne Hodgins

Standards, Processes and Marketplaces for e-Knowledge

Every organization needs to prepare for the implications of advances in Internet technologies and standards, and the extended sharing of e-knowledge through partnerships and marketplaces. The following two actions will prepare organizations for the seamless internal and external sharing of knowledge.

9.

Standards

Monitor the latest developments in standards and processes for information sharing. Translate into clear explanations of the implications of e-knowledge standards for your enterprise. Develop organizational stories of e-knowledge transformation.

Your organization should be aware of technology and standards developments and their implications relating to the following key areas:

- e-learning and e-knowledge
- Internet/Semantic Web/Grid
- Web services (XML, SOAP, UDDI, WSDL)
- "Disruptive" technologies as they emerge

Translate these new and prospective developments into succinct and believable descriptions of organizational transformation.

a. Cross-functional Working Teams and Web Sites for Pooling Insights. This is an important role for a small working team in your organization, with membership drawn from across the enterprise. In a university, this would involve participants from the CFO, library, IT Division, and academic affairs areas. In a trade association, tech-

nology, marketing, membership, product development, and publications would need to engage. Corporate working groups would need to reflect the full spectrum of players. The arcane details of standards development are well beyond the interest of all but a few, but the implications touch every part of the organization.

b. Engage Broad Cross-Sections of the Enterprise in Storytelling about e-Knowledge. Don't just share stories (of successes and failures); get people to tell *their* stories. Get them to talk about the use of e-knowledge in their words as a way to discover the importance of standards. Use the enterprise portal/intranet to share stories, ideas, and perspectives, and to stimulate dialogue with broad cross sections of the organization. The consensus-building phase of standards development and understanding e-knowledge is all about developing common understanding based on industry requirements and input.

c. Participate in External Working Groups. If your organization has a stake in the outcomes of standards development then it needs to discern a point of engagement in the process. Possible choices include IMS, W3C, IEEE LTSC, GKEC, PROMETEUS, or national standards bodies.

Exemplary Resources:
Articulating the Importance of e-Knowledge for an Enterprise

Many organizations have touted the importance of these developments for their stakeholders. Check out the following examples of organizational documents:

- e-Learning Technical Standards. NHSU Project Management Group. www.doh.gov.uk/nhsuniversity/
- Standards Australia Knowledge Portal. knowledge.standards.com.au
- World Bank Web site for insights on storytelling in knowledge management. www.worldbank.org

10.
Knowledge Sharing

Develop policies, protocols, and infrastructures for knowledge asset management (KAM) and external knowledge sharing. Participate in internal and external e-knowledge sharing to acquire experience and to develop and hone these capabilities.

Identify the elements needed for your organization to recognize, digitize, and manage its knowledge assets and make better use of internal and external knowledge resources. Develop processes that enable you to monitor, meter, and exchange learning objects and other digitized content internally and with external parties and marketplaces. Key considerations include:

- Legal issues, digital rights management (DRM) policies and processes;
- Relationships with publishers, repositories, and marketplaces, and other digital rights management partners;
- Technical infrastructures and processes;
- Best practice business models from learning object trading exchanges;
- KAM and DRM specification progress from appropriate standards bodies; and
- Cost accounting capabilities to measure the cost of e-knowledge and drive progressive reduction in these costs.

To develop perspective on these issues, check what leading organizations or consortia are doing—IMS, MERLOT, OKI, ADL co-labs, COLIS, and national learning object exchanges, such as the Australian Learning Federation.

Knowledge asset management must also include knowledge embedded in communities of practice and accessible through interaction with them.

Plan for and develop the infrastructures, policies, and procedures that will enable your organization to participate in e-knowledge marketplaces. Work to find ways to leverage your organization's existing disparate collections of digital knowledge (in learning management systems, CRM systems, and the many databases it depends upon, as well as within communities of practice) to develop capabilities in managing e-knowledge.

a. Early Adopters Have Developed Policies and Procedures. Few organizations have adequately developed the policies, procedures, and infrastructures necessary to participate in e-knowledge marketplaces. These need to deal with the elements of authentication, authorization, access, rights management, and financial transaction. Over time, standard policies, contracts, and terms will emerge. Digital rights management will be an increasingly important function for learning organizations of all kinds. Once again, a small working group can be utilized to assess the enterprise's current state of development, future needs, and means of closing the gap.

b. Participate in the Development of Repositories and Marketplaces. Organizations should develop the necessary capacities and relationships to make their e-knowledge available to repositories, marketplaces, and other digital rights management partners. This will enable organizations to develop competencies in effective digital rights management. It will also expose them to emerging best practices. Moreover, it will hone their skills in digitizing content, context, pedagogical notes, insights, managing metadata, and all of the components of effective learning experiences.

Exemplary Resources:
Enterprise Policies, Procedures and Infrastructures

See resources referenced in Chapter 5.

Inevitably, across society, large-scale shifts to electronic formats will occur. In the publishing world, the big questions centers on whether these shifts will be driven by publishers acting alone, or will the shift to digital publishing result from collaboration with other institutions, companies, and cultural entities yet to be developed.

Gordon Freedman

Summary: Ten Ways to Accelerate Your Organization's Readiness for e-Knowledge

Best Practice, Business Models, and Strategies

1. *Engage the enterprise on the subject of e-knowledge. Use storytelling to explore how individuals already experience knowledge. Mobilize energies from grassroots to CEO and Board.*

   Organizational storytelling about experiencing e-knowledge is the way to engage your enterprise in understanding the changes and challenges of the next decade, Conversation is the coin of the realm of the Internet culture, But it's not just about talk. You must also "walk the talk" by deploying technology tools that change the manner in which you use knowledge in decision making and in your core enterprise processes.

2. *Develop a knowledge strategy for the enterprise that brings into alignment: 1) management of the enterprise's knowledge assets, and 2) the enterprise's business plans to achieve mission and goals.*

   A concise, cogent strategy sets the stage for more effective knowledge management and for initiatives that establish competitive advantage. Knowledge strategy must be explicitly stated in business plans.

3. *Support a wide variety of knowledge management and community of practice pilots throughout the enterprise. Enable different expeditions and multiple trajectories, operating in parallel.*

   While the organization needs an integrated enterprise applications infrastructure for knowledge sharing, the practice of knowledge management may vary among different process teams and communities of practice. Your enterprise should encourage expeditionary experimentation and sharing of success stories among different communities of practice.

4. *Scan the environment for examples of changing best practices, business models, and strategies; collect competitive intelligence on market leaders and innovators both from inside and outside the industry. Energetically benchmark e-knowledge practices.*

   Enterprises cannot afford to leave knowledge strategy and e-knowledge best practices to chance. Since most paradigm-busting innovations come from outside the circle of market leaders, enterprises must scan the e-knowledge horizon broadly for emerging concepts, innovations, best practices, business models, and strategies.

5. *Establish reducing the cost of knowledge sharing as an important enterprise goal. Begin to put in place the infrastructures, policies, processes, and mechanisms place to achieve that goal*

   Reducing the cost of knowledge and enhancing knowledge sharing experiences are long-term goals but enterprises must begin to develop cost accounting capabilities immediately.

Organizational Infrastructures, Processes, Competencies, and Cultures

6. *Take a "Value on Investment" (VOI) perspective to planning for your organization's ICT infrastructure and knowledge ecology. Develop visions, plans, and strategies for your Enterprise Applications Infrastructure and Solutions (EAIS), shaped by VOI and guided by perspectives on potential e-knowledge jump shifts.*

   VOI is a facile instrument for focusing your enterprise on the innovative and transformative uses of ICT. It attracts attention to infrastructure, applications, and solutions development as an essential strategic issue. See Chapter 5 for details.

7. *Focus on key elements of Enterprise Applications Infrastructure and Solutions" (EAIS): a) Web site and portal capabilities to create the "experience gateway," enabling progressive discovery of WINWINI; b) fusion of mission-central applications; c) progressive implementation of Web services; and d) wireless initiatives and mobile work/learning pilots.*

   These elements of EAIS are high priority and must engage a broad cross-section of the enterprise community; it's too important to be left to technologists, alone. See Chapter 5 for details.

8. *Initiate change in the enterprise knowledge ecology: a) process reinvention and innovation; b) change the knowledge culture; c) elevate the understanding of knowledge flows, communities of practice, and knowledge as social interactions; d) make the enhancement of individual and enterprise e-knowledge capabilities an organizational priority for human resources development.*

   Enterprise knowledge ecology will be one of the most important topics of the next decade. Changing the culture requires identifying specific, concrete ways of using e-knowledge to build competitive advantage, then using examples to engage people and change how they feel about their behavior. Knowledge ecology is best changed through specific initiatives that improve an important process rather than broad enterprise-wide attempts at cultural change. See Chapter 5 for details.

Standards, Processes, and Marketplaces

9. *Monitor the latest developments in standards and processes for knowledge sharing. Translate into clear explanations and stories about the implications of e-knowledge standards for the enterprise.*

   Developments in standards, technologies, and marketplaces provide a small working group with a sterling opportunity for storytelling. See Chapter 4 for details.

10. *Develop policies, protocols, and infrastructures for knowledge asset management and external knowledge sharing. Participate in internal and external e-knowledge sharing to acquire experience and develop and hone these capabilities.*

    Enterprises need to roll up their sleeves and dig into the nuts and bolts of e-knowledge repositories and external knowledge sharing. See Chapter 4 for details.

Mobilizing Leaders, Policy Makers, and Practitioners

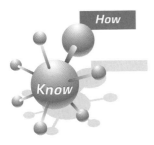

Mobilizing the enterprise community on the subject of e-knowledge is the most important of the ten immediate actions. Before this can occur successfully, we must understand the art of communication and change in the Internet culture. It's not about pushing a powerful message and strategy, fully formulated and ready for action. It's about storytelling, adding value, and changing how people *feel* about change and the future.

> *The reason so many change initiatives fail is that they rely too much on data gathering, analysis, report writing, and presentations instead of a more creative approach aimed at grabbing the feelings that motivate useful action.*
>
> *John Kotter, 2002*

Learning from The Cluetrain Manifesto

This book with the peculiar name was written by four practitioners specializing in new media and communicating via the Internet. It started out as a Web site, attracting interested participants who offered their perspectives on how the Internet was changing the rules and routines of business communication. Eventually, the *Cluetrain Manifesto* Web site grew to contain 95 theses about communication and commerce in the Internet world and a wealth of insight about how practices are changing. The book was merely a printed version of the nuggets that were found in the stream of conversation that ran through the Web site.

The Cluetrain Manifesto offers a simple thesis: The Internet is a throwback to the days when commerce was conducted in the bazaar. Commerce was about the conversations through which everything was discussed and negotiated: the nature of the product, its value, its price, and its terms of exchange. Over the course of time, the conversations shaped and personalized product offerings and what individuals thought of the products and those whose mark was upon them. Voice—the authentic expression of the individual that is present in the work of our hands and our minds—is as present in the Internet as it was in the commerce of the bazaar. The work of the Internet is carried on through conversation—Web pages, e-mail, discussion groups, blogs, klogs, product offerings, and communities of practice—that give new forms of expression to the human voice in our organizations, be they colleges and universities, corporations, trade associations, government agencies, or philanthropies.

> *We don't know what the Web is for but we've adopted it faster than any technology since fire.*
>
> *David Weinberger*

To be effective, communication in the Internet Age must engage people in authentic conversations through which they discover meaning, especially for new ideas and concepts. These concepts can be put to work in our enterprises, to understand the potentials of e-knowledge. The liberating impact of Internet culture is not limited to people's interactions via the Internet; it influences other interactions as well.

> *Successful change leaders identify a problem in one part of the change process, or a solution to a problem. Then they show this to people on ways that are as concrete as possible . . . But whatever the method, they supply valid ideas that go deeper than the conscious and analytical parts of our brains—ideas with emotional impact.*
>
> *John P. Kotter and Dan S. Cohen*

THE SEVEN HIGHEST VALUE FORMS OF ORGANIZATIONAL STORYTELLING

If your objective is:	You need a story that:	Your story will need to:	You will also need to take these actions:	Your story will use or inspire these phrases:	When successful, your story will have the following impact:
1 To communicate a complex idea and spark action	- is true - has single protagonist who is prototypical of your audience	- focus on the positive outcome - be told in a minimalist fashion	- frame the story so that the audience is listening - provide "guide-rails" that help direct the listener towards the hoped-for insight	"Just think . . . " "Just imagine . . . " "What if . . . "	your audience will "get" the idea and be stimulated to launch into action
2 To get people working together in a group or community	- is moving - is interesting to the listeners - is a story about a subject that the listeners also have stories	- be told with the context	- establish an open agenda - engender a process of story swapping - have an action plan ready	"That reminds me . . . "	your audience will be ready to be working together more collaboratively
3 To share information and knowledge	- includes a problem, the setting, the solution, and the explanation - captures the granularity of the relevant area of knowledge	- reflect multiple perspectives - be focused on the difficulties and how they were dealt with	- verify that the story is in fact true - cross-check with other experiences	"We'd better watch that in future!"	your audience will understand how to do something and why
4 To tame the grapevine and neutralize negative gossip	- reveals humor or incongruity either in the bad news, or in the author of the bad news, or in the storyteller - is true	- be amusing or satirical - be a blend of truth and caring for the object of the humor	- make sure that the bad news is indeed untrue - commit yourself to telling the truth, however difficult	"You got to be kidding!" "That's funny!" "I'd never thought about it like that before!"	your audience will realize that the gossip or the bad news is either untrue or unreasonable
5 To communicate who you are	- reveals some strength or vulnerability in your past - is true - is moving	- be told with context	- make sure the audience has the time and the interest to hear your story	"I didn't know that about you!" "How interesting?"	your audience will have a better understanding of who you are as a person
6 To transmit values	- exemplifies your values in action - is relevant to the "here and now" - is moving - is believed	- provide context - be consistent with the actions of the leadership	- make sure your actions are consistent with your story - make sure the context of your story fits the listeners	"That's so right!" "We should really do that all the time!"	your audience will understand how things are done around here
7 To lead people into the future	- is about the future - captures the basic idea of where you are heading - focuses on a positive outcome	- be told with as little detail as needed to understand the idea - be evocative - resonate with the listeners	- provide context from past and present - make sure that people are ready to follow (if not, use type #1 story, i.e. a story to spark action)	"When do we start?" "Let's do it!"	your audience will understand where they are heading for

*Excerpt from a forthcoming book by Stephen Denning, entitled *The Squirrel: The Seven Highest Value Forms of Organizational Storytelling*, of which advance chapters are available at www.stevedenning.com/squirrel.htm.

Engaging Conversations, Revealing Stories, Expeditions of Discovery

The scene has been repeated in enterprises of all kinds, from Sydney to San Francisco to South Hampton. Individuals, teams, and communities of practice confront the future through conversation and a spirit of expeditionary discovery. Communities at the World Bank share stories to reveal old insights in order to understand fresh challenges. Cross-campus teams at Eastern Michigan University answer the question, "How will the university portal enable me to experience the University if I am a student, a faculty, an employee, a parent, an alumni, or legislator?" Member leaders and staff at the American Association of Pharmaceutical Scientists tell stories about the ecology of interactivity at their annual meeting in order to understand how to extend and enhance the meeting through e-knowledge.

The first challenge for enterprise leadership is not for the management team to make the right decisions about e-knowledge. Rather the challenge is how to engage the enterprise community in revealing conversations and storytelling, focused on real issues, challenges, and opportunities, so that the right decisions can be illuminated and emerge. Engaging the enterprise on the subject of e-knowledge, through storytelling and conversation is an indispensable strategy.

In his forthcoming book, *The Squirrel: The Seven Highest Value Forms of Organizational Storytelling,* Stephen Denning describes the range of uses to which storytelling can be put in the course of organizational change. Denning's perspectives can be deployed in any setting to provide the experiential, emotional, and factual foundations needed for people to engage and discover the future.

The tension between innovation and stability means the application's portfolio of a company's information infrastructure is constantly churning.

C.K. Prahalad and M.S. Krishnam

Developing a Knowledge Strategy that Drives Enterprise Initiatives

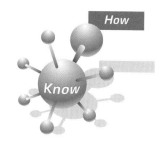

One of the ten immediate actions involved is developing a knowledge strategy. Enterprises should develop an explicit knowledge strategy in order to focus attention on the e-knowledge imperative. This strategy cannot be voluminous if it is to succeed in capturing attention and evoking the imagination of the enterprise's stakeholders. Indeed, some of the best examples of knowledge strategies are concise statements that may not even be labeled by such a grand term as "knowledge strategy."

Knowledge Strategies in Different Settings

Many of the enterprises already cited are guided by knowledge strategies or some equivalent, explicit statement. Consider the following examples from corporate, education, association, and governmental environments.

- Boeing Corporation's use of wireless technology to bring design and assembly knowledge to the manufacturing floor has created an "augmented reality" environment for its assembly workers that will only increase with the introduction of ambient technology. Moreover, the use of "smart manufacturing" has transformed many aspects of the assembly of large aircraft parts from a "cut and fit art" to a technology-driven science. Boeing and other firms in this industry know that knowledge drives every aspect of the design and manufacturing of their products and is fundamental to competitive advantage.
- The University of Southern Queensland has clear strategies for using knowledge as a differentiator in its learning experiences. These understandings are supported by Professor Taylor's seminal article, "Fifth Generation Distance Learning," which cogently articulates

the centrality of e-knowledge in the new "killer apps" for fifth generation distance education.

- The American Association of Pharmaceutical Scientists develops its products, services, and experiences around the strategic insight that personalized, satisfying access to current, continuously evolving knowledge is an indispensable resource for pharmaceutical scientists and those who want to associate with them.
- The Knowledge Network launched by the UK government has been guided by the simple understanding that many government services require cross-departmental conversation and rationalization, based on the sharing of knowledge and insight during policy and service development.

A cogent, explicit knowledge strategy shapes business plans and initiatives, as in the following example.

The American Health Information Management Association (AHIMA) AHIMA's motto is "quality healthcare through quality information." AHIMA represents 40,000 professionals serving the information needs of the U.S. healthcare system, as manifested by managing, analyzing, and utilizing the data used in a patient's record. Clearly, this association must be a leader in information and knowledge if it is to meet its members' needs, plus the needs of its members' supervisors, clients, and patients—the true source of indispensability to its members

AHIMA engaged in a strategic planning process that set the goals of establishing indispensable relationships with members, customers, makers of health care policy, and other stakeholders. The planning process launched four expeditionary initiatives that would be used to position AHIMA for competitive advantage and discover a new level of relationship with its members. Two of these expeditions explicitly dealt with creating and sharing knowledge with members, non-member customers, and other stakeholders.

- *Defining, Mapping, and Providing the Body of Knowledge (BoK) for the Profession.* AHIMA's CEO and Board recognized that its stature as a renowned knowledge provider was a benchmark of its value to members and its perceived standing in the health care field. So they made knowledge a strategic imperative.

First, they stated their strategic intent to define the "body of knowledge" for health information management and to access that BoK from the AHIMA Web site and portal, offering some elements for members only. In the process of defining the BoK and linking to its components, AHIMA affirmed its concern that it did not own an iconic text for Health Information Management (HIM). Therefore, over the course of two years, AHIMA completed a comprehensive, contemporary text for two-year programs and commissioned a similar text for four-year programs.

Second, AHIMA made the provision of knowledge and participation in co-creation and learning a centerpiece of its portal experience. Its value proposition positions knowledge sharing at the heart of its aspiration to become indispensable to HIM professionals.

- *Growing Communities of Practice.* AHIMA explicitly decided to redirect the energies of staff and members from its governance model to a community of practice model. Two forces motivated the change: 1) the existing governance model was overly complex, draining the association's energies, and 2) the association's opportunities were found in mobilizing its members' expertise in the emergent practice areas of the profession. To become indispensable to its members, AHIMA needed to become the place where the conversations of greatest meaning to practitioners were convened, with members and non-member customers being co-creators of value, not just consumers.

AHIMA developed an enterprise portal that transformed its Web site (www.ahima.org) into the gateway for members, non-member customers, and other stakeholders. Several geographical communities continued to exist, leftover from the geographical base of AHIMA's governance model. But the new communities of practice that have evolved have been allowed to emerge biologically, in response to the developing trends and interests in the field, not a predetermined architecture, established by staff or member leaders. As a result, the new communities of practice reflect a combination of traditional topics like Medical Records Coding (6,812 participants), and emergent interests like Home Coding (800 members who work from home offices), JCAHO Accreditation Standards, APCS (2,501 participants), and Acute Care (1,673 participants).

A case study describing AHIMA's knowledge strategy, its expeditionary initiatives, and its prospects for the next several years may be found at www.transformingeknowledge.info.

In explicitly stating the centrality of knowledge, AHIMA shaped all four of its expeditions, plus all of its tactical business plans for both ongoing operations and new initiatives.

Becoming a global company once meant penetrating markets around the world. But the demands of the Knowledge Economy are turning that strategy on its head. Today, the challenge is to innovate by learning from the world.

Yves Doz, Jose Santos and Peter Williamson

Most strategic planning involves preparing dense documents filled with numbers and jargon. But building the process around a picture yields much better results.

W. Chan Kim and Renee Mauborgne

A company that builds a portfolio of initiatives in areas in which it enjoys advantages of familiarity can prosper even amid uncertainty.

Lowell L. Bryan

Focusing on Sources of Competitive Advantage

In *The Discipline of Market Leaders*, Michael Treacy and Fred Wiersma (1999) describe how an assortment of iconic enterprises achieved long-term success. Traditionally, market leaders assess and respond to the strategic opportunities in their marketplaces, selecting the one essential strategic element for their business. Then they focus their energies and special, proprietary tacit knowledge on that single element to achieve world-class performance. For some enterprises, their key was operational excellence, resulting to competitive advantage in cost and timeliness; others chose to create great products, becoming recognized as leaders in innovation and quality; still others focused on customer intimacy, developing intimate relationships with customers and other stakeholders. While the other two elements of performance are important, intelligent enterprises found ways to deliver world-class performance through outsourcing and strategic alliances with partners who possessed special tacit knowledge on how to excel along that particular vector of performance.

Examples of Competitive Advantage.
In developing a knowledge strategy, individuals should focus on each of these three elements of performance to determine how e-knowledge could deliver competitive advantage for your enterprise, given its particular set of opportunities and challenges. What would such an analysis have yielded for some of our examples?

- Boeing's products are world class, but in the hypercompetitive aircraft industry, with a few massive competitors, intelligent manufacturing has come to be a powerful differentiator, leading to revolutions in cost control, timeliness, and

The Lenses of Competitive Advantage

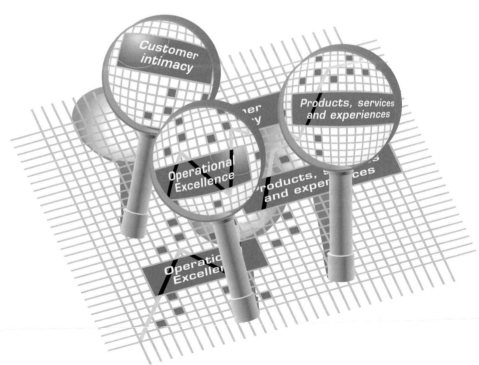

customization of products. However, other differentiations could emerge on the product side. For example applying intelligent manufacturing to the ergonomics of the cockpit could create a new standard for usability.

- AHIMA and AAPS would most certainly have found that their relationship with members and customers (customer intimacy) was their most strategic asset, but only if they could use that relationship to engage the members and customers to be both consumers and co-creators of knowledge and insight in their fields.

- The University of Southern Queensland enjoys several vectors of competitive advantage. First, its relationships and reputation with satisfied students, educators and guidance counselors, and civic leaders (distributed across Australasia) provide the basis for a pipeline of future learners. Second, the nature of USQ's learning experience (either purely virtual or blended learning) provides a distinctive, engaging, convenient learning experience that involves learners as co-creators and offers a highly competitive price.

- The Knowledge Network in the UK thrives based on developing a world-class product, public policy based on cross-departmental conversation and rationalization and the capacity to engage citizen feedback to tune and co-create effective policy and implementation.

Changing Market Leadership. Taken a step or two further, such an analysis suggests that e-knowledge is changing the dimensions of market leadership and competition advantage.

First, e-knowledge is an important instrumental factor in the creation of products, services, experiences, and knowledge. It can be leveraged to reduce costs, improve quality and timeliness, and personalize offerings.

Second, as products and services become more and more defined by the experience in which they are embedded or through which they are engaged, e-knowledge and interactivity become even more essential competitive factors.

Third, many e-knowledge-rich products, services and experiences are produced through co-creation with learners, customers, members, citizens, suppliers, alumni, and other kinds of stakeholders. Co-creation causes an irrevocable blurring of the boundaries between customer intimacy; products, services, and experiences; and operational excellence. New competitors can take advantage of the power of co-creation to unseat market leaders that do not provide the capacity to create indispensable relationships based on co-creation through communities of practice.

Making e-Knowledge Part of Enterprise Plans and Initiatives. The worse thing that can be done with e-knowledge is to create a set of stand-alone knowledge initiatives. Within many enterprises, that is what has happened to knowledge management and enterprise learning. They have become initiatives in themselves, not a strategic element of the enterprise's workflow and business plans.

Experience dictates that e-knowledge must be part of a unified, varied toolkit that includes infrastructure development, process reinvention, knowledge management, enterprise learning, and fostering communities of practice. If effectively mobilized, the concept of e-knowledge can muster strategic support and generate a knowledge strategy that drives identifiable elements in the enterprise's business plans and initiatives.

Co-creation Fuses the Lenses

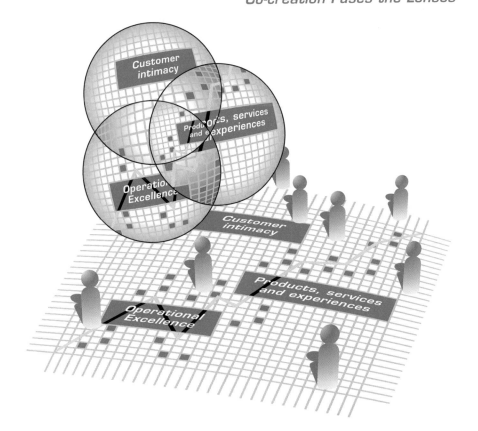

Proponents of e-knowledge need to be hard-nosed, focusing on solid VOI and ROI. During economic downturns, e-knowledge can provide efficiencies, cost containment, and operational excellence that are highly useful in a tactical way.

Moreover, truly strategic initiatives can result from understanding how e-knowledge is key to co-creation of customer products, services, and experiences and other the vectors of competitive advantage. During a downturn, such initiatives can be used to position the enterprise to capture market share both during the downturn and when the economy improves.

Simultaneous Parallel Processes of Action and Reflection. Achieving success in the e-knowledge future requires an understanding of multifaceted change. Think of parallel actions operating on a range of fronts driving cascading cycles of reinvention, measurement and reflection. Crafting enterprise vision, mission, and knowledge strategy is intertwined with storytelling, conversation, and environmental scanning. This in turn is supported by the continuous development of infrastructures, applications, and enterprise-wide solutions in compliance with emergent standards. Such a knowledge strategy drives enterprise initiatives and business plans, guided by pilot projects and initiatives that change how knowledge is used in the co-creation of experiences and the forging of new relationships. A new round of refinement begins with storytelling about concrete examples, measurement of results, and forging of new relationships, which all the while enhance and reshape the capabilities of individuals and organizations in an atmosphere of confidence and trust. This ongoing process of transforming e-knowledge engenders wider communities of reflective practice. Such communities become the stewards of the processes, applications and tradecraft necessary for success in tomorrow's Knowledge Economy.

Building the Reflective 21st Century Enterprise. This brings us full circle. Back to our core assumption that e-knowledge will usher in a new era of success and competitive advantage for those individuals and enterprises that learn how to enhance their knowledge sharing capacity by an order of magnitude. This is not wishful thinking, nor does it require Star Wars technology. Leading-edge enterprises and new innovators are already setting new benchmarks for leveraging knowledge. The signs are in plain view. Every enterprise aspiring to succeed in the 21st century global economy must make certain that it becomes both a reflective practitioner and an ardent student of e-knowledge.

Companies spent the 20th century creating and managing efficiencies. They must spend the 21st century creating and managing experiences.

C.K. Prahalad and V. Ramaswamy, 2002

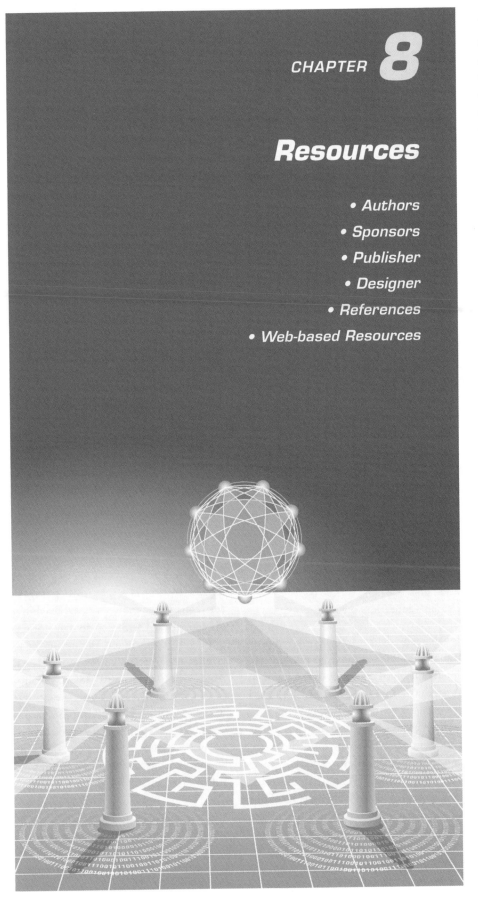

CHAPTER *8*

Resources

- Authors
- Sponsors
- Publisher
- Designer
- References
- Web-based Resources

Transforming e-Knowledge has been made possible by an assemblage of governmental and corporate sponsors whose support has sustained our publishing and distribution. education.au limited, SCT, WebCT, Knowledge Media, and the MOBIlearn Project are committed to the advancement of e-knowledge. They have contributed to the concepts, content and case materials in the text.

Design concepts, layout, and illustrations are by Phil Taylor of Global-ID Pty Limited.

The Society for College and University Planning (SCUP) is the publisher of *Transforming e-Knowledge*.

A list of primary references is included in *Transforming e-Knowledge*. In addition a Web site containing materials supporting this subject is available at www.transformingeknowledge.info. The site includes a full bibliography, searchable glossary and who's who in e-knowledge, case studies and vignettes, and other resource materials, including a full bibliography.

Readers are encouraged to simultaneously use the online resources and print version of *Transforming e-Knowledge*. Use these tools in tandem to enhance your capacity to absorb knowledge and insight on these issues.

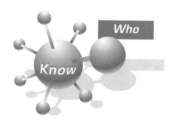

Authors

Donald M. Norris
President, Strategic Initiatives, Inc.

www.strategicinitiatives.com
dmn@strategicinitiatives.com
703.450.5255

Don is well known as a thought leader, researcher, and consultant. His book, *Transforming Higher Education: A Vision for Learning in the 21st Century* (1995) was instrumental in providing a framework for advancing the concept of transformative e-learning in the late 1990s. Dr. Norris has also written *E-Business in Education: What You Need to Know* (1999) and *Expeditions in E-Business for Association*s (2000 and 2001 editions). He consults on knowledge transformation strategies with a leading-edge set of educational institutions, technology-enabled solution providers, and professional societies and non-profit organizations. He is a frequent speaker at educational and professional meetings on the subject of organizational transformation, expeditionary strategy, and the realignment of enterprises to Knowledge Age imperatives.

Jon Mason
Executive Consultant, education.au limited and Assistant Director, IMS Australia

jmason@educationau.edu.au

Jon has an advocacy role in developing interoperability standards relevant to Internet-enabled education and training in Australia. Through education.au limited his focus is on supporting collaborative initiatives and building knowledge networks aimed at achieving mutual benefit. Jon's responsibilities have recently included Acting Director, IMS Australia; co-Chair, the Dublin Core Metadata Education Working Group; member of the IEEE LTSC; Australian delegate, ISO/IEC JTC1 SC36, IT in Learning, Education and Training; Chair, Standards Australia IT-19-1; Member, Standards Australia Knowledge Management Reference Group; Member, Australian ICT in Education Committee, Standards sub-Committee; co-lead, IMS Global Learning Consortium, Digital Repositories Interoperability Working Group; and, member of the MOBIlearn Advisory Group. Jon is well respected for his perspectives on e-learning, interoperability standards, and knowledge networks.

Paul Lefrere
Director of Networking and Partnerships, Centre for Educational Technology Interoperability Standards, University of Wales and British Open University

P.Lefrere@open.ac.uk

Paul is widely recognized for his insights on reusable information objects and related tools; knowledge creation, innovation, and exploitation; and Web-based learning services. Dr. Lefrere's association with the British Open University has led to a variety of new, mass market Open University courses and other breakthroughs in technology-based teaching. He has worked with a wide range of relevant organizations, including IMS Global Learning Consortium, IEEE LTSC, CEN/ISSS, NSF, JISC and European Commission's PROMETEUS. He has worked with many European corporations. Dr. Lefrere frequently is invited to speak on topics relating to e-learning and knowledge management at international meetings.

Sponsors

education.au limited
www.educationau.edu.au

Established in 1997, education.au limited is a non-profit company limited by guarantee and owned by the Australian education and training Ministers. education.au limited collaborates with numerous stakeholders in education and training communities, "building Australia's knowledge networks." It works with, and services, the early childhood, schooling, vocational training, adult and community education, and university sectors. The primary business of the company is to develop and manage online services that are of benefit to the education and training sector and are national in scope. It does this through the use of collaborative and consultative processes with the aim of building knowledge networks and a collective approach to meeting the challenges and opportunities presented by the Internet and information economy.

SCT
www.sct.com

SCT is a global information technology solutions company, serving nearly 1,500 clients worldwide. It is a recognized leader and innovator in the markets it service— both education and energy and utilities. In education, SCT is leading the way in transforming administrative systems into e-education infrastructures, promoting solutions and services that provide a strong value on investment for its clients. SCT is a leader in Web managed services and in enhancing the knowledge asset management capabilities of its clients.

WebCT
www.webct.com

WebCT is the leading provider of e-learning solutions to the global higher education market. WebCT's vision is to work in concert with leading institutions to go beyond online course delivery and actually transform the educational experience. To that end, they deliver state-of-the-art educational technology that supports a full range of teaching and learning styles and optimizes intellectual and technical resources. WebCT is a leader in academic services solutions that advance the institution's e-knowledge capabilities.

Knowledge Media, Inc.
www.knowledge-media.com

Knowledge Media is a global leader in e-knowledge infrastructure software for the extended knowledge enterprise. An award-winning leader in strategic e-knowledge management, e-learning and learning management, KMI's over 300 global clients have included US Federal agencies, Fortune 500 companies, universities, local governments and major associations. KMI's mission is to deliver the right knowledge, at the right time, in the right context.

Knowledge Media is the developer of SYNERGY 3.0 Knowledgeware™, a revolutionary e-knowledge management suite that produces award-winning e-learning, knowledge portals, learning portals, performance support, e-newsletters, virtual conferences, and automated workflow control processes to radically enhance knowledge work.

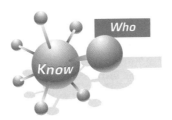

MOBIlearn Project
www.mobilearn.org

The MOBIlearn project, co-funded by the European Commission (IST Program), and with supporting actions by NSF/USA and DEST/AU, is exploring new ways to use "ambient intelligence for mobile learning", which encompasses key advances in teaching and learning technologies and new forms of working to meet the needs of learners, working by themselves and with others. The project involves more than 24 partners and 150 leading organizations coming from a broad range of technology companies, universities, and other partners from across the World. MOBIlearn is coordinated by GIUNTI Ricerca .

Publisher

Society for College and University Planning
www.scup.org

The Society for College and University Planning (SCUP) is committed to promoting the advancement and application of effective planning in higher education. SCUP was established in 1965 as a planning resource for public and private two-year and four-year institutions, college and university systems, governing boards, and commercial organizations that support the higher education community. The mission of the Society for College and University Planning is to promote the practice of comprehensive planning in higher education by developing and disseminating planning knowledge.

Designer

Design concept, layout and illustration by *Phil Taylor* from Global-ID Pty Ltd.

phil@global-id.aus.net

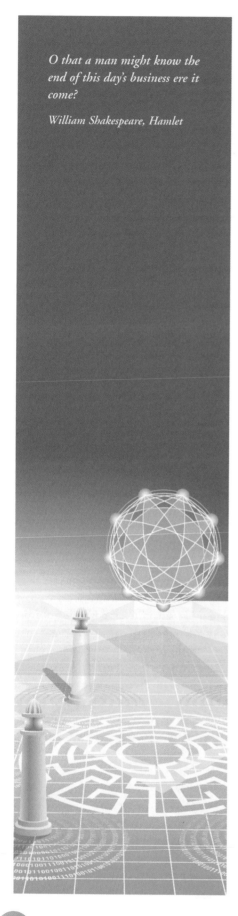

O that a man might know the end of this day's business ere it come?

William Shakespeare, Hamlet

References

The following references are those that were quoted or cited. They are only a small fraction of the resources used in the creation of this book. You will find a complete set of resources at www.transformingeknowledge.info.

American Productivity and Quality Center. www.apqc.org.

Arthur, Brian W. 2002. Is the Information Revolution Dead? If History Is a Guide, It Is Not. *Business 2.0,* March, 65–72.

Australian Government/World Bank. *The Virtual Colombo Plan 2002.* www.developmentgateway.com.au/vcp.html

Berger, Carl. 2001. *The Next Killer App: And You Thought Administrative Computing Was Expensive.* EDUCAUSE, www.educause.edu/asp/doclib/abstract.asp?ID=EDU0139

Berners-Lee, Tim, James Hendler and Ora Lasilla. 2001. The Semantic Web. *Scientific American,* 5:1.

Brown, John Seeley. 2000. *The Social Life of Information.* San Francisco: Jossey-Bass.

Castells, Manuel. 2001. *The Internet Galaxy: Reflections on the Internet, Business and Society.* Oxford: Oxford University Press.

Community Intelligence Labs (CoIL). 2002. www.co-i-l.com/coil/

Collier, Geoff, and Robby Robson. 2002. *eLearning Interoperability Standards.* Sun Microsystems.

Collins, Jim. 2001. *Good to Great.* New York: HarperCollins.

Crow, Raym. 2002. *The Case for Institutional Repositories: A SPARC Position Paper.* Washington, DC: The Scholarly Publishing & Academic Resources Coalition. www.arl.org/sparc/IR/ir.html

Davenport, Thomas H., and John Glaser. 2002. Just-in-Time Delivery Comes to Knowledge Management. *Harvard Business Review.* July, 107–111.

Deloitte & Touche Consulting. 2001. *From e-Learning to Enterprise Learning.* New York, Deloitte Research, 112–115.

Denning, Stephen, Michel Pommier, and Lesley Shneier. 2002. Are There Laws of Knowledge Management? Connecting the Future: Global Summit of Online Knowledge Networks. Adelaide: education.au. March 4–5.

Denning, Stephen. *The Squirrel: The Seven Highest Value Forms of Organizational Storytelling* (forthcoming)

Downes, Larry and Mui Chunka. 1998. *Unleashing the Killer App: Digital Strategies for Market Dominance,* Boston: Harvard Business School Press.

Drucker, Peter F. 1995. *Managing in a Time of Great Change.* New York: Penguin Books.

————. 1999. *Managing in Turbulent Times.* New York: HarperCollins.

Ducatel, K., M. Bogdanowicz, F. Scapolo, J. Leijten, and J-C. Burgelman. 2001. *Scenarios for Ambient Intelligence in 2010.* February, IPTS-Seville, 7.

Ferguson, Glover T. 2002. Have Your Objects Call My Objects. *Harvard Business Review,* June, 138–143.

Foster, Ian. 2002. The Grid: A New Infrastructure for 21st Century Science. *Physics Today,* February.

Freech, Vincent. *Parasitic Computing.* www.nd.edu/~parasite

Garreau, Joel. 2002. Cell Biology: Like the Bee, This Evolving Species Buzzes and Swarms. *Washington Post,* July 31.

Gartner. 2001. Changing the View of ROI to VOI—Value on Investment. *Gartner Research Note, SPA-14-7250,* November 14.

Gleason, Bernard W. 2002. Integrating to the Max. *NACUBO Business Officer,* September, 28–36.

Green, Kenneth C. 2002. *Campus Computing Survey.*

Grove, Andrew. 1999. *Only the Paranoid Survive: How to Exploit the Crisis Points that Challenge Every Company.* New York: Random House.

Hall, Brandon. 2001. *Learning Management and Knowledge Management: Is the Holy Grail of Integration Close at Hand?* www.brandon-hall.com

Hagel, John, and John Seely Brown. 2001. Your Next IT Strategy. *Harvard Business Review*, October 105–113.

Hames, Richard. 2002. *Cathedrals and Cafes.* Unpublished PowerPoint presentation.

Hoffman, Jennifer. 2002. Peer-to-Peer: The Next Hot Trend in e-Learning? *Learning Circuits*, February 16.

Holtshouse, Dan, Christopher Meyer, and Rudy Ruggles. 1999. *The Knowledge Advantage: 14 Visionaries Define Marketplace Success in the New Economy.* Chico, CA: Capstone Publications.

Hunter, Richard. 2002. *World Without Secrets: Business, Crime and Privacy in the Age of Ubiquitous Computing.* New York: John Wiley & Sons.

Irvine, Martin. *Elearning and the Coming Revolution in Higher Education.* Unpublished PowerPoint slides.

Jacobsen, Carl. 2002. Web Services: Stitching Together the Institutional Fabric. *EDUCAUSE Review*, March/April, 50–51.

Jarmon, Carolyn. 2002. Redesigning Learning Environments: Round 1 Final Results, Round II, Round III. *The Pew Learning and Technology Newsletter*, June.

Kvavik, Robert B. and Michael N. Handberg. 2000. Transforming Student Services. *EDUCAUSE Quarterly*, Volume 23:2, 30–37.

Kelly, Kevin. 1997. New Rules for the New Economy. *Wired*, September, 140–143 and 186–197.

Locke, Christopher, Rick Levine, Doc Searls, and David Weinberg. 2001. *The Cluetrain Manifesto: The End of Business as We Know It.* Cambridge: Perseus Publishing.

McDermott, R. 1999. Learning Across Teams: How to Build Communities of Practice in Team Organizations. *Knowledge Management Review 8*, May–June, 32–38.

McElroy, Patrick and Barry Beckerman. 2002. *Developing an International Learning Object Economy: A New Industry Model for the E-Learning Market.* LCX Corporation, White Paper, www.lcxcorp.com/

———. 2002. *Managing Digital Learning Content in Higher Education Institutions,* White Paper, www.lcxcorp.com/

Milstein, Sarah. 2002. Scholarly Reviews Through the Web. *New York Times*, August 12.

Nilsson, Mikael, Matthias Palmér & Ambjörn Naeve. 2002. Semantic Web Metadata for e-Learning—Some Architectural Guidelines. *WWW2002 Proceedings*, Honolulu, May, kmr.nada.kth.se/papers/SemanticWeb/p744-nilsson.pdf

Nonaka, Ikujiro. 1999. The Dynamics of Knowledge Creation. In *The Knowledge Advantage: 14 Visionaries Define Marketplace Success in the New Economy.* edited by DanHoltshouse, Christopher Meyer, and Rudy Ruggles. Chico, CA: Capstone Publications.

Norris, Donald M. 2002. *Assuring Value from Your Technology Investment.* White Paper, October.

Partington, George. 2002. Blogging: Electronic Postings and Links Push Information to the Surface. *Worldcom.com*, July 26.

Prahalad, C. K., and M. S. Krishnan. 1999. The New Meaning of Quality in the Information Age. *Harvard Business Review*, September–October, 109–118.

Prahalad, C.K. and Venkatram Ramasdwarmy. 2002. The Co-Creation Connection. *Strategy & Business,* Issue 27, 50–61.

Por, George. 2001. Management Education and Knowledge Ecology. *BizEd*, November–December.

Port, Otis. 2002. The Next Web. *Business Week*, March 4, 96–102.

Prensky, Mark. 2001. Digital Natives, Digital Immigrants. *On the Horizon*, NCB University Press, v9n5, October.

Quinn, James Brian. 2002. Strategy, Science and Management. *MIT Sloan Management Review*, Summer, 96.

Rao, Madanmohan. 2002. Mobilizing Knowledge Workers with Wireless Solutions. *CRM Magazine*, July 27.

Ready, Douglas. 2002. How Storytelling Builds Next-Generation Leaders. *MIT Sloan Management Review*, Summer, 63–69.

Redeen, Bill. 2002. SCORM 1.2/1.3: Knowledge Reuse, Constraints and Recent Case Studies. *ADL Plugfest 6 Presentation and Webcast.* Defense Acquisition University, August 3. www.adlnet.org/index.cfm?fuseaction=Plugfest6Schedule

Sawnhey, Mohanbir and Deval Parikh. 2001. Where Value Lives in a Networked World. *Harvard Business Review*, January, 79–86.

Shank, Roger. 2002. *Designing World-Class E-learning.* New York: McGraw-Hill.

Slaughter, Richard A. 2002. Foresight in a Social Context. Paper presented at an international conference at the University of Stratclyde Graduate School of Business. July 11.

Snowden, Dave. 2002. Complex Acts of Knowing: Paradox and Descriptive Self-Awareness. *Journal of Knowledge Management* (Special Edition), v6n2: 1–14.

Tapscott, Don, David Ticoll and Alex Lowy. 2000. *Digital Capital: Harnessing the Power of Business Webs.* Boston: Harvard Business School Press.

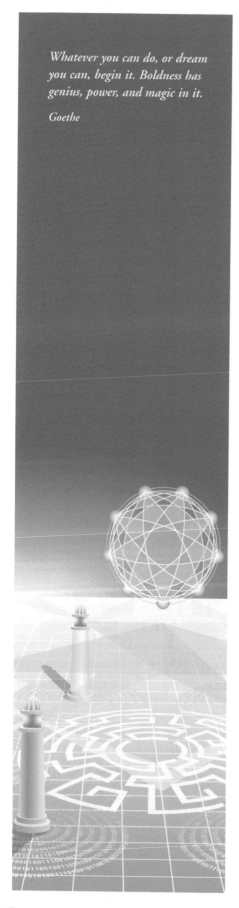

> *Whatever you can do, or dream you can, begin it. Boldness has genius, power, and magic in it.*
>
> *Goethe*

Tarlow, Mikela. 2002. *Digital Aboriginal—The Direction of Business Now: Instinctive, Nomadic, and Ever-Changing.* New York: Warner Books.

Taylor, James C. 2001. *Fifth Generation Distance Education.* Australian Department of Education, Training and Youth Affairs, Higher Education Division, Higher Education Series, Report No. 40, June.

Treacy, Michael, and Fred Wiersema. 1997. *The Discipline of Market Leaders.* Cambridge: Perseus Publishing.

Twigg, Carol. 2001. *Innovations in Online Learning: Moving Beyond No Significant Difference.* Pew Learning and Technology Program. www.center.rpi.edu/PewSym/Mono4.pdf

UNESCO. *Education For All—Grassroots Stories.* www.unesco.org/education/efa/know_sharing/grassroots_stories/

United States Department of Commerce. 2002. *Visions 2020: Transforming Education and Training Through Advanced Technologies.* Washington DC, September 17. www.ta.doc.gov/reports/TechPolicy/2020 Visions.pdf

Weigel, Van B. 2001. *Deep Learning for a Digital Age: Technology's Untapped Potential to Enrich Higher Education.* San Francisco: Jossey-Bass.

Wenger, Etienne, William N. Snyder, and Richard A. McDermott. 2002. *Cultivating Communities of Practice: A Guide for Managing Knowledge.* Cambridge: Harvard Business School Publishing.

Wenger, Etienne. 1999. *Communities of Practice: Learning, Meaning, and Identity.* Cambridge: Cambridge University Press.

Woelk, Darrell and Shailesh Agarwal. 2002. Integration of E-Learning and Knowledge Management. *Proceedings of E-Learn 2002.* (World Conference on E-Learning in Corporate, Government, Healthcare, and Higher Education, Montreal), Association for the Advancement of Computing in Education (AACE), Norfolk, VA.

Young, Jeffrey R. 2002. Superarchives Could Hold All Scholarly Output. *Chronicle of Higher Education,* July 5.

Web-based Resources

A toolkit of Web-based resources may be found at www.transformingeknowledge.info. These resources will be regularly updated and refreshed and they can be used in tandem with reading the book, providing additional perspective. Transforming e-Knowledge is a manifesto, a resource, and a guide to a wide range of issues relating to the strategic use of knowledge. Select resources as your interests dictate.